ORGANIZING FOR COMMUNITY WELFARE

ORGANIZING FOR

EDITED WITH AN INTRODUCTION BY

Chicago

COMMUNITY WELFARE

Mayer N. Zald

Quadrangle Books 1967

Library of Congress Catalog Card Number: 67-12356

Acknowledgments

These essays originated in a curriculum development grant from the Office of Juvenile Delinquency and Youth Development, Welfare Administration, Department of Health, Education and Welfare. They are part of a series of studies which has been coordinated by Professor Morris Janowitz of the University of Chicago and which deals with the application of social science concepts to youth and welfare problems.

The curriculum development grant was part of a larger grant (HEW No. 62216) administered through the Division of Social Science, University of Chicago. I wish to thank Morris Janowitz, Director of the Center for Social Organization Studies, for his perceptive advice and his support throughout the period of the grant.

The essay by Martin Rein and S. M. Miller was presented at the Columbia University–Mobilization for Youth Training Institute Workshop, April 30, 1964. My own essay contains material published under the title "Organization as Polities: Concepts for the Analysis of Community Organization Agencies," *Social Work,* October 1966.

MAYER N. ZALD

Vanderbilt University, 1967

Contents

ORGANIZING FOR COMMUNITY WELFARE

Mayer N. Zald
Introduction

Throughout this book we assume that sociology and social psychology can help to illuminate social welfare problems. Without always posing specific solutions, these analyses permit us to see problems of human welfare from new perspectives, to separate components of problems, and to anticipate problems that arise from the implementation of social policy. This is a broad analytic approach to welfare problems and the institutions and processes aimed at eliminating or alleviating them. We offer neither "comprehensive plans" nor limited evaluations of specific attempts at change. Instead, our purpose is to highlight dilemmas, point to limitations, spell out assumptions, examine variation, and even to account for the very definition of what becomes a welfare problem.

Our work has explicitly been conceived as an example of applied or policy science. "Applied sociology" and "sociology as a policy science" are two names for the application of sociology to practical problems. The former term applies to any responsible attempt to use sociology as a tool to solve man's problems. People who use the phrase "policy science" usually mean both a broader and narrower task. Sociology as a policy science is broader than applied sociology in that it takes a basic science approach to the problem with which it deals. Sociology as a policy science analyzes problems whole and does not always attempt to specify immediate strategies for change. On the other hand, sociology as a policy science is narrower than

applied sociology because it sees as its major audience bureaucratic and governmental decision-makers. Applied sociology
sweeps across the range of situations where sociological knowledge can be useful—from family counseling, to resolving or
creating community conflict, to international relations. But as
a policy science, sociology tends to deal with problems that
are handled in large and purposive organizations.

It is a sign of maturity that some sociologists now enter into
a dialogue with men of affairs without feeling they are losing
their souls, or, as important, without their colleagues turning
a suspicious eye. On the surface, social scientists' engagement
with practical domestic problems might appear to be only a
fad related to the growth of the civil rights movement and the
emergence of the war on poverty. Such a view ignores an important transformation in the organization of sociology: the social
sciences are experiencing a fundamental institutionalization of
the social scientists' concern with social problems and social
policy.

Contrast the situation today with that of twenty years ago.
Then many sociologists had just finished using their skills to
further their country's cause in World War II. They had engaged
in a range of applied efforts—from sample surveys of enlisted
men's attitudes, to labor mediation, to attempts to impose price
control, and to intelligence surveys of the social structure and
morale of the enemy. After the war two social scientists edited
a book called *The Policy Sciences: Recent Developments in
Scope and Method.*[1] Its avowed aim was to show how social
science perspectives could inform the intelligence of national
decisions, although most of the essays were, in fact, conventional social science. The volume had little impact on the
behavioral sciences, even if it did anticipate later concerns. Of
course, many social scientists studied social problems, and an
important group of them, the Lewinians, attempted to implement techniques of social change at the level of the small
group. Nevertheless, the historic distinctions between pure

and applied research were still emphasized, to the disadvantage of the latter.

What has changed? First, the definition of the massive domestic problems of poverty and civil rights has been built upon, and in turn called forth, social science–related social criticism. But the growth of policy-oriented concerns precedes the upsurge of these interrelated social movements, so that its roots must be found elsewhere.

The bases of the institutionalization of policy or action concerns can be found in two related phenomena affecting social science—a dialectic of intellectual development, and the transformation of occupational opportunities. The dialectic of intellectual development involves the generational cycle that takes place in any developing discipline. Sociology has always attracted people who wanted to help change the world; but as the field developed, the attempt to master scientific techniques of measurement and, more important, the supposed detachment and objectivity of the scientist made scholarly concern with policy problems seem inappropriate. Only as a "second generation" in the social scientific community became confident (justifiably or not) of the scholarly and scientific basis of its analysis, did individual sociologists throw off the yoke of neutralism.

Changes in the occupational affiliations of sociologists may be even more important for the institutionalization of action concerns. It appears that sociologists are increasingly locating outside of the traditional liberal arts college and graduate department setting.[2] In the last two decades, medical schools, law schools, schools of social work, mental hospitals, general hospitals, schools of education, schools of nursing, city planning agencies, public housing authorities, and others have, for a variety of reasons—sometimes for purposes of prestige and public relations, sometimes because of real problems in social measurement and social relations—found it useful to employ sociologists. It is inevitable that sociologists in these settings will be concerned not only with basic science aspects but with the policy implications of their research.

Several other types of evidence indicate that the current pre-occupation with policy is more than a fad. First, more and more scholarly journals are directly concerned with the policy problems and perspectives that can be illuminated by the scholarly analysis of social scientists. E. A. Shils edits *Minerva*, an international journal dealing with such questions. Daniel Bell and Irving Kristol edit *The Public Interest*; Alvin Gouldner was instrumental in starting *Trans-action,* and Alfred deGrazia started *The American Behavioral Scientist.* Although these journals differ widely in dedication to scholarship, quality, substantive content, and style, they indicate a deep commitment to the application of sociological and social science perspectives to policy issues.

Second, the Society for the Study of Social Problems, the association of sociologists most directly involved with applied and policy concerns, has shown a steady growth—from 500 in 1953, two years after its inception [3] and the year that *Social Problems* was first published, to about 1,000 in 1965.[4]

Third, distinguished members of the profession have turned their attention to the arena of social problems and social policy. Several former presidents of the American Sociological Association have, within the last five years, edited books dealing with related themes.[5]

Fourth, there is a growing number of courses about the problems of using sociological knowledge to change social structures and processes.

Fifth, in conjunction with program grants, federal legislation for mental health, education, poverty, and civil rights has begun to build into the law research and evaluation requirements. Thus, to some extent, new programs will build in social science expertise and perspectives.

In light of this institutionalization, can we say anything about the distinctive provinces of the sociologist? First, of course, social scientists have competence in evaluation research, both in designing the research and in specifying the evaluative problems and relevant variables. More important for the essays presented here are the concerns of modern society that seem to require sociological imagination.

It would be presumptuous, indeed, to assert that sociology has any unique competence to deal with a particular welfare problem. Confronted with intractable societal problems, the sociologist reaches into a mixed bag of variables, concepts, and strategies of change. It is true that sociologists have spent more time thinking about the measurement of such factors as social class or the impact of subcultures than most social scientists; yet even here their work overlaps with others. Certainly interest in income inequality and the distribution of wealth has been more characteristic of economists than of sociologists, and the anthropologist shares with the sociologist an interest in subcultural variation.

Whether or not sociology and social psychology have a distinctive province, they have concentrated upon certain aspects of welfare problems in modern society. Sociologists have concerned themselves with aspects of our differentiated and bureaucratized society which are crucial to the sophisticated understanding of the opportunities, constraints, and dilemmas of welfare policy. They have faced the enormous complexity of modern communities and their interdependence. Without in any way claiming our list to be exhaustive, let us briefly mention several features of modern society which have been noted by students of welfare problems and which are foci of interest in the essays in this book.

The Web of Interdependence and Influence

The establishment of multiple, overlapping, and even conflicting centers of power is often referred to as the Jacksonian tradition in American society. Because of our Protestant distrust of centralized power, we have developed a social system which sharply limits the discretion of central authority; as many decision centers as possible are linked to the local populace. Even without the Jacksonian tradition, however, the differentiation of complex societies leads to many institutional agents having overlapping responsibilities for and conceptions of welfare-related problems.

Within sociology more attention has been given to intra-institutional developments, patterns, and processes than to inter-institutional processes. Yet the latter clearly are of more interest to sociologists than to other social scientists; and the concepts of role, status-set, inter-institutional exchange, professional ideology, client-professional relations, and the like are the tools necessary for analysis of such processes.

Among the essays included here, that of Elaine Cumming deals most directly with such problems. Basing her paper on a set of empirical studies she has made, Dr. Cumming analyzes the processes by which people with mental problems are identified and allocated among various agencies and professionals. She suggests that basic American values of individualism, openness, and equality have shaped the development of the system for allocating services, and that our system can be seen as an analog to a pinball machine rather than a central dispatcher model. She also notes the way our market mechanisms interact with our stratification system to relate types of personnel to types of patients.

Universalistic Tendencies of Politics and Social Status

Modern society not only is differentiated but also has strong universalistic tendencies. Political rights have slowly been extended to all adults. The notions of equal treatment before the law, of equal access to medical and educational facilities, and of equal welfare benefits under similar disability contingencies are all part of a growing tendency of universalism. In its most general terms, universalism is a function of the spread of legal-rational society. Stated somewhat differently, the tendency of our society is toward the incorporation of the dispossessed. This seems to be a long-range trend of modern societies.

Sociologists are interested in two aspects of the trend which are particularly relevant to welfare problems: the sources of resistance to incorporation which exist in the institutions of society, and the sources of resistance to incorporation among the dispossessed themselves. (Interestingly enough, aside from a few like Reinhard Bendix and T. H. Marshall, they are interested less in the roots of the basic tendency toward universalism and incorporation.) In examining sources of resistance to incorporation in the institutions of society, the sociologist looks to the stratification system of the society as a whole and to the internal control and economics of particular institutions. For instance, how is it that middle-class neighborhoods get good schools, while lower-class neighborhoods settle for exaggerated custodialism? On the other hand, the sociologist does not assume that the dispossessed can use facilities whenever they are available, or that universalism is an unmixed blessing. The concepts of the values, perspectives, and knowledge contained in subcultures becomes relevant here.

As a further aspect of the trend toward universalism, William J. Goode points out in his essay that the incorporation of the dispossessed leads us to see social problems where none was defined before. When Negroes were outside of society, who in the society worried about the legitimacy of children born to them? At one time most Negro births were illegitimate. A problem emerges only as societal agents take responsibility for these births, consciously pay the bills for them, and attempt to change Negro family structure in a way more compatible with dominant societal values.

Goode proceeds to show how illegitimacy rates are a function of both the lower enforcement of norms of social control in the more deprived strata of society, and the "role bargains" with men that poor girls, both Negro and white, must make. His essay concludes with some searching remarks on the changes that must occur if illegitimacy rates are to be affected by social policy.

Incidentally, the problems of incorporating the dispossessed are also linked to some aspects of the Jefferson-Jackson persuasion touched upon earlier. In particular, as we move beyond the problem of legal rights to actual citizenship participation, we confront the problems of full and equal participation in a stratified society. The ideal of an alert and active citizenry stumbles against the realities of wealth and power.

Large-Scale Organizations

Not only is modern society becoming increasingly differentiated and universalistic, it also does more and more of its work through large-scale organizations. Sociologists have systematically analyzed both the gains and the pathologies of bureaucracies. They have examined the sources of organizational flexibility and inflexibility, of organizational character and commitments, and of differences in structure and performance. At the center of welfare policy are the mechanisms for administering and formulating them. Large-scale organizations and their internal processes play a crucial role at all levels in the welfare process—from the formulation of new policy, to the allocation of legally defined benefits, to the aggregation of demands for changes in policy.

Three of the essays in this book analyze problems related to the functioning of large-scale organization in a community context. David Street notes that the desire to make the school system responsible for socialization of the urban working class is an old one, and that the schools have long represented a hope at the same time that they have been blamed as a failure. Using "character analysis," he shows how the potentialities of the school system as a central agent in incorporating the dispossessed are limited by the basic organizations, resources, and perspectives of key personnel in the educational system and by the tasks that have been assigned the schools by the society. His general analysis is illustrated by a case analysis of vocational education and concludes with a program of institutional change. For Street, the problem of the educational system is not one of developing innovations—there are plenty of those; the problem is one of institutionalizing change.

Street's emphasis is on the explanation of the pathologies and rigidities of one of the central institutions of the society, the educational system. He asks why this institution does not easily accommodate welfare goals. The essays by Martin Rein and S. M. Miller and by me approach a different kind of organizational form than the schools. These essays explain the character of organizations designed explicitly to realize welfare goals. The essay by Rein and Miller centers on the demonstration project as an innovative mechanism for achieving high performance and a maximum spread of services for specific welfare programs. The demonstration project is a tool used by philanthropic foundations, professions, and the federal government to test and spread innovations in service in local communities, especially the large cities. As the attempt is made to build support within the community and its organizations, the demonstration project runs into pitfalls which either thwart the quality of service, limit its impact and continuity, or reduce the possibility of transfer and spread.

I deal less directly with policy questions than Rein and Miller or Street. My purpose is to account for the variation in strategies and modes of operation of community organization agencies, a class of organization whose purpose is to mobilize community resources for self-help and changes. The essay analyzes these kinds of agencies as miniature polities, showing how constitutions and constituencies shape practice.

The Social Psychology of the Recipient of Service

With the increased differentiation of society and the growth of large-scale organizations has come a complex process of defining who and how the organizations are to serve. A prime task of social science in the service of welfare objectives is that of understanding the entire social matrix surrounding the target population of welfare policies—the recipients of service. A social psychological approach can illuminate at least three major topics. First is the classification of the process, by which people in similar situations are somehow labeled as deviant in some specific way and in need of help. Social psychologists out of the symbolic interaction tradition have been especially alert to the complexity of this labeling process. Elaine Cumming and William J. Goode are sensitive to this problem, but it becomes a major analytic focus for Edwin Thomas and Robert D. Carter. Among their main contributions is an understanding of how the social category of the "poor" is created.

A second major, though related, task involves understanding the interaction of client with agencies and society. How does one became a client? How does a client wend his way among agencies? What determines the agencies' and society's classification and reaction to different contingencies of client life?

A third major task of social psychology is understanding the life situation of the client. What maintains him in his societal position? The notion of a culture of poverty, for instance, is an attempt both to explain the life situation and understand what maintains the poor in poverty.

Thomas' and Carter's essay most consciously utilizes formal social psychology to analyze a welfare problem. In their consideration of both the social process of defining the poor and the factors maintaining people in poverty, they are able to illuminate the problem of the poor and synthesize a large amount of the relevant literature. Noting that poverty is relative to its social context, they begin by discussing the differences between material inequality and poverty and psychological inequality. They attempt to specify conditions for perceptions of poverty and, importantly, the inequity of poverty. They then turn to the problem of how people are assigned to different social positions by both personal and impersonal agents.

Finally, they turn to the societal context and the different principles—exchange justice, reciprocity, and responsibility— under which assistance is given the poor.

We have touched on salient aspects and trends of modern society that are peculiarly relevant to the work of the sociologist *cum* policy scientist, and which are reflected in the essays that follow. Of course, there are other observable trends—the transformation of the family system, the rise of a youth culture, the internal differentiation of professions, changing community structure, and so on. Furthermore, sociologists' historic concern with specific social pathologies—for example, juvenile delinquency, narcotics addiction, and alcoholism—makes the work of these "pathology experts" relevant in specific cases. But the ones we have listed give some sense of the special contribution of the sociologist to the analysis of system-wide problems in implementing welfare policies.

Although it is clear that the talents of the sociologist are becoming increasingly relevant to a wide range of applied situations and decisions, the limits of sociological knowledge in seriously appraising policy decisions also have become painfully clear. To the old question, "Can science save us?" many sociologists are answering, "Not very likely!" The limitations in the application of sociological knowledge and perspectives stem both from the inadequacies of knowledge and the complexity of the process of formulating and implementing policy decisions. Without discussing the former limitation, let us note some of the limits stemming from the policy process.

Policy formulation in the United States proceeds largely by the method of "disjointed incrementalism," as contrasted with the method of "rational-comprehensive planning." The phrases are those of the economist Charles E. Lindblom,[6] who feels that intellectuals have tended to be oversympathetic to the benefits of the latter, to the neglect of the virtues of the former. Disjointed incrementalism is a reasonable strategy of policy formulation when there are many conflicting values to be maximized, when there are multiple centers of power each with a commitment to a specific goal or aspect of policy, and when there are many factors or variables which can affect policy outcomes, many of which may be unknown. Disjointed incrementalism allows the policy-maker to start from a known base—the effects of ongoing programs, which, after all, represent previous decisions of how and where to commit resources. Thus, rather than formulating policy on the basis of a total analytic scheme, the policy-maker starts from a narrower range of alternatives and options.

Whether we agree with Lindblom's belief that this is an optimal way of making policy in a pluralist complex society, as a description of the actual process it seems to be correct. For our purposes what is most relevant is that the broad analytic schemes of the sociologist will often have but marginal relevance to the incremental decision-maker. Any one incrementalist will often have only a few factors that he can effect, and these may or may not be those relevant to sociological analysis.

Nevertheless, sociological analysis can serve as a tool and counsel to the incrementalist. Sociological investigation and analysis can help to improve the wisdom of decision. By pointing out the limitations of social structure or specific policies, the sociologist adds realism to the expectations of policy effectiveness. By pointing out intervening processes, the sociologist provides the grounds for more differential and sophisticated policies and also points to additional levers for change. By providing broad perspectives, the sociologist helps the decision-maker to trace out the limits and opportunities of the present situation and to take a longer view of the directions of policy.

Furthermore, by exposing contradictions and dilemmas, a more rational assessment of priorities becomes feasible. All of the essays in this volume seek to contribute to this more limited goal of policy science.

Notes

1. Daniel Lerner and Harold Lasswell, Stanford, 1951. The article by Lasswell, "The Policy Orientation," pp. 3-15, remains a remarkable statement on social science as a policy science.

2. Calculations from the data presented by Matilda White Riley indicate that in the period 1950-59, liberal arts positions increased 62 percent while positions in professional schools and other settings increased 132 percent. From a base of 1,466, liberal arts positions grew to 2,381; the "applied" sector grew from 658 to 1,526. See her "Membership of the American Sociological Association, 1950-59," *American Sociological Review*, XXV, No. 6 (December 1960), 921. It should be noted that the Riley work, as well as that of Janice Hopper, "Sociologists in the 1964 National Register of Scientific and Technical Personnel," *The American Sociologist* I, No. 2 (February 1966), 71-78, is concerned with the more educated segment of the profession. Eldridge Sibley's study of the occupations of terminal M.A.'s indicates that many more of these are in applied settings. See Eldridge Sibley, *The Education of Sociologists in the United States*, New York, 1963, p. 56.

3. *Social Problems*, I (January 1954), 114.

4. *Social Problems*, XIII (Winter 1966). 356.

5. Robert K. Merton and Robert A. Nisbet, *Contemporary Social Problems*, New York, 1961. See also the forthcoming volume, *The Uses of Sociology*, edited by Paul F. Lazarsfeld, Harold Wilensky, and William Sewell.

6. See his "The Science of Muddling Through," *Public Administration Review*, XIX (Spring 1959); *The Intelligence of Democracy: Decision Making Through Mutual Adjustment*, New York, 1965; and with David Braybrooke, *A Strategy of Decision: Policy Evaluation as a Social Process*, New York, 1963.

I. ORGANIZATIONAL STRUCTURE: CONSTRAINT AND OPPORTUNITY

Mayer N. Zald
Sociology and Community Organization Practice

In the last few years the intellectual and action horizons of community organizers have broadened. Once they were largely involved in helping voluntary agencies to coordinate plans, avoid duplication of effort, and mobilize the community for specific, limited, and generally accepted goals. Today some community organizers are interested in fomenting broad social change.

The proliferation of tasks and settings presents both difficulties and opportunities for those who wish to understand the profession and improve its effectiveness. Competent teaching and practice forces us to transform our base of knowledge, broaden our concepts, develop new techniques, and examine a wider range of situations.

Just as the sociology of medicine and the sociology of education are amplifying our understanding of those fields, so too can a sociology of community organization illuminate community organization practice. Indeed, more so. After a brief description of the major elements of such a sociology, we shall develop

I am indebted to Martin Rein, Thomas Sherrard, John Marsh, Richard Murray, and John Tropman for reactions to various versions of this essay.

some concepts from organizational theory which apply to one part of a sociology of community organization practice—the analysis of community organization agencies.

I. Toward a Sociology of Community Organization

A sociology of a profession or institution comprises at least three relatively distinct areas: (1) the explanation and description of its historical emergence and development; (2) the explanation and description of the social structure and operating system of the field; and (3) the description and analysis of the object of the field—in this case communities and their specific problems.

THE EMERGENCE OF COMMUNITY ORGANIZATION PRACTICE

The growth of community organization as a separate field is a relatively recent development. An explanation of its growth depends partially on a definition of the field. If "community development" is defined differently from "community organization" (the former being broader, more ambitious, and usually referring to changes in total communities, the latter being more segmental, restricted, and partial in its goals), then the explanation of the incidence and growth of the field is likely to be different. If one takes the narrow view, analysis is probably restricted to the North American continent and advanced industrial societies. Here the field of community organization practice is defined as the organizations and professions whose primary goals are to mobilize and coordinate members and agencies of communities to solve community problems. Under this definition, when work on a community problem is routinized or no longer requires that community resources be mobilized, it would be considered the province of other, specialized agencies. For instance, an air pollution problem might involve the field of community organization practice only until specific institutional solutions were adopted. The broad definition we have adopted allows us to include both community development and traditional community organization approaches in our discussion.

If we accept this definition, it is difficult to explain the growth of the field. Some easy explanations can be rejected. For example, the emergence of the field is not just a function of the rapidity of change in communities, for some societies have had rapidly changing communities without having community organizers. Nor is it a function of complexity, because many societies with highly differentiated communities have not developed community organization specialists. Nor is the emergence of community organization a function of advanced affluence, for some affluent societies do not seem interested in developing community organization. Nor is it a function of poverty and a desire for change, because there seem to be better routes to prosperity than through community organization. Nor is it a function of rationality, because many sound programs get along quite well without community organizers. Nor is the ideology of the value of self-help required, for community organizers sometimes operate in settings where this ideology does not exist.

Careful examination will probably lead us to several explanations rather than one. Furthermore, if we examine ancient civilizations we shall probably find historical analogs to community organizers in many societies, and the conditions for their growth will throw light on community organization practice in our own time. The development of a sociology of community organization practice awaits such studies.

THE SOCIAL SYSTEM OF COMMUNITY ORGANIZATION

If a sociology of community organization is to be of use to the practitioners, it must focus on the distinctive social attributes of the field and its characteristic problems and dilemmas. Further, on the one hand, it must articulate the mechanisms for resolving dilemmas and problems and, on the other hand, clearly specify the limits of community organization action.

Analyzing the social system of an institution or field embraces the following topics: (1) the recruitment, socialization, and careers of key participants in the system; (2) the interaction and interdependence of organizations and actors within the field; (3) the ties linking agencies within the field with other institutional areas (e.g., how does the community organization agency and practice affect the economy, and vice versa); and (4) the internal variation in types of community organization practice as related to variations in goals and settings.

What are some of the distinctive features of the community organization field?

1. The client is never an individual. If the client is conceived as the whole community or as a part of the community, the professional must deal with conflicting interests and groups. This is certainly different in degree from social casework or from such other professions as engineering and medicine. If the client is conceived as whoever pays for services, there may be conflict between clients, professional values, and community goals.

2. The "case" or project may take years. For most agencies, developing a community is not a short-term task. Only the community organization teacher called in as a consultant has a brief relationship with the project. The fact that most projects take a long time has several consequences for the professional field. First, the professional may "over-identify" with the community

or agency and lose his ability to compare different situations. The development of adequate diagnosis demands comparative knowledge. Second, because the task takes many years, the professional may be evaluated by *how* he accomplishes things, not by *what* he achieves. Competence is measured in terms of personality and style, not ability to effect change.

3. The skill and diagnostic base of community organization practice is an amalgam of many disciplines. Practitioners draw upon a range of disciplines, from small-group and psychodynamic theory to economics and political science.

4. The institutional structures and patterns of community organization practice are emergent. In many respects community organization practice is in a pre-institutional phase. The training patterns and requirements, the structure of occupational roles, the web of relations with distinctive groups and other institutions are now being formed.

5. The community organization practitioner often wants to change the structure of community decision-making and participation, but he must do this through specific projects. The community participant may be unaware of or uninterested in the more general goals.

6. The professional cannot impose his own conditions of work on settings. Because the image of his skill is not sharp and because he does not have a monopoly of required skills, the professional is often not in a position to impose conceptions of goals and means. The principle of client self-determination not only is a part of the ideology of community organization practice but also is often a necessary reaction to the clients' unwillingness to allow the profession authority.

7. Related to the preceding point, the professional is bound by his agency context. Compared with other professions, his practice is more determined by organizational than professional standards and expectations.

This list of distinguishing characteristics of the community organization field is by no means exhaustive, nor are these features exclusive to the field. Nevertheless, the list points up some of the factors that might be stressed in an analysis of the social system of community organization.

KNOWLEDGE BASE FOR THE ANALYSIS OF COMMUNITY PROBLEMS

Besides analyzing the social structure and operating system of the field, sociology also attempts to contribute knowledge about social problems and community structure, the target problems of the field. The literature on social problems is vast and confusing, but certainly we can easily identify the proper and necessary knowledge for an analysis of the specific community and social conditions which the community organization practitioner confronts. Whether it is the level and nature of delinquency, the rate of illegitimacy, or the organization of health services, the sociologist can point to a somewhat relevant body of descriptive and analytical literature.

The situation is less optimistic when we turn to the analysis of community structure and operation. Although the field of community studies is rich and varied, dating back to the classic works of the Lynds and enjoying an amazing resurgence in the last decade and a half, our knowledge about community structure has rarely been translated into a form useful to the community organizer. Sometimes the only advice we get is "look for the real power structure"—the motto of the Floyd Hunter–C. Wright Mills school of thought. Of course, this is an oversimplification. For example, Roland Warren's recent book. *The Community in America*,[1] especially in the later chapters, begins to spell out both the strategies for community change and the range of variables necessary for really useful analysis of community systems. But his analysis is only a beginning for a fully developed sociology of community organization practice.

II. Some Concepts for the Analysis of Organization

The analysis of the variation in community organization agencies is crucial for such a sociology because community structure and social problems are defined in the context of organizational goals and needs. Furthermore, it is impossible to consider the community organization practitioner without considering the agency context in which he is employed. Indeed, compared to many professions, a much greater part of the variety of practices is determined by the organizational context for the profession. This assertion has important consequences for both the theoretical base of the field and the nature of its curriculum. We shall summarize briefly the current level of conceptualization of community organization practice, then discuss the kind of organizational theory needed to analyze properly these agencies. We shall present four broad concepts and related propositions which help to explain the kinds of problems and organizational styles found in different community organization contexts.

APPROACHES TO CONCEPTUALIZING
COMMUNITY ORGANIZATION PRACTICE

As in any emerging discipline or profession, especially when knowledge is not clearly linked to practice, the first stage in thinking about community organization is the "cookbook" stage. In the classroom, after a brief attempt to discuss the evolution of the field and to define it, the teacher moves to a "how-to-do-it" course in techniques that "work" in the field. How to run a committee meeting, how to attract top leadership, how to run a finance campaign are typical of the topics discussed. Such techniques are stated normatively—that is, in terms of correct procedures garnered from experience. Differential techniques or strategies for achieving goals under differing situations are not given or are given only as asides. The techniques are not related to a more general theory of community organization practice.

The second stage in the thinking about community organization is the development of general models of the enabling process,[2] or, if you prefer, planned change through client-change agent relations.[3] Ross and Lippitt, Watson, and Westley have presented normative theories (theories prescribing right practice) based on social-psychological assumptions about the way people can be mobilized and changed in the absence of strong external inducements (for instance, coercion, threats, or money).

These approaches are limited in three major ways. First, they tend to ignore or play down the role of differential diagnosis and differential treatment. Second, they do not allow the community organization practitioner to use external inducements to create and maintain change. Third, they tend to analyze professional practice as if the change agent (community organization practitioner) had no restrictions and ministered to a client on the basis of his knowledge, without considering the parent organization, the problems, and the community.

With regard to the first criticism, it seems clear that the user of the "enabling processes" might often employ means not foreseen by the proponents of this theory. If the only way to mobilize lower-class slum dwellers is to agitate and create hostility against external agents, is this method to be included in the treatment? It certainly seems to be an enabling process. Just as in medicine or psychiatry differential diagnosis requires differential treatment techniques, so too do different community diagnoses require different approaches.

Second, too often it is assumed that the only tools the community organization practitioner employs are his knowledge and his professional self-presentation. This situation may have been true of community organization practice often in the past, but now both in America and the old-new nations, the agencies that employ community organizers are increasingly equipping them with external sanctions and inducements to gain community allegiance and change. Often they can help obtain money, educational programs, or other specific advantages. Sociology and social psychology should include such external factors in their formulations.

Third, theories of the enabling process and of client-professional relations focus on a "micro" as opposed to "macro" framework. Although such a framework has the advantage of delineating narrowly the immediately relevant factors in the client-professional relation, it does so at the cost of the full range of determinants. It focuses on the client-practitioner relation *in vacuo*. It ignores the complexity of the client system or, for that matter, the problem of defining exactly who is the client. It ignores the constraints and capabilities of the practitioner which are set by his organizational and community context.

No matter how we define the client, the "needs" and "problems" to be worked on in the community are not defined by the mutual agreement of the practitioner and relevant members of the community. In fact, they are defined and shaped by the employing agency. The techniques selected to deal with them also depend upon requirements of the organization. Whether the practitioner facilitates, fund-raises, or foments, whether he plans, serves as a resource expert, counsels, or agitates is determined by the structure, aims, and operating procedures of the organization that pays the bill. Any useful theory of community organization practice must include concepts and propositions about how community organization agencies shape practice, how such organizations are themselves constrained, and what kinds of problems and communities can be shaped and affected by what kinds of agencies.

ORGANIZATIONAL ANALYSIS OF COMMUNITY ORGANIZATION AGENCIES

The sophisticated reader immediately asks, "Which organizational theory or concepts?" for there are many of them. The general approach followed here is that often called "organizational analysis." [4] It considers the entire organization, and not some subpart, as its object of analysis. Typically, the analysis examines the relation of goals to structure, the pressures to change goals arising from the environment, and the internal arrangements of the organization. The analysis focuses on the way organizational processes give power to different groups and how, in turn, subgroup loyalties and power affect the operation and direction of the organization. Organizations are seen as developing "distinctive characters"—styles and strategies of coping with recurring dilemmas. In contrast to the Weberian analysis of bureaucracy, this mode of analysis can be applied to any complex organization. Compared with public administration approaches, it de-emphasizes the description of formal structure and formal rules and requirements to concentrate instead on the multiple dependencies of organizations, the development of organizational commitments to groups and policies with varying consequences.

Often only implicitly treated in organizational analysis is the polity of organizations—the patterns of authority and influence and the mechanisms for their generation and use. This paper explicitly uses a quasi-political frame of reference. Community organization agencies are among a class of organizations in which goals are often in flux. The ebb and flow of power and influence are central to understanding the problems of these organizations. Conflict is sometimes covert, sometimes overt, but almost always present. The relationships of the organizations to their environments are unstable. Thus it seems warranted to give explicit attention to problems of power and the modes of binding people together for collective action. Community organization agencies can be analyzed as miniature polities.[5]

Four interrelated concepts form the core of our analysis.

1. Organizations have *constitutions,* that is, specified kinds of activities, general goals, and norms of procedure and relationships which are more or less institutionalized in the organization and which are changed only with great effort and cost.

2. Constitutions are linked to the *constituency and resource base* of the organization. The constituency is not the clientele; rather, the term refers to the groups and individuals who control the organization and to whom the agency executive or executive core are most immediately responsible—boards of directors, key legislators, office-holders, or major fund-raisers or grantors.

3. Community organization agencies wish to affect *target* populations, organizations, or decision centers.

4. Finally, community organization agencies exist among, and interact with, other agencies. They have *external relations* which can facilitate, impede, or leave unaltered the accomplishment of operative targets.

CONSTITUTIONS, CONSTITUENCY, AND GOALS

In a sense, the constitution of an organization represents its social contract—the basic goals and means to which the major supporters and staff of the organization are committed.[6] When attempts are made to change the constitution of an organization, unless clear benefits accrue to the major supporters the agency can expect conflict and disaffection.

When we speak of the constitution of an organization, we mean, of course, more than just the formal or written statement of goals and procedures; in some cases these may have little to do with the actual constitution. On the other hand, many patterned aspects of agency operation may not be part of the constitution because they may not concern basic agreements about goals and means.

An analysis of constitutions is important for a sociology of community organization practice because it clarifies the problems agencies confront when they attempt to change goals and structure, the chances of attaining specific goals, and the styles of work of the professionals. To be fruitful, constitution analysis must be reduced to more specific analytic problems. Let us treat two: agency goals, and constituencies and agency autonomy.

DIMENSIONS OF GOALS

Usually organizations come into being and are maintained to pursue collective ends. A central part of the constitution of any organization is the sets of agreements about goals which are understood by major constituents. Organizational goals, with beliefs about how to attain them, set tasks and problems for personnel.

Although there are several conceptual and methodological approaches to the study of goals,[7] two aspects are especially crucial here. First, the goals of the organization determine some of the basic types of community organization work. For example, they determine whether the task is to gain consensus among disparate agencies or to mobilize the poor for self-help. Second, attempts to shift the objectives of the organization can threaten the body politic of the organization. For example, changing from an organization devoted to educating the public to one running action programs might lead many supporters to question their allegiances.

The goals of community organization agencies can be classified along three distinct dimensions. (1) Change orientation or service orientation. The community group or individual either is given a specific service or is to be changed in some way. A community research bureau would be a provider of service, whereas an agency attempting to increase the power and participation of a group in a community would be change oriented. (2) Institution orientation or individual and group orientation. For example, some community organizations work mainly with other agencies and their representatives, such as local welfare agencies, whereas others, such as community centers, work with individuals and groups. (3) Member (internal) orientation or non-member (external) orientation. For example, a settlement house often works with members, whereas a governmental community development agency works with groups outside of the government bureaucracy.

The dichotomous cross-classification of these three dimensions yields the typology presented in Figure 1. The purpose of the typology is to highlight similarities and differences in the constitutions of organizations within the community organization field. Most of the major types of community organization work are shown.

The examples in Figure 1 are illustrative. In actual instances, a given organization might be classified in a different cell than indicated here. For example, some national health agencies (cell H) may be more institution (hospital and profession) oriented than individual oriented. Furthermore, in empirical cases an agency might be oriented to both institutions *and* individuals, it might aim at change *and* service, and it might work with both members and non-members. It is clear that some of these organizations are more likely to involve group work than community organization practice. But community organizers can be found in all of these types of settings.

Cell A includes organizations aimed at changing institutions that are members. For example, if a regional hospital planning group included most of the hospitals in the area as members and tried to get them to change or adopt new policies, it would

FIGURE 1

GOAL DIMENSIONS OF COMMUNITY ORGANIZATION AGENCIES
A Typology Based on Change or Service Goals
Applied to Internal or External Targets that
are Either Institutions or Individuals and Groups

	Change Oriented		Service Oriented	
	Institution	Individual and groups	Institution	Individual and groups
	(A)	(B)	(C)	(D)
Internal (member)	Regional planning groups for specific areas. New style welfare councils (planning change oriented).	Neighborhood block clubs. Settlement houses.	Old style welfare councils (coordination and discussion of plans).	Community centers. Adult education.
	(E)	(F)	(G)	(H)
External (non-member)	Lower-class social movements. Governmental community projects.	Agencies working with street gangs. Community mental health programs.	Regional or community research agencies.	National health agencies (excluding research).

be categorized in cell A. Cell B includes organizations aimed
at getting individual members to change practices. An agency
with rehabilitation goals aimed at members would be classified
in this cell. Neighborhood and block clubs that attempt to
change members' behavior—home maintenance, political participation, etc.—would be placed in this cell. On the other hand, to
the extent that they are oriented to getting new or expanded
services, they would be placed in cell E. Cells C and D include
those agencies that provide a routine program of service to
their members. For instance, many welfare councils largely
serve as a forum for discussion of common problems of member agencies (cell C). Community centers (cell D) provide a
meeting place and recreational and club facilities for members.
Community organizations attempting to get families and employ-
ers to relate in more helpful ways to ex-mental patients would
usually be classified in cell F. On the other hand, where the
agency provides a service, such as information, research, or
specific materials and goods that are well accepted by the recipients, they would be placed in cell G or H.

This typology points up similarities of problems in practice
shared by agencies "located" in the same cell and differences
between agencies in different cells. We can hypothesize about
some of these similarities and differences.

Community organization agencies aimed externally, aimed
at change, and aimed at institutions (for example, changing
the school system) must find a way to penetrate the decision
processes of organizations. They may do it by persuasion, but
if that fails, sanctions—bad publicity, control of monies and
personnel—may be utilized. On the other hand, organizations
aimed at providing services to individual members (for example, community centers) must develop attractive programs to
bring people in the door—no question of conflict or of mobilizing sanctions arises in such cases.

In general, the more change oriented the goals, the greater

the sanctions needed by the practitioner and his agency to accomplish his goals. (Of course, incentives can come from within the target or client group—for example, an alcoholic may strongly desire to be cured.) Furthermore, the more an organization is member oriented, the greater the likelihood of a consensus on action because the act of joining implies some agreement about goals. Member-oriented agencies are more likely to use persuasive statements about the relation of the proposed action to goals than are non-member-oriented organizations. The latter must more often use either appeals to self-interest or specific incentives and sanctions.

Finally, when a community organization agency deals with other agencies, it cannot expect to gain the loyalties and commitments of the personnel of these institutions. On the other hand, where members are individuals, the agency may build up a backlog of loyalty and commitment which can be used in sustaining itself.

These dimensions also relate to the problems of organizational maintenance in the face of attempts to attain specific goals or to change goals. We have said that the constitution of the organization consists of a set of expectations which, if ignored, threaten the maintenance and stability of the organization. For example, Peter Clark has discussed the case of a local voluntary organization composed of businessmen interested in taxation and governmental efficiency.[8] The standard activity of the organization was information gathering and education on different tax and governmental programs. Clark found that when any specific tax legislation or assessment was proposed it was difficult to get the organization to take a definite stand on the proposal. Instead, a group of businessmen who favored or opposed the tax would often form a specific ad hoc committee to lobby for or against the issue. Clark concluded that although the organization was concerned with taxation, any specific piece of legislation tended to have differential effects on members, and a definite stand by the organization would lead to internal conflict. To avoid dissension, members took action outside of the organization. Clark's example represents a situation in which the organization's constitution did not allow for attempts at change. The point is that as an organization begins to change its basic goals (for instance, along the dimensions discussed in the typology in Figure 1), constitutional problems emerge.[9]

CONSTITUENCY AND AGENCY AUTONOMY

Some community organization agencies have goals of integrating and coordinating major constituents, and constituency relations are obviously a central part of their activity. Even for those agencies whose basic goals are not these, the question of constituency-agency relations is important. A pattern of normative expectations develops about consultation, discretion, and the locus of initiation of agency goals and programs. This pattern is largely a function of the resource dependency (sources of money and legitimacy) of the agency.[10] To the extent that an agency is heavily dependent on its constituency, it is likely to develop a constitution allowing little discretion to officers and key personnel.[11]

Constituency-agency relations are crucial in understanding executive roles. Executive roles vary in terms of how much and how often the executive must report to the constituency. The executive may be little more than a facilitator of constituency decision-making, or he may be the major decision-maker.[12] What determines this variation?

Three factors (excluding personality style, appear to be important in affecting the level of executive discretion—the fund-raising base, the role of the constituency in accomplishing organizational goals, and the knowledge base differential between constituency and staff. First, the more the agency's fund-

raising base is routinized and relatively independent of its
constituency, the less likely is the staff to consult systematically
with and involve the constituency in decision-making. Thus,
agencies that have an immediate and vital appeal to the public
(such as the national voluntary health organizations), or have
legal and routinized access to funds, are less likely to have
broad participation of constituency in decision-making.

Second, when the agency is directly dependent on its constituency for achieving organizational goals, greater attention will
be paid to constituency wishes and participation. An agency is
dependent on constituency for achieving goals when the prestige
and influence of the constituency must be utilized to mobilize
other segments of the community. After all, the moderate prestige and influence of community organization professionals is
usually insufficient to generate widespread community support.
An agency is also dependent on the constituency when it is
their change that is sought (when the constituency and the
target group is the same).[13] Although an agency's attention to
its constituency may only be formal or slight, nevertheless it
affects the conduct of office.

Finally, the greater the knowledge gap between staff personnel and constituency, the more likely is the staff to operate
autonomously, consulting the constituency only on "boundary"
conditions—changes that affect the relation of the agency to the
community. In general, the more decisions are defined as "professional" problems, the less likely are constituencies to be
involved.

It would be wrong, however, to assume that an executive
cannot influence agency-constituency relations. Constitutions
are not immutable. Furthermore, the executive may not want
autonomy; the constituency may represent a resource which
can usefully be cultivated but which retains responsibility for
all action.

CONSENSUS AND CONSTITUTIONS

Underlying many of the propositions just discussed is the problem of organizational consensus; indeed, the notion of a constitution assumes consensus about major means and goals. Moreover, how organizational power relations manifest themselves—whether they lead to conflict or to alienation, whether the organization is able to pursue goals effectively or is immobilized—is partly a function of the level of consensus. The basic shape that an organization takes—the constitution of decision-making and action-taking and the role of the professional within the organization—is partly a function of the level of consensus within the organization.

In a perceptive essay titled "Strategies, Structures and Processes in Decision-Making," James D. Thompson and Arthur W. Tuden offer a sociological analysis of the consequences of consensus for organizational constitutions.[14] Thompson and Tuden argue that the basic shape of organizational structure and styles of decision-making is limited by the level of agreement about outcomes (ends or goals) and the level of agreement about means (beliefs about causation, what will lead to outcomes). They suggest the following typology:

In Figure 2, the first two lines in each cell are those designated by Thompson and Tuden. The first line refers to the most efficacious strategy (or style) for decision-making that is likely to result from a given combination of levels of agreement. The second line refers to the most likely structure for handling such decisions. The third line, which is our extension of Thompson and Tuden, refers to the professional role that a community organizer or other leader is likely to take in such an organization.

The collegium (cell B) is an organization in which major participants agree about goals but not about means. It has a

FIGURE 2

CONSENSUS PROBLEMS IN ORGANIZATIONS:

Structures, Strategies of Decision-making, and Professional Roles*

	Level of Agreement About Ends	
	Disagreement	Agreement
	A	**B**
Disagreement	1. Inspiration	1. Judgment
	2. "Anomic structure" (searching sect)	2. Collegium
	3. Innovator, new alternatives (charismatic leader)	3. Discussion leader
Level of Agreement About Means	**C**	**D**
Agreement	1. Compromise and bargaining	1. Computation
	2. Representative assembly	2. Bureaucracy
	3. Mediator	3. Planner, action initiator

* Adapted from Thompson and Tuden, ibid.

decision style that has sometimes been called participant democracy, in which everyone must rely on judgment. It is a style
common to social work agencies in which professionals are
the major participants and share common goals, but in which
the technology is imprecise. Consensus is reached only after
much discussion; case conferences are the rule. This is also
likely to be the form taken by new community councils with
relatively limited goals, or in community mental health programs, for these programs are relatively untried. Since there is
a high degree of consensus on ends, the good faith of the participants is assumed in discussion, and the process facilitates
the sense of good judgment. Discussion is continued until a
consensus is reached.

The representative assembly (cell C) differs from the collegium
in that major participants do not share ends, except possibly
the goal of remaining in the organization and keeping it going.
When means are known but ends are not shared, it is difficult
to get consensus through persuasion and debate, no matter how
long the discussion goes on. Thus consensus is reached through
an exchange and bargaining process in which major participants
enter into coalitions, compromise their goals, and bargain over
present and future issues. If the participants are only weakly
tied to the organization, veto power may be granted to major
participants to prevent their ends being so threatened that they
leave the organization. In this kind of organization, such as an
omnibus community council, the professional role may resemble
that of a mediator. Often when an organization is made up of
participants with incompatible goals it solves problems by
settling for a narrower agenda compatible with almost everyone's ends.

A bureaucratic structure supports a "computational approach"
(cell D) when there is high agreement on ends and the means
are relatively well specified. This is the ideal case for rational
coordination because such organizations can develop special-

ized roles clearly linked together. Community organizers are occasionally involved in true bureaucratic structures as planners or as executives. Furthermore, in some of the new nations, agencies devoted to community development are part of the governmental bureaucracy and take on bureaucratic characteristics. But such organizations are not typical of the community organization field because a bureaucratic structure assumes specific and consensually agreed-upon goals and a routinized or clear technique to achieve ends. Possibly the national health agencies most approximate these, although some urban planning agencies and housing agencies that employ community organizers may also have essentially bureaucratic structures.

Finally, cell A contains what we have labeled the "searching sect" (Thompson and Tuden call it an "anomic structure"). Sometimes organizations are composed of people grappling with some problem or situation only negatively defined—they know they do not want anarchy, or they know they want to escape a present situation, but true operative goals cannot be agreed upon. Such an organization may be close to disintegration, and only a radical or charismatic solution which finds some basis for common interest or common means seems to be a solution. In such a situation the posing of radical innovations solves the problem of group action. It may be that the recent growth of lower-class action organizations in urban slums has some of this quality—they develop operative ends and means which were previously not part of the repertoire of the participants. Furthermore, they do it among people who rarely participate in organizations. Whether the searching sect can be transformed into another type depends on the organization's ability to reward participants and thus change its level of agreement on ends and means.

Thus, the constitutions of organizations are in part adaptations to the level of consensus among major participants, and the structures discussed represent different ways of binding people or groups into organizations. The community organizer faced with varying degrees of consensus about ends and means is forced to recognize that both his role and the operation of his agencies depend upon finding a viable mode for reaching consensus.

It should be clear that consensus and power are complexly related. Operating consensus can be bought by judicious use of incentives. If a community organization agency controls enough incentives, it can impose a computational decision style on the situation. On the other hand, many community organization agencies do not control incentives, and therefore inspirational, judgmental, and compromising decision styles develop.

CONSTITUENCY CHARACTERISTICS AND AGENCY OPERATION

The constitution of an organization emerges and is maintained partly to satisfy the constituency. At the same time that they give the organization its continuing mandate, the characteristics of the constituency partly shape goals and means. Two characteristics of great importance are the social class background of the constituency and the extent to which the constituency consists of individuals or organizations.

A large body of literature testifies to the greater difficulties of involving working-class as compared to middle- or upper-class individuals in voluntary organizations.[15] Extending these findings to community organization agencies, the following proposition emerges: the lower the socio-economic status of the constituency, the more difficult it is likely to be to maintain interest and participation. In other words, the community organization practitioner with a lower socio-economic constituency will devote more of his energies to motivating the constituency than he would in other organizations.

Not only is level of participation affected by the socio-economic basis of the constituency, but also the style of participation is likely to differ. In general, we would expect that when a community organization agency aimed at changing some aspect of the community has a middle- and upper-class constituency, it will more likely attempt to gain its ends through persuasion, informal negotiation, and long-range harmonizing of interests. On the other hand, the more an organization has an essentially lower-class basis, the more it will resort to direct action, open propaganda, and agitation (when it takes action at all).[16]

The higher we go in the stratification system, the more likely it is that the constituency has easy access to officeholders, can command respect from them, and can threaten to use sanctions which the target person will recognize. Thus the more elite the constituency, the more likely it is that informal negotiations will take place and can be fruitful.

Moreover, people from higher socio-economic groups have organizational experiences at an earlier date. The higher the status, the more likely that the constituency will have had experience in organizational negotiation, the more time they can comfortably spend in organizational participation, and the more rewarding to them is such participation.[17]

Obviously, the community organization practitioner in organizations with different constituencies must take these factors into account. His methods of getting concrete results, the amount of time he spends in agitational versus more neutral types of activities, and the way he involves the constituency will differ depending upon the class base of the constituency.

For many community organization agencies the crucial characteristic of the constituency is not so much its class base but its individual versus organizational basis. Everything else being equal, the more an agency has a constituency of smaller agencies, the harder it is to get commitment to an action program which does not have widespread societal consensus, and the more likely the agency serves as a clearing house for information and coordination.[18]

One of the advantages of a constituency made up of organizations is that the community organization agency then has a built-in multiplier effect. Once programs are agreed upon they can be disseminated through a wide range of other organizations—the population that can be reached is greater. On the other hand, a constituency of organizations requires the agency to work through the problem of new and extreme programs with all constituent agencies. If the new program threatens the autonomy of the organizations or challenges *their* constituencies, there will be little incentive for commitment. Because of the desire to protect organizational autonomy, agencies made up of organizations are more likely to have a structure like a representative assembly, which permits veto powers, whereas agencies made up of individuals are more likely to have either straight majoritarian or oligarchic structures.[19]

The "everything else being equal" clause in this proposition is especially important. If the organizations have joined the community organization agency with the expectation that extreme programs would be proposed, then such an organization might be as likely as one made up of individuals to initiate rapidly new and extreme programs. Thus some community councils organized for neighborhood protection and development have grown out of organizations and still have initiated "radical" action programs.

TARGET GROUPS AND COMMUNITY ORGANIZATION PRACTICE

The purpose of the professional and his agency is to improve the "functioning" of groups, individuals, and communities. To do this he attempts to change individuals, the relations among individuals, and the relationships among groups. His goal may be reached not only by changing relationships and attitudes but also by changing the facilities—hospitals, schools, trading associations, etc.—through which people carry out their daily lives.

Thus he may be attempting to mobilize the community for a relatively specific substantive proposal, and the target group may be changed only insofar as it has reached a fairly specific decision. Values, norms, and social relations may not be changed, and only questions of efficiency may be involved. Differential diagnosis of target problems has important organizational implications. Let us examine two aspects of agency-target relations—the role definitions of line workers and the tactics of institutional penetration.

The problem can be posed as a question: Should line workers be specialists or multi-purpose workers coached by specialists? Should the worker be a technical expert, knowledgeable in the specific problems of the community, or should he be a generalist, knowledgeable about how to relate to communities?

The answer depends at least partly on the extent to which the target group accepts and is committed to the purposes of the agency. To the extent that an organization's goals are accepted and its functions in a community understood, a specialist organization can most efficiently communicate information and methods which can then be utilized by a target group. However, to the extent that members of a target group are suspicious of an agency, communication channels will be blocked. In such a situation a "multi-purpose" worker will be necessary. His main job will be to establish linkages between the organization and the target group. As these linkages are established, it becomes possible to reintroduce specialists, now trading on the multi-purpose workers' relations.[20]

But what of the qualifications of multi-purpose workers? Who should they be? To the extent that the target group is difficult to penetrate because of problems of distrust, and to the extent that major sanctions are not controlled by the organization, the most effective multi-purpose worker is likely to be one who minimizes social distance at the same time that he represents the "ego-ideal" of target group members. "Personalistic" as opposed to "professional" criteria become crucial. As many field workers have noted in working with lower-income ethnic groups and with delinquent gangs, and as Katz and Eisenstadt have suggested for Israeli administrative agencies, the overcoming of distrust may require the worker to appear to identify more with the problems and perspective of the target group than with the problems and programs of the agency. But as the level of distrust decreases, the target group becomes amenable to the norms and procedures of the agency, and more normal agency-client relations can be established. Thus, in order to be effective, community organization agencies must evaluate the extent to which target groups are receptive to their policies. Staff role definitions must be fitted to this diagnosis. Sometimes, however, community organization diagnosis involves the question of how to get specific decisions made, not of how to reach a group. A new set of practice questions emerges when the target question switches to that of penetrating institutional decision centers.

Many community organization workers and others who are trying to change communities seem to say, "If you want something done, you must get the power structure behind you." The power structure on the community level is seen as the heads of the largest firms, or, if absentee owned, the managers. If you want a new hospital built, if you want the city police to hire Negroes, if you want a fluoridation bill passed, if you want to eliminate "blockbusting," you are told to find the power structure. If community organizers followed this dictate, they would find themselves pursuing a chameleon. If they tried to mobilize the same elite on every decision, they would fail both to mobilize them and to attain their objectives.

Though some communities may have monolithic power structures, recent research suggests that these are more likely to be smaller cities. Moreover, some of the findings of a monolithic structure now appear to rest on methodological errors.

The power structure can be somewhat irrelevant, for many decisions come out of isolated and official decision centers, or are most sharply affected by the sentiments of a diffuse voting populace. Thus the job of analyzing decision centers requires the most precise diagnoses of the chain of influence and mechanisms of decisions.

If the decision involves a referendum, different kinds of issues appeal to different groups. Machiavellian advice to a community organizer interested in promoting school bonds is to keep the vote low, for a low vote means that the middle class will be overrepresented, and its members tend to vote for school funds. On the other hand, when, as in some states, referenda are held on welfare matters, the lower class should be gotten out, for its members tend to vote "yes" on welfare measures.[21] It appears that the best way to get a fluoridation issue defeated is to have it debated: it will be passed if the decision is made by a small closed group which meets in relative isolation and is relatively ignored by the community. The best way to lose a fluoridation vote is to get a lot of people interested and excited.[22]

In mobilizing a target group, the community organization practitioner and agency must squarely face the dilemma of his relative commitment to "the democratic process" versus his commitment to specific social values. The sample advice just given obviously conflicts with faith in the democratic process. This is a dilemma not only for community organization practitioners but for all advocates of social welfare. In part, however, the choice between pursuing specific goals regardless of the democratic ideal resolves itself according to agency goals and mandates. For instance, the more specific and concrete an organization's objectives, and the greater the demands on the organization by the constituency, the more likely the workers' concerns about the democratic process will be relegated to the background.

EXTERNAL RELATIONS

In mobilizing a target group, in reaching a specific objective, or in integrating services, community organization agencies must interact with other agencies. The community organization agency may be but one among many, and without a mandate to guide, direct, or lead the other agencies. Often a community organization agency has as part of its mandate the integration of the disparate agencies in the community, although sometimes the mandate is more formal than real.

One of the basic premises of organizational analysis is that only under very special conditions do organizations actually admit that they are ineffective, willingly give up turf, and purposefully attempt to reduce their size. These special conditions involve low ideological or career commitment to the organization on the part of staff, an increasingly difficult fund-raising problem, and a constituency that increasingly finds better alternative uses of time and money. As a working assumption, it is reasonable to assert that most organizations will attempt to maintain autonomy and increase their scope.[23] Even when it is obvious that one agency is better capable of achieving a shared goal than another, it would be rare indeed for the latter to donate its income for the expansion of the other agency. And it is rarely obvious that one agency performs much better than another.

Given the assumption that agencies generally wish to increase autonomy and scope, the integration and coordination of agency policies and programs depends on the enlightened self-interest of the independent agencies. Coordination, facilities sharing, and proper integration are likely to occur only when both of the autonomous agencies stand to "gain." Here are some specific conditions: [24]

1. If two agencies are competing with each other for funds, for constituency, and for staff, full-scale coordination and merger

of programs is unlikely. Given the nature of our funding processes, in which multiple appeals for money increase the total
amount of funds available for the welfare sector, a merger of
identities would not necessarily lead to a more effective welfare
economy.

2. The greater the marginal cost of coordination and integration, or the lower the marginal profit, the less chance of integration and coordination of programs. (Cost and profit are not
necessarily money costs and profits; there can be costs of time
and energy, for instance.) It follows that coordination will be
most easily achieved on problems which are least expensive
to both parties. Coordination is more easily achieved for a
specific problem than for overall organizational programs.

3. The greater the organizational commitment to a fixed program or style of operation, the less likely the coordination and
integration. An agency develops a commitment to a certain
program because it is compatible on ideological grounds and
because it helps the agency solve problems of identity. The
program then becomes part of the organizational character.[25]
To the extent that such a program must be changed by a
merger, costs increase.

Stated somewhat differently, some of these illustrations indicate the conditions that contribute to coordination, cooperation,
and integration.

1. The greater the symbiotic relation between agencies, the
more likely the coordination. For instance, in the area of juvenile delinquency the police and a street-worker agency have
more to gain from cooperating than a family service agency and
a street-worker agency. The street-worker agency can only occasionally contribute to aiding the family agency with its caseload; and at best, the casework agency can only help "cool
out a troublemaker." On the other hand, the police and the
street worker have a strong relation. The street worker gains
status with the gang by being able to negotiate with the "fuzz"
while the police get quieter streets. The same principle applies

to the relation of membership groups to the Y.M.C.A., or of mental hospitals to general hospitals.

2. The greater the marginal profits, the more likely the co-ordination. Sometimes funds are granted only to cooperating agencies. If the funds are large enough they offset the costs of integration or joint planning. Marginal profits of coordination occur when there is a crisis in facilities. When programs become overburdened, when facilities are inadequate and multiple expansion funds are not available, a negotiated settlement may allow specialization among agencies, reducing overall financial needs and creating a profit of coordination. Robert Morris has discussed cases where hospitals have benefitted from such marginal profits of coordination.[26]

Some evidence also suggests that overlapping constituencies contribute to coordination.[27] The less constituencies overlap, the more likely they are either to be neutral to or to distrust each other, and thus the more time it will take and the more difficult it will be to gain cooperation.

This last point suggests that external relations may also be related to the concepts we discussed earlier, that is, costs and profits are defined in the context of and affected by organizational constitutions and goals, constituency, and target groups.

SUMMARY AND CONCLUSIONS

We have discussed one part of a sociology of community organization practice—the organizational analysis of community organization agencies. A well-developed sociology of the field would also consider its emergence and growth, the operating social system, and the diagnosis of community problems and community structure.

Some concepts and propositions have been developed—in a quasi-political way—about the determinants of agency processes and problems and, consequently, the styles and problems of professional practice. Because it seemed to be the least de-

veloped area of analysis, the concept of organizational constitution has been most fully stated—it is the social contract of the
organization. The discussion concerned the relative autonomy
of organizations *vis-à-vis* their constituency and some dimensions of goals. Some consequences of varying characteristics
of the constituency—social class and organizational versus individual status—for agency operating problems were set forth.
The discussion of target groups focused on problems of staff
role definition and of diagnosing decision centers and the chain
of influence necessary to reach them. Finally, in regard to
external relations of agencies, the cost-benefit conditions of
coordination attempts have been specified.

Each section has presented several testable propositions about
the conditions under which different kinds of community organization agency problems and processes arise. But this essay
has not presented a complete analysis of community organization agencies because it has ignored the internal role structure
of agencies. There are not enough empirical studies of these
agencies to develop firm propositions. Nevertheless, analysis
along these lines will have a rich reward both for sociology
and for community organization practice. For sociology, studies
of sets of organizations will allow us to examine problems of
mobilizing support and community consensus; for community
organization, we can use an analytic and differential basis to as-
sess community organization agencies and evaluate practice roles.

Notes

1. Chicago, 1963.
2. Murray G. Ross, *Community Organization: Theory and Principles*,
New York, 1955.
3. Ronald Lippitt, Jeanne Watson, and Bruce Westley, *The Dynamics of
Planned Change: A Comparative Study of Principles and Techniques*, New
York, 1958.
4. For work utilizing the perspective, see Philip Selznick, *T.V.A. and the
Grass Roots*, Berkeley, 1949; *Leadership in Administration*, New York,

1957; and *The Organizational Weapon*, Rand Corporation, 1952. See also Burton Clark, *The Open Door College*, New York, 1960, and Charles Perrow, "The Analysis of Goals in Complex Organizations," *American Sociological Review*, XXVI, No. 6 (1961), 854-866. David L. Sills, *The Volunteers*, Glencoe, 1957; Martin Rein and Robert Morris, "Goals, Structures and Strategies for Community Change," *Social Work Practice*, 1962, National Conference on Social Welfare, pp. 127-145; and Robert D. Vinter and Morris Janowitz, "Effective Institutions for Juvenile Delinquents: A Research Statement," *Social Service Review*, XXXIII (1959), 118-130.

5. Using political metaphors leads us away from traditional concepts of organizational structure. Although it would be possible to consider some of the usual concepts such as staff-line, hierarchy, etc., these are of lesser importance for our analysis. First, since community organization agencies usually control few incentives, organizational structure is less a function of the rational (efficient adaptation of technology to goals) and more a function of the constituency and constitution of the organization. Second, these are usually small organizations with little internal specialization—either by departmentalization, professionalization, or technology. Thus the standard analysis of intra-organizational relations—departmental competition, lateral and vertical communication, staff-line conflicts, and the like—are of lesser importance for community organizations than for other organizations. Third, social psychological questions about commitment often are more important to the analysis of community organization agencies than structural questions about hierarchy and authority.

6. Not much attention has been paid to organizational constitutions by sociologists, because they often work in organizations whose constitutions are not problematic. First, they work with organizations with relatively clearly defined goals. Second, they work with organizations in which the participants are paid money, insuring at least a minimal commitment to the organization and giving the executives control of the constitution. Third, they work in organizations in which the means of the organization are dictated by technology—that is, there are clear dictates as to means, to behaviors necessary to achieve goals. To the extent that any one of these conditions is not met or is under question—incentives to commitment, ambiguity of means, agreement and specificity of goals—the constitution becomes subject to debate and, as changes occur, commitment to the organization is subject to change. E. Wright Bakke uses a conception of constitution or "charter" which is even broader than ours but has the same intent. See his *Bonds of Organization: An Appraisal of Corporate Human Relations*, New York, 1950, especially Chapter VI, "Organizational Charter," pp. 152-179.

7. See Mayer N. Zald, "Comparative Analysis and Measurement of Organizational Goals: The Case of Correctional Institutions for Delinquents," *Sociological Quarterly* (Fall 1963), pp. 206-230.

8. See his unpublished Ph.D. dissertation, *The Chicago Big Businessman as Civic Leader*, University of Chicago, 1959.

9. On the succession of goals in organizations, see David L. Sills, pp. 146-158, in A. Etzioni, ed., *Complex Organizations*, New York, 1954. See also Mayer N. Zald and Patricia Denton, "From Evangelism to General Service: On the Transformation of the Y.M.C.A.," *Administrative Science Quarterly*, VIII, No. 2 (1963), 214-234.

10. For one treatment of the problem of organizational autonomy see Charles Perrow, "Organizational Prestige: Some Functions and Dysfunctions," *American Journal of Sociology*, LXVI (1961), 854-866. See also Selznick, "Leadership in Administration," *op. cit.*, pp. 120-133.

11. Note that the proposition does not apply to the formal or stated charter of the organization alone, but rather to the expectations that develop out of the actual dependency bases of the organization. The point is important, for many organizations (notably business corporations) formally "decentralize" and on paper sometimes resemble what are called "federated" systems. Yet through the judicious—and sometimes injudicious —use of central power these corporations never really build a constitution of federalism.

12. See Rein and Morris, *loc. cit.*, and Sills, *loc. cit.*

13. It should be clear, however, that there is an analytic difference between a target group and a constituency. A target group or institution is the change object of the organization. The target group is not directly involved in the choosing of the means, the personnel, or the goals of the agency. Target groups become part of the constituency when they become part of the decision-making apparatus of the agency.

14. In *Comparative Studies in Administration*, ed. by James D. Thompson, Peter B. Hammond, Robert W. Hawkes, Buford H. Junker, and Arthur Tuden, Pittsburgh, 1959, pp. 195-216.

15. For a careful summary of much of this literature and an attempt to understand the dynamics of the phenomena, see William Erbe, "Social Involvement and Political Activity," *American Sociological Review*, XXIX, No. 2 (April 1964), 198-215.

16. See the discussion in Herbert Gans, *The Urban Villagers*, New York, 1962, especially Chapter V, "The Community," pp. 104-120. The necessity of active and direct modes of expression in the appeal to lower socio-economic groups is one of the essential elements in Saul Alinsky's approach to community organization.

17. Catherine Richards and Norman Polansky have shown that, among adult women, those who participated in organizations as adolescents and whose parents also participated were more likely to participate in voluntary associations than those who did not have either of these characteristics in their background. The overall rate of parent and adolescent participation is, of course, directly related to socio-economic status. See their "Reaching Working Class Youth Leaders," *Social Work*, IV, No. 4 (October 1959), 31-39.

18. I have less confidence in this proposition than I do in the previous one. For one thing, it may cause us to compare unlikes—for instance, neighborhood block clubs with welfare councils. Ideally, to test such a

proposition we would take community organization agencies in similar types of communities with similar types of goals and see if variation in their constituencies did in fact lead to different types of action programs. Such a design might be difficult to realize.

19. See Rein and Morris, *op. cit.*, for a discussion of the problems of agencies whose constituencies are made up of organizations.

20. Cf. Albert Mayer and associates, in collaboration with McKim Marriott, and Richard Park, *Pilot Project India: The Story of Rural Development in Etawah, Uttar Pradesh*, Berkeley, 1958. See also Elihu Katz and S. N. Eistenstadt, "Some Sociological Observations on the Response of Israeli Organizations to New Immigrants," *Administrative Science Quarterly* (1960), pp. 113-133, Herbert Gans, *op. cit.*, Chapter 7, "The Caretakers: Missionaries from the Outside World," pp. 142-162, and Eugene Litwak and Henry J. Meyer, "A Balance Theory of Coordination Between Bureaucratic Organizations and Community Primary Groups," *Administrative Science Quarterly*, XI, No. 1 (June 1966), 35-39.

21. For a study that looks at the relation of income and ethnicity to "public" and "self"-interest voting on referenda, see James Q. Wilson and Edward C. Banfield, "Public Regardingness as a Value Premise in Voting Behavior," *American Political Science Review*, LVIII, No. 4 (1964), 876-887.

22. See Maurice Pinard, "Structural Attachments and Political Support in Urban Politics: The Case of Fluoridation Referendums," *American Journal of Sociology*, LXVIII, No. 5 (1963), 513-526. See also William A. Gamson, "Community Issues and Their Outcomes: How to Lose a Fluoridation Referendum," pp. 350-357 in Alvin W. Gouldner and S. M. Miller, ed., *Applied Sociology: Opportunities and Problems*, New York, 1964. Pinard argues that higher turnouts lead to more defeats, while Gamson argues that the social process must also be taken into account in understanding defeats of fluoridation proposals.

23. Aside from the Perrow article cited earlier, see also the paper by Norton Long, "The Local Community as an Ecology of Games," *American Journal of Sociology*, LXIV (1958), 251-261.

24. Our discussion draws on the following set of articles which have recently discussed problems of coordination and inter-organizational relations: William Reid, "Interagency Coordination in Delinquency Prevention and Control," *Social Service Review*, December 1964; Eugene Litwak and Lydia Hylton, "Inter-Organizational Analysis: A Hypothesis on Coordinating Agencies," *Administrative Science Quarterly*, March 1962; Sol Levine and Paul E. White, "Exchange as a Conceptual Framework for the Study of Inter-Organizational Relationships," *Administrative Science Quarterly*, March 1961.

25. On the concept of organizational character, see Philip Selznick, *Leadership in Administration*, New York, 1957.

26. See Robert Morris, "New Concepts in Community Organization Practice," *The Social Welfare Forum*, New York, 1961, pp. 128-146.

27. *Ibid.*

David Street
Public Education and Social Welfare in the Metropolis

Introduction

In 1931 W. I. Thomas stated what we can now consider a classic sociological critique of the schools of the metropolis:

An organic connection with a larger community is necessary to the maintenance of moral standards and fine sentiments. If we look, therefore . . . for a social agency whose influence may penetrate the family we find it in the school. The school is not a natural organization like the family, but an artificial organization capable of rapid changes and adjustments. In this respect it has almost the freedom of a scientific laboratory. It receives all children early and keeps them a relatively long time. Its function is the setting and solving of problems and the communication of information. Its representatives are far superior to the average parent in intelligence and understanding. If we invented any device to replace social influences lacking at other points it would be the school. It is probable that the school could be a sort of community forming the background of the family and the child and could supply the elements lacking in the home, at least to the degree of preventing in large measure delinquency and crime, if it exercised all the influence it could conceivably exercise, and that it could, more than any other agency, socialize the family.[1]

Thomas goes on to extol the virtues of the then-promising visiting teachers movement, but then he expresses his sociological reservations about the school:

But while in the present condition of society there is no point at which the prevention of delinquency and the socialization of the family can be undertaken so successfully as in the school, the school itself has very grave defects of character, and the question of its adaptation to the welfare of the child involves at the same time the question of change and reform in the school itself. Many educators will agree that if we attempt to measure the influence of the school with reference to its efficiency as a factor in personality development we are confronted at once with the following conditions:

1. The average school, like the old community, works on the assumption of uniformity of personality and presents the same materials and plans in the same order to all. The assumption is that children react in the same way to the same influences regardless of their personal traits or their social past, and that it is therefore possible to provoke identical behavior by identical means. "Nature," says Dr. Jennings, "has expended all her energy in making our little flock of children as diverse as she possibly can; in concealing within it unlimited possibilities which no one can define or predict. It sometimes seems as if we parents in our process of educating them were attempting to root out all of these diversities, to reduce our flock of children to a uniform mass. . . . The only way in which appreciable progress can be made in the attempt is by cutting off, stunting, preventing the development of the special and distinctive qualities of the individuals. Un-

fortunately, this can be done to a certain extent, but only by a process which may rightly be compared with the taking of human life."

2. The creative or plan-forming interest of the child is an expression of the phase of new experiences which is based on curiosity and appears very early in the child. The child expresses his energy and secures his recognition, favorable or unfavorable, mainly along this line. Response and security do not mean so much to him yet. The fact that the school work is detached from activity and not related to the plan-forming and creative faculty explains its failure to interest the child. An investigator took five hundred children out of twenty factories in Chicago and asked them this question: "If your father had a good job and you did not have to work, which would you rather do, go to school or work in a factory?" Of the five hundred children, between the ages of fourteen and sixteen, 412 said they would rather work in a factory . . .

3. There is therefore a question whether as a device for plan-forming by presenting the right material and definitions at the right moment, the school is not inferior to the world at large, at least when its influences are protracted. The school presents indispensable information, a technique for handling problems, such as reading, writing, and ciphering, and presents the solution of the innumerable problems which are already solved and which it is unnecessary to solve again. But the school works injuriously on personality development and creative tendencies. By presenting the whole body of cultural values in a planless way, planless so far as schemes of personal development are concerned, it tends to thwart and delay the expression of the plan-making tendency of children until physiological maturity approaches and the energetic, plan-forming creative period is passed. . . . In measuring the influence of the school we must recognize two types

of success in the adaptation of the individual to life, the one based on his assertion and realization of wide and original claims, the other on contentment with limited claims. If he is contented with claims which are more limited than his powers justify, his adaptation is success through relative failure. To the degree that the school treats children as identical it produces a maximum number of relative failures. To some extent the genius is regarded as a prodigy because so much spontaneity is repressed by the school.

4. Clinicians and case workers who handle successfully difficult children taken from the schools report that the schools tend to accentuate rather than obviate the difficult features. Some of them feel that where unsocial and neurotic tendencies have begun to appear through bad family conditions the school is an additional influence for evil to be overcome. . . . It is desirable that the school should eventually supersede the juvenile court and replace other welfare agencies concerned with the child, but in adapting itself to this task and to the task of general education it will be compelled to make provisions for the development of the emotional and social life of the child as well as the information. . . .[2]

Thomas' analysis of the bureaucracy of the school is incisive and eloquent, as is his statement of hopes for the school. These themes were not unique, however. Ever since the school began to serve the children of the urban working classes, it has been both praised as the key instrument for socialization to American culture and blamed as a rigid institution unwilling or unable to attend to the human problems of its individual pupils. "Do-gooders" without and reformers within education have forever pressed for a broadening of the goals of education, for a greater outreach toward the psychological and social problems of the child, his family, and the community.

These demands have never been greater than they are today. A set of familiar problems conspire to produce a crisis in public education in the large cities. Just how unprecedented this crisis may be need not be argued here; it is grossly overstated in the popular image of the blackboard jungle, but it is real and serious. The crisis is in part a result of the fact that in the last decade and a half there have been tremendous increases in the school populations of the large cities and great changes in the racial and, to some extent, the socio-economic composition of these populations.[3] The typical pattern of the big cities has been an overcrowding of schools and concentration of poorer Negro or Puerto Rican populations in the older, central neighborhoods, where the older school buildings are located; an imposition of higher age minimums for leaving school, which threatens the schools with assuming a more custodial role; a decline in academic performance in the areas undergoing change; a demoralization of staff and the movement of teachers who have seniority to outlying areas; an increase in the difficulty of recruiting new staff into the changing neighborhoods; and the development of frantic efforts to build new schools and otherwise redress inequalities for these changed populations.[4] A related aspect of the crisis is economic. Increases in the school population and in the educational needs of deprived groups have not been accompanied by increases in resources and, in some cases, have gone hand in hand with an absolute loss in resource base because of urban clearance and the outmovement of industry, business, and middle-income residents.

The crisis is also political and moral. The rising tide of militant demands for equality, for compensatory action, and for racial integration has challenged the basic operating philosophies of the schools. Sometimes it also has generated substantial white backlash. In many cases the result has been conflict and polarization within the community and the school board, polemic and recrimination, protests, stalemate, and a situation in which it is difficult or even impossible to mobilize community consensus to pass needed school referenda. Caught in the middle have been the school boards and school administrators.[5]

To a significant degree the crises relate to the issues involved in broadening the goals of education in the inner city. Objectively, despite the glaring educational problems of the metropolis, the schools may be doing roughly as well or better than ever before, as measured by such indices as drop-out rates. But in the society as a whole there has been a revolution of rising expectations about social justice and what is to be accomplished, not only for Negroes but for all groups that do not share adequately in the general rise in affluence and rectitude. Under this revolution the school system is seen not only as the institution which principally must make up for all deficiencies in education, but also as a strategic social agency in alleviating poverty, reducing delinquency, integrating a segregated community, and correcting other social ills. In part, these expectations turn upon the school system because it is so visible—so much more amenable to attack and demands for reform than diffuse institutions such as property rights and usages. Of course, the demand that the schools become much more effective in their strictly educational task has a great deal of realism. The upgrading of skill or educational requirements for participation in most parts of the labor force, especially in the face of the uncertainties of automation, increasingly means that in American society the undereducated will become the permanently unemployed. The fact that children in the ghetto are academically several years retarded at the time of their entry to high school can no longer be tolerated.

The broader demands made upon the big city schools, whatever their merits, provoke even further turmoil. As never before, the schools are called upon to humanize, to "open up," to coordinate with, to become the "cutting edge." Robert Havighurst has expressed the demand dramatically in his call for the schools Yet Havighurst recently has written a paper indicating that the to become the major instrument of "social urban renewal."[6]

schools in at least one large city, Chicago, are less, not more, involved in the social welfare business now than they were decades ago.[7]

This essay is policy-oriented and partially speculative. It is my contention that many of the current demands made upon large city school systems, particularly those which seek to use the schools as the major instrument for the solution of urban social problems, are unrealistic. These demands reiterate the American tendency to prescribe "education" for all ills. The demands are unrealistic in that they ignore the character of the school system as a complex organization, or ignore the actions necessary to produce a change in organizational character sufficient to address these demands.

The empirical basis of this essay is a study of the organization of the Chicago public school system, augmented by observations in several other large cities.[8] Many of the observations have focused on various experimental efforts located in the schools of disadvantaged children in the urban ghetto. In many respects these observations stimulate an inductive pessimism about the potentialities for greatly expanding the social welfare component of the large city schools, no matter how promising the innovations are for education itself. One does see slum schools where, with or without foundation support, dedicated staff members have labored hard to rejuvenate the curriculum, to produce materials more appropriate to the children, to introduce team-teaching or non-grading, or to broaden the cultural horizons of the child. The observer finds exciting models under development, as, for example, in Chicago where the teachers at Doolittle School have worked hard to conceive of what really must be done to help the slum child develop self-esteem, and where a flexible work-study program for drop-outs seems to produce good results; or in Detroit and Philadelphia, where there are exciting ventures in restructuring school-community relations. The visitor sees that experiments previously tried only in the Scarsdales of our land can work in the slums, too.

Positively, these efforts have stimulated and reflected a great improvement in the educators' understanding of the educational problems of these children. It has come to be understood that these boys and girls do not meet the ordinary assumptions and expectations of the school, and the educators have come more fully to believe that educational retardation is not the child's or his family's fault alone. Although the educators see that the life of poverty, discrimination, the ghetto and the slums, the transplantation from the rural South to the urban North, and the experience of growing up in a household without books all take their toll, it is also recognized that the "middle-class" character of the school itself can be deleterious. It is "middle-class" in that the school—its texts, its curriculum, its graded organization—is geared to conventional techniques and conventional standards for the conventional children who are to come with the language skills, motivation, demeanor, and general cultural preparation that are generally assumed by the school. The educators have come to understand that the disadvantaged students pile up in the lower tracks of an academically oriented system in which, from the beginning, they cannot compete. Most importantly, the schoolmen have begun to view the task of bridging the gap between the "have" and "have-not" schools not only as one of helping the youths make up for their deficiencies but also as one of revising the format of the school so that it will be more appropriate to the childrens' needs.

Significant as these efforts have been for the educators' thinking about the problem and as models for future action, they do not provide a solution. The large city school systems continue to react to current crises with essentially piecemeal and ephemeral reform. This is a time of great innovation but very little change. There is a proliferation of projects,[9] but the many projects reach only small proportions of the children they aim to help. Most of these efforts are quite small-scale, and many last only a few months or years. Schools two blocks from the experiment may be untouched. The new ideas may pass on when the grant runs out, when the principal moves to another school, or when the key teacher retires. Often the new practices suffer death by incorporation: they are so successful that they are "phased out" to other schools or to the whole system, where they may operate without the special resources or careful understanding involved in the original effort, or where they may become "standard operating procedures" embodied only in aging memoranda. Often the innovations are applied mechanically, as when new monies are used only to lengthen the standard school day, and often the character and results of new practices are so poorly researched that no one can find what has (or has not) been done or accomplished. In general, the schoolmen operate under the implicit notion that change comes about additively, on the basis of numbers of projects, and give little serious consideration to how to cross thresholds or produce multiplier effects. There are few ways to communicate and aggregate piecemeal innovations to make them part of the system.

The difficulties of innovating in the schools are most glaring when the change requires developing cooperative arrangements with other agencies in the metropolis. In part, this problem simply reflects the general governmental chaos of the city, as when brand new schools must be torn down to make way for expressways or urban renewal. But it also reflects the educators' special defensiveness and attention to keeping the boundaries of the school system impermeable. This can be seen clearly in the great difficulties which developed in New York, Chicago, and other cities when federally sponsored juvenile delinquency projects sought to involve both schools and social welfare agencies in joint planning and operations. In many cases these negotiations turned into notorious political fiascos in which the schools in the end simply refused to give up any autonomy in the interests of cooperation with social workers and other outsiders.

The Organizational Character of the Large City Schools

The difficulties in adapting the schools to broader goals, special populations, and cooperation with other agencies are not isolated instances of failure. They reflect some profound constraints built into the organizational character of the large city school system. By "character," a term elaborated for organizational analysis by Philip Selznick,[10] I refer to the distinctive sets of commitments, predispositions, capacities, and incapacities possessed by a given organizational type. The specific question here is what is the school system's capacity for change to meet altered conditions expectations, and demands? To understand the school system's character, we must look more carefully at its goals, particularly as these are changing and are affected by the organization's interrelations with its environment. We also must look at a number of constraints which are built into the organization: a circumscription of activities by legal, quasi-legal, and traditionalist criteria, an inflexible commitment to universalism in both ideology and operations, weaknesses in organizational control mechanisms, the limiting characteristics of personnel, rigidities in the division of labor, deficiencies in the relationship between the local school and its immediate community, and inadequacies in research and development operations.

ORGANIZATIONAL GOALS AND ENVIRONMENT

The schools of the large cities show in exaggerated form what many analysts have seen as the central organizational problem of education: the difficulty in settling on goals given the ambiguity of the term "to educate," the multiple constructions placed upon it, and the lack of consensus about it found both within and without the schools. All school systems face a conflict between those who define the organization's task narrowly in terms of specified amounts of subject matter and those who define it broadly as the production of intellectual, moral, religious, social, and emotional growth. On various sides, groups cry for greater emphasis on patriotism and the evils of communism, alcohol, nicotine, sex, and the United Nations, or for new programs of vocational training, advanced technical training for the post-Sputnik era, more psychological counseling, a renewed emphasis upon the three R's or the teaching of moral habits, more driver education, and so on. Not only is there considerable doubt and dispute about what the goals and priorities for resource allocation should be, but even given a set of goals, there is great difficulty in deciding whether or not the school is meeting them. Like other organizations that work on people rather than material objects, the schools face great difficulty in establishing objective measures of success. It is theoretically possible to find high consensus on the goals and means of the school, and this can be seen in some small and homogeneous communities. Ordinarily, however, a great deal of board and administrative effort must be directed toward mediating among conflicting definitions of goals and technologies and toward achieving some kind of viable definition of the organization's task adequate to conduct on-going operations. For the educators, this problem is not made much easier by the existence of other than traditional educational philosophies; progressivism, whatever its virtues, obscures the limits of educational goals even further by saying, in effect, that everything is education.

In the schools of the large city, the task of settling on goals has always been especially difficult because of the heterogeneity of the pupils and of the groups that provide support and make claims upon the schools. In the United States an important aspect of the definition of the goals of public education has been that education is to be provided not for an elite but for all. Presumably this commitment was made once and for all in the victory of the "common school" movement over the separatist, European-style "Latin Grammar School." But the real test of the common school in the big cities may be developing only now. In decades past, not enough members of the middle classes (except those using parochial schools) withdrew their children and put them in private schools to embarrass the idea of the democratized school, while not enough members of the lower classes stayed in school long enough to raise serious questions about their curricular needs. The schools could provide a pre-academic training from which lower-class youths would presumably derive some benefit until the nearly inevitable day when, except in unusual cases, they would drop out.

Since World War I, however, the mass high school has developed into a reality, and compulsory school attendance laws plus the relative drying up of youth employment opportunities have insured that the high schools will be brimming with students in at least the freshman and sophomore classes. High school graduation rates have risen greatly, and for several decades the high school diploma—whatever its validity as an index of learning—has served as a useful aid to the employability and mobility of working-class youth. With the general rise in education, college enrollment has become an object for an increasing number of these graduates. The new relevance of college admission and performance standards has turned attention toward the *quality* of the secondary training received by working-class youth, a smaller consideration when the high school diploma was the final product.

Thus the schools are faced with an increase in the disparity of the cultural levels of the groups that will be with them the full twelve years, and with a diversification and strengthening of expectations for performance. Especially significant is the impact on school goals of the growth of the civil rights movement and its focus on public education. Yet, while the requirements of Negroes and the lower classes must be taken more fully into account, it is not at all clear whether the increase and redirection of resources this requires (much less school integration) can be reconciled with the continuing and upgraded demands placed on the school system by the remaining middle-class and white groups.

Emerging federal programs promise to provide new resources conditional in large part on the school systems' commitment to enlarging programs for their deprived populations. In the long run this development, with other national movements (for example, the emergence of high-prestige curriculum revision groups), may dramatically alter the resources and goals of the schools. But at present the schools remain in a stressful situation: they are still basically tied to local constituencies and resource bases and to the fluctuating characteristics of this environment; federal, state, and local resources remain inadequate to the heightened demands; and the schools often must operate in a situation of political stalemate, one that is increasingly racial. Further, the schools still must submit to periodic local referenda. At the extreme, in Detroit, a third of the standard operating budget must be voted upon at each school election. A few years ago the Detroit schools lost one of these plebiscites when both civil rights and anti-Negro groups protested against the system's integration policies. Three grade levels had to be put on half-day sessions until a new referendum could be held.

Divisions in the community tend to be reflected in divisions among the members of the school board. Techniques for selecting board members vary from city to city, but in general either electoral or appointive procedures generate a board loosely representative of major and often polarized elements of the community: business, labor, professions, and major ethnic and religious groups. Outside the large cities, the schools have often allied themselves with business and professional interests as a means of gaining political support. In the metropolis, the tempting alliance has been with the dominant political organization. Yet this alliance time and again has brought cries of favoritism in hiring and promotion, of graft in building programs, and of general corruption, and has resulted in cycles of reform. Despite the ups and downs, the secular trend is toward nonpartisanship (which probably has the usual effect of limiting the rising influence of working-class groups) except as *sub rosa* connections are made for mobilizing support at times of crisis or bond issue.

It is in these contexts that the definition of the school system as the strategic organization for producing desired changes which would eliminate poverty, ignorance, delinquency, segregation, and prejudice provokes further crisis. While the clamor goes up for the schools to articulate with the "Great Society" and the poverty program, to employ social work and psychological services on a large scale, or to engage in large-scale social planning, the educators honestly but uncertainly complain that these roles "are not part of education."

The schoolmen are not powerless, of course. Their ideological commitment to lay control of education prescribes considerable professional "guidance"; and on the majority of school decisions their control of information, their technical knowledge, and their appeals to conventional or "good" practice are paid deference by the school board. Further, they can mobilize a variety of pressure groups—PTA's, Mother's Clubs, *ad hoc* groups, and so on—for action. On such issues as integration, however, the schoolmen have no more marketable claims to professional expertise than does anyone else, nor do they have an ideology conducive to exercising leadership in this area. This is indicated in a recent study of civil rights protest and public school integration policies in eight northern cities. In most of the cities the superintendents initially took a very negative stand against civil rights demands. In all eight cities, following various protest demonstrations, the superintendents then found themselves moved out of the forefront by the decision-making activities of the school boards.[11]

Obviously, the schools are undergoing some broadening of goals. The character of the change and the eventual outcome are unclear, but some of the terms of change can be suggested: "color-blind" versus bi-racial; equalitarian or open opportunity

versus compensatory opportunity; the "four walls" school versus
the "open doors" school; the schoolhouse versus the settlement
house; academic emphases versus social-intellectual emphases;
and "school-keeping" versus "problem-solving" education. For
the time being, the professional educators react in a conservative
way, falling back on the traditional definitions of competent
school administration as "sound planning," good buildings, and
"professional" staffing. In some cities, especially Chicago, the
professionals' reaction has been quite defensive. Such reactions
are partially understandable, however, by virtue of the fact that
the professional group has had to bear so much external hostility
in recent years. Behind the conservative reactions has been a
search for new ideologies and formats for reconciling traditional
operations with the new demands. Among the many problems
is whether staff members brought up through traditional operations are capable of handling programs addressed to new goals.

INTERNAL CONSTRAINTS

Some basic characteristics of the structure and culture of the
large city school system set further limits on its present adaptability to new demands. In many respects these characteristics
induce the kind of bureaucratic rigidity at which Thomas, in
the quotation opening this essay, was hinting. These constraints
include the following:

1. *Legal, quasi-legal, and traditional bases of operation.* While
the goals of the school system are fluid and subject to controversy, actual conflict over goals occurs principally at the mar-
gins of organizational effort and in periodic fits and spurts about
particular programs or policies. On a day-to-day basis these
organizations operate in a highly routinized way. Students
pledge allegiance, do push-ups, take exactly two courses in
history and three in English (or exactly four in English, two
in history, and one in physics), memorize the Preamble to the
Constitution, the distance to the moon, or the number of feet

in a mile, and go out for basketball or band with little questioning. Practices involving curricula, programing, and allocation of personnel largely proceed on traditional bases. And in the principal's office and classroom, the model of obedience to headmaster and teacher is usually questioned only in the breach.

In part, traditionalism and rigidity come from a plethora of statutory, quasi-legal, and professional restrictions built up externally over the years. The setting of minimum legal standards necessary to keep the schools honest, to integrate local educational programs with other local, regional, and national systems of education, and to force or induce laggard school districts to improve programs has produced tremendous limits upon flexible operations. These limits include, for example, the 180-day school year for paying state aid and regulations about what courses are to be taught. Schools are also constrained toward standardization by the activities of regional and national accrediting associations, textbook and test publishers, and college admissions officers.

These activities tend to reinforce the organization of education around an inflexible system of grade levels and units, a system presupposing that students will learn similar amounts in similar times. With very heterogeneous student bodies, such a system cannot operate without developing elaborate systems of homogenous grouping and more or less formal track systems. Often these systems rigidify the school further: they tend to have a self-fulfilling character in terms of what they do to the students. Attempts made to guarantee mobility between groups or tracks often fail.

Concern with revision of the basic premises of the system is diverted by the legal provisions under which school boards must make decisions. These provisions ordinarily place on the board members responsibility for passing on the most minute aspects of school operations—with the result, Joseph Pois argues, that attention is diverted away from major policy questions.[12] These provisions divert the administrators in the same ways. My observations indicate that adaptiveness often requires and receives actions in opposition to bureaucratic regulations. For example, in Chicago many administrators have been "flexible" in their administration of school attendance rules because of their insight into the problems caused for the child when residential moves require school change during the academic year. But it took a careful study by our project, documenting the negative effects of frequent school changes and showing that many residential changes requiring school changes were of only very short distances, before the question of officially changing the rules could be broached at the top administrative level. In New York City one of the guiding motifs of good school administration is to "fight 110 Livingston Street," the central headquarters. As some principals explained to me, the only way to get their jobs done is to fake requisition slips and other forms.

2. *The commitment to universalism.* The large city schools are highly committed to the universalistic treatment of students, personnel, and neighborhoods. This commitment has constituted a significant advance in freeing education from the pressures of politics, ethnic groups, and special interest groups. It has come largely as an attempt to "clean up" the schools in various periods of scandal. Universalism has become a major ideological theme of the schoolmen and board members, and it has become embodied in a variety of day-to-day operating practices. Equality of treatment of different populations has been far from fulfilled,[13] but in the big city schools, especially since the great reduction in racial gerrymandering of attendance areas in the last few years, it is a profound theme. The importance of this theme has been clearly shown in the defensiveness of the typical schoolman's response to civil rights demands. This response is understandable in that the demands give the lie to the assumption of equality and begin to challenge the notion that equality itself is morally adequate. These civil rights changes have brought the counter-response that racial demands are themselves a case of special pleading.

Beyond the issue of whether the commitment to universalism disables the schools in developing adequate compensatory programs, one can see that universalistic practices constrain the schools in a number of other ways. First, most large city school systems have been left with unwieldy practices of teacher recruitment, placement, transfer, and promotion. These practices are highly dependent on rank-order placement on various kinds of written and oral tests, on graduate training received, on seniority, and on the detailed fulfillment of various bureaucratic procedures. At its extreme, in New York City, over a thousand different types of tests and certificates are given for supposedly different types of teaching positions. Universalistically, seniority and amount of graduate education received become almost the only legitimate bases for allocating rewards. Except for the few who can aspire to administrative position, rewards are little differentiated, limited principally to standard movements in income and, frequently, opportunity to move to schools in "better" neighborhoods.[14] Movements to develop less ascriptive and arbitrary standards for judging and allocating personnel are resisted, as are efforts to attract teachers to the more difficult schools by providing them with higher pay.

Second, universalism is expressed among neighborhoods in administrative formulas which set specific numerical ratios of pupils to teachers to principals to specialists, thereby greatly restricting the school system's flexibilty in adapting to special needs. Given the great difficulties in recruiting enough teachers to the difficult schools, the administrator's frequent question, "Have we got enough bodies in that school?" becomes understandable. Universalism also is expressed in the standardized curriculum, which allocates particular courses, texts, and other materials to each school in identical fashion, or in a fashion varied again usually only on standardized criteria—test scores showing the presumed merit (or, as compensatory education becomes more fashionable, demerit or social disorganization) of the student body.

3. *The inadequacies of control mechanisms.* The schools are over-centralized in the sense that universalistic practices, the standardized curriculum, and the conduct of programs of school-community relations from the central office and board result in obvious difficulties in adapting to the different problems of varying neighborhoods. Further, attempts to introduce decentralization formally—through, for example, the creation of subdistricts having their own superintendents, as in Chicago— have not met the problem because few resources and little fiscal and administrative autonomy have actually been given to the decentralized personnel. In part, these difficulties reflect a tendency to bifurcation in the perceptions of "educational" and "administrative" decisions. In Chicago the local area superintendent is to "run his own district," but control over budget, staffing, and so on is still kept downtown.

The schools are also under-centralized, in the sense that it is difficult for decisions made at the top of the organization to be activated lower in the organization. Efforts at decentralization and the creation of specific operations often create fragmentation, as in New York City, where there is a proliferation of un-coordinated bureaus and projects. There are few control mechanisms which could promote changed behavior on the part of operating personnel. In any organization staffed primarily by persons presumed to be professionals, one would expect direct supervision to be less important than prior training and processes of persuasion, manipulation of rewards, and continuing professional socialization as means to control behavior. This is precisely the case in the schools, where, especially at the level of the relationship between the principal and the fully certified or tenured teacher, real supervision is considered inappropriate except for those teachers presenting exceptional behavior problems.[15]

The alternative control mechanisms are also weak, however. With rewards tending to be ascriptive, persuasion usually is limited to generalized exhortation. And socialization generally is given over to external units—schools of education usually little oriented to the problems of the large cities or to a confrontation of the issues involved in shifting to new goals. This applies both to socialization received prior to taking the teaching position and graduate education pursued while a teacher or an administrator. In sharp contrast to, for example, the military, where officers spend over a quarter of their careers in in-service training, the schools tend to depend on outside agencies for voluntary re-tooling and limit their in-service efforts to short-term and occasional workshops.

The comparative lack of in-service socialization procedures seems especially important in the schools because teachers, as contrasted to most other professionals, operate mainly as "solo practitioners," with little on-the-job lateral communication and few peer supports. Such collegial communication could provide the opportunity not only for needed respite but also for "carrying the news" of innovations from one teacher or classroom to another. This may be one reason why professional commitment seems to be relatively low in education—especially in the large cities, where, because of dispersed living patterns, off-the-job contact cannot be relied upon to provide professional contacts and to build morale. Yet intensive in-service training might be crucial for the kinds of changes in teacher attitudes and behavior necessary if the schools are really to broaden their goals.[16]

The problems of organizational control over teachers' behavior find many parallels, and very crucial ones, at the middle level of administrators and principals. Again, the school system relies primarily on external activities—work on graduate degrees in education—for socialization, and again lateral communication tends to be low. Supervision of principals is often a dilemma. Many systems suffer from the fact that principalships are more or less permanent, allowing personnel to become entrenched. Other systems rely on a fluid system of movement and reward by frequent promotion, which reduces familiarity with the neighborhood and may induce a hyperconformity. All systems also rely on a stream of rules and orders from the central office, conformity to which may substantially reduce long-run capacity for performance.

4. *Characteristics of personnel.* One reason that the underdevelopment of in-service training seems to be a crucial deficiency is that the general characteristics of the personnel are limiting. The available labor pool for qualified teachers has become limited in most of the large cities, in part because of financial and social limitations in competing with other communities, and because of the opening of other opportunities for groups which previously furnished most of the teachers. Persons recruited to the teaching profession often are women who are primarily committed to their own roles as wives and mothers. Male recruits often have outside commitments too, for they frequently must "moonlight" on the side to support their families. Recruits are often marginal members of the middle class, perhaps insecure in their positions and clearly largely conventional in their attitudes. Even young teachers raised in the inner city may have quite hostile attitudes toward teaching in its problem schools.[17] Further, the teacher population changes slowly: most big city school systems have a teacher turnover rate of only about 15 percent per year, and this mainly at the younger levels. In one large city the median age of teachers is reported to be over fifty. In many ways the rise of militant teacher unionism in the large cities in recent years, whatever its positive outcomes for employee salary, self-respect, and morale, threatens to further restrict flexibility, control, and change in the schools by heightening universalistic demands.

Except for the superintendents, large city administrators are almost totally inbred, and they tend to organize into informal or formal mutual associations protective of the status quo. Further, the credentials of the superintendents may be impressive but often do not portend leadership in changing the goals of education in the metropolis. A great many of the large city superintendents grew up and first taught in small towns, gained their major administrative experience in rural America or in the affluent suburbs, and have reached an age where educational reformism is not to be expected.

5. *Rigidities in the division of labor.* Perhaps even more limiting than the characteristics of personnel are the rigidities in the schools' division of labor. Teaching continues to involve the simple pattern in which teachers work alone with groups of pupils. Efforts to develop team-teaching practices or to bring "master teachers" into the classroom to aid inexperienced teachers fail outside of exceptional cases. As solo practitioners, teachers are resistant to anyone who would "interfere" in their classrooms.[18]

The most significant result of this resistance is the pressure built up in many cities against bringing volunteer and paid subprofessionals into the schools as teacher aides. Given limited financial resources, the use of such personnel might provide the only way to increase staffing dramatically. At the same time, it could raise the teachers' professionalism by providing a lower-status group to which more routine tasks could be delegated.

6. *The relationship between school and community.* Except in upper- and middle-class areas, the relationship between the local school and its immediate community usually is highly attenuated in the city. Neither the "neighborhood school" nor the broader "community school" models hold in communities where pupil and teacher transiency is high, where personnel live physically removed from the local setting, and where boundaries are kept impermeable. Usually the inner city school erects many barriers to outsiders, facilitated by the fact that in the school the visiting adult is so obviously a stranger. In the Chicago schools, any visitor must always report to the principal's office, perhaps to be taken only on a short and guided tour or sometimes to be denied admission completely. The strength of these boundaries becomes very apparent in the difficulties encountered in collaborative ventures between schools and social workers.

While some school systems, notably those of Detroit and Philadelphia, have experimented with keeping their schools open at all hours, reaching out to community residents, and creating a new "school-community coordinator" who makes up for the lack of an indigenous staff, most inner city schools have little contact with the families of their children. Consequently, the development of loyalties to the school is quite limited except in cases of special efforts or special luck (as in Chicago's Carver High School, where the drop-out rate among an all public-housing population dropped greatly when the school won the state basketball championship).

The result has been to allow for the development of great apathy about the schools, despite the general high valuation placed on education itself, in the poorer neighborhoods, and to stimulate great hostility toward the schools in many of these areas. To the extent that broadening the goals of the inner city schools requires extensive cooperative efforts between educators and local residents, these patterns also place great limits on the potentialities for change.

7. *The weakness of research and development.* Compared with other organizations of comparable size and resources, the large city school systems are "primitive." There is a deficit of operational information and a clear absence of adequate mechanisms for central planning. These systems are essentially reactive rather than anticipatory. Research and development are non-existent or weak in most of the systems, and, even when sophisticated computer operations exist, "research" often consists only in the collection of student attendance data required to receive state aid.[19] Millions of dollars have been spent across the nation on experiments for deprived students, but there is almost no information about the research or the results which is truly adequate to make decisions about future programs.

My observations of experiments for the "culturally deprived" in various cities clearly indicate that there are certain conditions under which innovations can more successfully be developed in the schools. First, change is maximized when the innovators are given a really meaningful degree of autonomy, particularly freedom regarding budget and staffing. Second, the chance for change is enlarged when leadership is given sufficient play. In several of the more successful operations, "charismatic" leadership and the "Hawthorne" effect clearly were significant. The superintendent must be willing to risk possible dilettantism and even competition for charisma, and he must be able to tolerate backlash from troublesome principals. Third, for many types of innovation enthusiasm alone is not enough, and it is crucial to insure that innovations are done with sufficient intensity and rational planning. A good example is found in the Philadelphia schools, which have developed a model of in-service training for inexperienced slum-school teachers which completely rejects the notion that workshops or occasional observation-and-critique could do the job. Instead, the trainer and the teacher-trainee work together every day for a month, trading off the preparation of lesson plans and the actual teaching. Fourth, the innovations often are maximized when barriers between the school and community are broken down, so that outsiders—college students, housewives, indigenous leaders, paid teachers' aides, and persons from local social agencies—can be mobilized to come to the aid of the schools. Finally, innovation often requires that school administrators develop an enlarged capacity for disruptions and tolerance of criticism, especially when innovation requiring involvement of the community is likely to mobilize backfiring criticism.

The crucial deficiency, however, is not in the experiment but in the research and development mechanisms for diffusing the new practices without bureaucratizing or in other ways incapacitating them. In one city a promising experiment in developing a non-graded system for slum elementary schools, sensitive to individual differences and able to avoid labeling children as failures in their early years, has been made "standard operating procedure" for the entire system almost overnight. Some evidence is emerging that in those schools that actually try to effect the plan, children are more rigidly "tracked" than before. In the same city the idea that teachers should be involved in the construction of curricula has evolved into a highly bureaucratized system of "revision cycles" in which new curriculum manuals are adopted after teacher questionnaire plebiscites, sometimes tabulated only after the new manuals are in press.

It is true, of course, that many of the big city systems have been exceptionally adaptive in building and staffing new schools in the face of great changes in population. But it is in expansion to meet population increase that school systems are always most flexible, for these organizations grow basically by reproducing standardized units—new schools are in this sense similar to new branch stores—rather than by transforming the whole basis of operation.[20] With other internal constraints, the weakness of research and development makes the task of incorporating social welfare goals in the large city school system most problematic.

The Case of Vocational Education

Many of the problems of change in the large city schools are highlighted by the difficulties of and potentialities for developing improved curricula in vocational education for inner-city youth.[21] This type of education cross-cuts traditional academic and broader goals. Its difficulties reflect in many ways the limits of the organizational character of the schools.

The concept of vocational education has had an historic power in American education, for it has implied that schooling is not merely to be an exercise in the classics or sciences for the privileged or talented few—it is also to be a preparation for life for the many. In the development of agriculture programs for the boys who would be farmers and home economics lessons for the girls who would be their wives, vocational education added a fourth R: relevance. The growth of these subjects was powerful and exciting not only because of the fundamental democratization of education which it involved, but also because it was stimulated by two revolutions in rural life: for the males, the shift to scientific farming, and for the females, the change from wood stove to electric range and refrigerator. In the rural community, vocational training proceeded without splitting apart the comprehensive school. It was relevant for nearly all, from whatever social class.

But vocational education has not been able to play this role so well in the city. Although vocational educators have created praiseworthy programs in a few cities and for some particular occupations, they have had great difficulty in addressing themselves to training for the blue-collar occupational spectrum as a whole. Often, programs leading to craft or technical occupations have touched only a minority. For most students vocational education freqently has meant "industrial arts" or shop courses—an undirected, semi-skilled training for boys destined to be semi-skilled workers. In many cases the democratic thrust of the concept has been lost, as when the college-bound and vocational programs split the better students between themselves and, in separate schools or in a single building, become rigidly "tracked" from one another—and also segregated from the bottom third of the students, who often receive neither academic fish nor vocational fowl.

RELEVANT TRENDS

Going on now are a number of important social trends connected with the transformation of America into an advanced industrial society which threaten in the long run to undercut vocational enrollments and to make the task of developing ade-

quate vocational programs more difficult. These include technological change, the growth of large bureaucracies, automation,
and other changes which imply that we will have a highly
specialized occupational structure, a great upgrading of work
skill requirements, an increase in white-collar and service employment requiring social relations skills, and a general affluence. Yet in the midst of the general improvement, a sizable
group of persons is being left behind—and in the process its
plight becomes ever more noticeable, especially among Negroes
in the city. The person who fails to obtain a good education and
training early in life is increasingly unlikely ever to move very
high.

Also relevant is the tendency for the society to become more
"meritocratic." Under this development, particularistic criteria
for judging people, in terms of social background, sincerity,
warmth, initiative, or other personal characteristics, are wiped
away so that the only criterion left is "pure merit." In the education system this takes the form of an increasing reliance on
standardized test scores to judge pupils on the bases of presumed ability and achievement. As Michael Young suggests in
his negative utopian novel on this development,[22] the rise of
meritocracy is not an unmixed gain: a society is created in
which many members of the population, simply because they are
not in the high intelligence range, automatically become defined as being without merit. One of the key problems of such
a society is to help people to accept themselves once they have
accepted the system.

The tendency to meritocracy is related to a tremendous drive
for college enrollment which extends to all classes. In many
respects this represents a positive contribution, as a further
democratization of education and an adjustment to changing
technology. But it can also be quite unrealistic. Problems that
can flow from this are illuminated in Burton Clark's case study
of *The Open Door College*,[23] in which he found that the initial

aim of creating a junior college in California that would basically be an institute for training technicians and semi-profes-
sionals soon was subverted by the students' desire to use the
school for liberal arts preparation before transferring to a four-
year college or a university. This happened despite the fact
that many of the students had little chance to gain admission to
the other schools.

An unrealistic drive for college extends even to many of the
students who are poorest academically. Among those who also
are socially disadvantaged this is a healthy sign of renewed
hope in American society. Yet where the urge is unaccompanied
by realistic hopes for accomplishment, it becomes another confusing element in the students' lives, producing loosely woven
sets of aspirations and expectations. In a Negro slum high
school in Chicago, a number of the girls in the "basic" (lowest)
academic track say that they expect to be lawyers when they
grow up.

It is clear from the foregoing that more and more American
high school students will want to go to college and will do so.
The practical limit is the physical capacity of American higher
education, but planned expansions are tremendous. Another
enlarging group will want to go but will not make it there, will
not last long, or will get only terminal, two-year academic
training. As in the California model, when the academic college
experience has begun to pall, these young people will need the
intensive vocational training increasingly required in an advanced industrial society.

But what of the other groups left behind—groups whose college drive or abilities and resources are low, half-hearted, or
divorced from reality? Alienation is endemic in the schools of
the youths who are headed nowhere. In particular, it can be
found in the lower tracks of the urban Negro high school,
mitigated only by the fact that many (although not all) of the
most alienated youths drop out. The rising expectations can

stimulate disenchantment if the appropriate means do not become apparent. These youths frequently do not know why they are in school or where they are headed. They are often bored with the school. Partially, this is a result of a decade of unrewarding experiences in the school; partly, it is the weak opportunity structure that lies ahead. But partly, also, it is a negative misperception of this opportunity structure. Good jobs —for example, in para-medical occupations—go unfilled while these youths see no future. One reason for this is that the vocational educators have not been particularly adaptive to new occupational lines and to new opportunities for training which could communicate a true instrumental value to these adolescents. Moreover, vocational training generally has taken for granted rather than addressed the basic vocational problem of these youth: their attitude toward work.

ORGANIZATIONAL LIMITS

If vocational education has not been as responsive to opportunities as it could be, this is partially because of its own particular set of constraints—the inability to mobilize industry and labor sufficiently in cooperative arrangements, the limits set by statutory and fiscal arrangements, and a reliance on traditional curricula. Even more important, perhaps, is the fact that vocational education suffers along with other types of education from the rigidities of the standard educational format. And while the vocational educators have gained a greater foothold in the schools than persons focusing on the social and psychological aspects of education, they still have not gained the same legitimacy in education as have those concerned with academic training. Vocational training ordinarily is separated from other education but usually has had to be organized in the conventional academic format—with standard class periods and other provisions—a rigidity quite damaging when educational goals require that the student relate to the world of work outside of the school.

The students in greatest need of vocational skills and direction are those for whom the standardized format has failed. These adolescents need an educational experience very much addressed to their individual attitudes and needs. Yet revisions needed for effective vocational training depend on revisions in the educational system as a whole. Part of the answer would seem to lie in introducing greater flexibility into the school in general, and especially into the relationship between vocational and academic education. Literacy is still the best vocational training. Books and workplace need less separation by curriculum and track, and more integration by phasing them more flexibly: for a given student the appropriate course might be a year in the school, a year in the workplace, a semester in the school, four years in the workplace, a year back for retooling (and not just technical) in the school, and so on. The whole high school may need to become non-graded, and vocational education could thrive as part of this development. The youth moratorium must be paid heed: students who opt for college must not be foreclosed from the world of work, and those who choose early work must not be shut out from a change of mind or from the opportunity for retraining for the changing occupational structure.

CURRICULUM POSSIBILITIES

Consideration of program possibilities suggests the need for three major types of efforts which have ramifications for the entire big city school system. The first and most straightforward is the need for ever more adaptive high-skill programs tied to the emergence and growth of new technical occupations in the changing economy. Vocational and big city educators seem ready to assign these programs to the post-secondary level, in part because of the inertia of present vocational programs. Certainly, many of the more useful ventures in this area will come at that level, but to allow the majority of high-level programs to be developed there will only reinforce the notion that a college diploma or advanced training is needed for every complex work task, and thereby will produce further bias against those without the financial or personal resources for college.

For this effort the basic prerequisites include not only the need to develop greater flexibility in programing than the school format is ready to provide, involving cooperative ventures in work experiences or apprenticeships and internships with occupations and organizations which have never had these before; the effort also demands that educators come more fully to terms with the various issues involved in integrating the vocational and academic curricula. This becomes necessary as the target occupations become more demanding of intellectual skills and appropriate social attitudes. There is also the problem of attracting those youths who are not irrevocably committed to the academic college route to these programs. This is not just a matter of communicating the immediate instrumental value of the training. It also involves the task of beginning to develop an awareness of and aspirations for new types of technical occupations much earlier in the students' lives.

The second effort required is to develop a great variety of programs, including long-range and short-term and opportunistic, if vocational education is truly to address the needs of the pre-drop-outs and others in the bottom third of their classes academically. One major aspect of this effort is to take such steps as will prepare and recruit more of these youths for the high-level training already mentioned, steps which include the need to drastically upgrade literacy skills.

Another major aspect of this second effort is the realistic need to develop short-term programs of the most practical and immediate sort for those who are not able or ready for more extensive preparation. The program of one urban high school in training slum boys quickly and simply for the task of working in an automatic car wash seems shortsighted in terms of the kinds of generalized work skills and attitudes that will be needed in adult life. But at least it provides a first work experience, some pay, and a motive for work and learning which, if coupled with a flexible and receptive program of further training when the boy is ready, may be an important beginning.

Persons who work with delinquents have found that often the key problem is somehow to help the boy muddle through adolescence without his doing anything too serious or getting caught and stigmatized. Come age twenty and time for marriage, the boy is likely to leave his cronies and straighten out. Analogously, the high rates of unemployment for out-of-school youth drop substantially in early adulthood. Here the task is to help the youth grapple with the job market without increasing his alienation, so that eventually he will see the school or other institutions as able to help him "straighten out" occupationally. They must also give him the opportunity simply to learn what work is like and make up for the fact that the military is no longer prepared to act as a "second chance" educational institution. These problems cannot be left optimistically to any agencies that might deal with the youth after he leaves the school, for by then his attitudes toward work may be too rigidly set.

As in the case of the effort to upgrade technical training, this effort involves the need to break out of the rigidities of the conventional school format, as well as the need for ready adaptiveness to new possibilities for cooperation with industry and labor. It also requires imagination in finding new areas for programs—for example, in restaurant work or museum-guarding. It requires great attention to developing coordination with whatever vocational programs will continue to work with these youths in later life. Finally, it necessitates turning substantial attention to the long-run development of social skills and motivations of individual youngsters.

The third effort of vocational curriculum construction, as I see it, must be renewed attention to the youth who *are* college bound, some to be successful, some not. These youths need vocational education, too, in the broad sense of the term. If they do not need specialized skills, they at least need some manual skills for their leisure life. More importantly, they need a sense of what the world of work is all about. They need a feeling for what work is, what craftsmanship is, what the division of labor is, how production is organized, and so on. Currently they have a profound ignorance about these matters, matters which are crucial to understanding the economy and society in which they will live.

Perhaps most importantly, they need to appreciate how all jobs can be "vocations" in the moral sense. Social scientists are only beginning to relearn this, as they have overdrawn the distinction between the academically oriented student, supposedly concerned with general intellectual and moral considerations, and the vocationally oriented student, concerned with education only as the key to income and security. Findings based on a study of Chicago public college students by Roberta Ash indicate that the contrast has been drawn way beyond the differences that exist.[24] Her subjects, many at the bottom of the college student academic heap, may not be very articulate, and they *do* view education as an instrument to a better position. But the position is not just a job: it has a moral and altruistic component; it is a contribution to society in the eyes of these students. Youths of all backgrounds and futures need to learn this, and to learn about the workplace as a corrective to the move to greater specialization and separation by merit in our schools.

IMPLICATIONS

The case of vocational education illustrates many of the issues of pursuing broadened goals in the large city school format. Although clearly the school cannot solve basic labor force problems, compensate sufficiently for inadequacies in aptitude, knowledge, or motivation for work deriving from the home environment, or force cooperative ventures upon employing firms or agencies, certain redirections of effort are necessary and feasible. Vocational programs suffer from their lack of legitimacy in the schools, and also, parodoxically, from the acceptance by the vocational educators of a traditional academic outlook which is insensitive to social and psychological concerns. Vocational education cannot be improved without transformations in the school system as a whole, but the recent direction of national efforts at curriculum revision in this field has focused on post-secondary training, away from the students with the bleakest occupational futures and away from their recalcitrant schools. Realistic efforts require not only flexibility and imagination in developing new programs within the school but a more aggressive stance in playing a coordinating role in the community.

The Potentials for Change

Given the large city school system's environment and internal constraints, there is a great possibility that its involvement in social welfare will remain unclear for some time. This possibility risks a continuation of confusion and delay in rational planning to meet urban problems.

Certainly there is the possibility that some school systems, beyond Washington's, will become almost wholly Negro; eventually, they may also become almost wholly lower-class. The withdrawal of whites and of middle classes of both races from the city—or at least from the public schools—could continue, and it might be exacerbated by any large-scale programs of federal aid to parochial schools. This possibility carries the danger that the public schools, as the schools for the poor, would become more and more a minimally financed custodial program treated in much the same way as public assistance operations.[25] The clientele (the parents) of such a system would have minimum local resources and political skills to press for standards and improved programs, and the flight of middle-class clientele presumably would be accompanied by the flight of educational personnel. (By the 1950's the major "action" in education already had moved to the suburbs from the big cities, many of which were the site of educational experimentation and affluence in the 1920's.)

On the other hand, such a system probably would get massive amounts of federal aid, funds which could provide the opportunity to develop strong remedial programs for the deprived student populations and for an explicit emphasis on welfare goals, albeit in a counter-democratic system. There would be no guarantee that welfare goals would become well articulated, however: the administration of federal monies by Office of Education personnel might continue the traditional emphases on improved facilities and teachers' training and qualifications without substantially clarifying the goals or capacities of the inner-city schools.

I assume that such a development is in no way inexorable. More important are the questions of what it would take to reshape the schools to meet the broader demands and, lacking such a reshaping, what alternative social arrangements seem promising.

THE RADICAL TRANSFORMATION OF THE SCHOOL SYSTEM

Broadening of goals and capacities requires transformation of the organizational character of the schools. In an earlier paper,

Morris Janowitz and I have presented a preliminary strategy embodying changes we believe necessary if the schools are to meet their broader demands.[26] Briefly, the key elements of this strategy include:

1. *Genuine decentralization of school operations.* They would be decentralized not to a large number of localized districts, as is the fashion in some cities (but is inadequate because there is not enough money to provide adequate staff in a great many offices), but to a few major sectors of the city. In order to avoid developing an administration and curricula stratified by class and race, the sectors would be drawn in such a way as to be socially heterogeneous. Each sector would have a basic staff for operations in its own area, and an advisory board of sector residents. The central administration would concern itself mainly with very general policies, the monitoring of budgets, and negotiations with national curricular and other agencies.

2. *A sharp increase and a substantial qualitative change in in-service training and opportunities for collegial contact,* both for teachers and for principals and other administrators. Training would be much broader, including social science and social welfare content. The effort should include experiments in the intensive socialization of cadres with the aim of generating collegial solidarity, as might occur, for example, in experiments of training groups of new teachers in special dormitories set up near slum schools.

3. *Greater flexibility in the division of labor,* especially through the introduction of volunteer and paid sub-professionals.

4. *Launching major experiments in slum areas through the creation of very autonomous experimental districts.* The major targets would be comprehensive urban high schools and the elementary schools that largely feed pupils to them. Experiments would include efforts at intra-agency cooperations and the use of school-community relations coordinators.

5. *Changes in the approach to racial integration in most of the large cities,* including the development of open enrollment

policies with racial quota systems, provision of busing where appropriate, allocation of special resources to integrated schools, and the development of special experimental integrated schools where school personnel and social scientists can study the actual impact of integration on the pupils and communities.

Such changes as these seem feasible, no matter how much temporary resistance they might generate locally, and most could be at least partially induced through the introduction of conditions for receiving new federal monies that might be allocated. But their implementation also requires the generation of strong and non-traditional executive leadership in the large city schools.

A distinctive aspect of our approach is that it rejects what we call the "specialization" model, which seems to be the usual response to demands for a broadened capacity in the schools, in favor of the "integration" model. Under the specialization model, the tendency is to add specialists—psychologists, social workers, experts in given subject matter areas, and so on—to the standard format. The danger of this model is that it can undercut the authority, feelings of competence, and actual competence of the classroom teachers and administrators. The integration model seeks to combat these tendencies by enlarging the personal capacities of these personnel.

Commitment to the integration model says something directly about the issues of broadening the goals of the school, even given a radical transformation in organizational format. The assumption is that the schools cannot become "neighborhood service centers" or psychiatric clinics without destroying their fitness for their basic educational tasks. Transformation of the schools through the integration model seeks to broaden goals, but principally through enhancing the abilities and outlook of the school personnel. What it should accomplish is, first, to stimulate a great increase in differentiation and experimentation with a variety of educational programs for deprived and other populations, with a high probability, for example, that some of the vicious dilemmas of the slum school could be broken; second, to offer the possibility that academic learning could be improved greatly by freeing teaching personnel from routine duties to focus on these tasks; third, to help to humanize the schools, as personnel come to appreciate the social and psychological problems of their students and communities much more fully; and, finally, to increase the sensitivity and willingness to make referrals to and join in cooperative efforts with social agencies outside of the schools.

COROLLARY AND ALTERNATIVE STRATEGIES

Whatever actions are taken to transform the schools, it is apparent that they have limited purposes built into their character. Without help from changed housing patterns and from the suburbs, the schools cannot truly racially integrate the city. The schools are not "total institutions"; they are basically socialization rather than resocialization agencies. Assaults on the problems of the inner city will continue to require and will benefit from a pluralism of approaches, both within and without education.

Benefits have been apparent where the schools have been slow to adapt to the new expectations for compensatory education. In Chicago the voluntary tutoring movement has developed over 150 separate after-school study centers and has perhaps thrived precisely because of the resistance from the professional educators. The result has been not only a new enthusiasm but also the creation of an articulate body of knowledge about how to set up and manage such centers and about what results might be expected. Further, in the end, the schools are beginning to acknowledge that they have something to learn from these efforts.

Thus there seems to be substantial wisdom in the "competi-

tion" proposition of American educators that the decentralization of education to the local level, and even the existence of
private schools, makes for an ultimate gain because of the
amount of individual experimentation it permits. Yet in general
the supposed gains have been limited, especially in the cities,
because most public and parochial schools have lacked finances
for experimentation, and because other private schools, although
often very innovative, have worked principally only with elite
or upper-class children.

Given the proposition that many approaches are necessary
a more adequate test seems to provide a significant alternative
strategy. It is a strategy embraced in part in federal legislation
allowing the development of experimental urban schools by
coalitions of universities. But even these efforts seem too narrowly conceived, for they envision single large-scale experiments
in each major city and they assume that experimentation should
be conducted principally by the professional educators based
in the universities. The preferred strategy would assert that—
within the restriction that competing programs should not
jeopardize the basic resources of the public schools—new
resources directed at urban educational and education-related
problems need to be more widely dispersed. They should go
to a variety of university, private school, and social agency–
sponsored experiments, and for efforts both with and without
professional educators at the helm.

Studies of the relationship between socio-economic status and
family disorganization variables on the one hand and intelligence and achievement on the other might not show repetitive
high correlations if there were true variation in the circumstances of schooling. Results from a special summer school for
under-achieving Chicago high school pupils, involving small
class size, especially talented teachers, and college-student
teacher aides, indicate substantial potentials for reversing the
usual downward patterns of these youth.[27] Experiments in a

variety of settings could really test notions of individualized instruction, special motivational techniques, the use of gifted amateurs, and other possible means.

In lieu of any major adaptations by the large city schools, some social welfare efforts that depend on education may have to set up not just experiments but quasi-permanent educational efforts running parallel to school programs. Federal monies given to private agencies for "head-start" programs in many cities during recent years might much more appropriately have been given for competing kindergarten and primary programs for slum children. If the schools will not allow their buildings to be used for evening community organization activities, alternative facilities will have to be procured. "Community action programs" directed at pre- or presently delinquent youth may have to set up humanized and interesting high schools if the public schools will not adapt. The Labor Department may have to provide the basic vocational training programs for lower-class youth. One need not go so far as Milton Friedman does in proposing we junk the public schools and substitute stipends to parents to purchase whatever education they want for their children [28] to agree that limited experiments in granting subsidies for the private schooling of poor persons with unusual educational aspirations seem warranted. Hopefully, such activities would have the supposed theoretical effect, competition leading to true incorporation. If not, new institutions will be built.

Further, heightened communication and rapprochement between the schools and other social agencies are necessary. Some divergences in outlook on the current scene seem unbridgeable. For example, educators and "indigenous leadership" community organizers cannot now collaborate because the former assume the ignorance of the lower classes while the latter assume their wisdom. But intelligent and structural contact among these groups should strengthen an understanding of the overlap and differences between education and social welfare goals and therefore make collaboration more feasible.

In reality, both the attempt at a radical transformation of the schools and the pursuit of corollary and alternative endeavors will be necessary if the schools are to meet their broadened requirements. In these ventures social scientists can play a significant role. Their doing so will require a shift from an emphasis on analyses of the educational correlates of community and personal background attributes to a study of experiments in revising the format of schooling. In the process, both the essential and the potentially variable aspects of the social organization of education should become more clear.

Notes

1. *The Unadjusted Girl,* Boston, 1931, pp. 213-214.

2. *Ibid.,* pp. 216-221.

3. For example, in Baltimore between 1950 and 1960 the total city population decreased by 1 percent while public school enrollment increased by 43 percent. There was virtually no change in the numbers of whites in the school-age population but an increase of 85 percent in the numbers of non-whites.

4. As is well known, the change has brought the minorities into the majority in many large school systems or parts thereof, as in Washington, D.C., where the proportion of white students is diminishing toward 10 percent; in Chicago, where slightly more than half of the students now are non-white; and in Manhattan, where some 75 percent of the school population is Negro or Puerto Rican.

5. Often the political and moral crises have become personal crises as well. People have become willing to go to jail over issues involving the big city schools, and in Cleveland within the past couple of years, one protestor gave his life in an effort to halt school construction. Some large city school superintendents have needed bodyguards, and, if several usually trustworthy rumor mills are correct, one superintendent of a major system resigned in recent years because of politically inspired violence directed at his children.

6. Robert J. Havighurst, "Urban Development and the Educational System," in A. Harry Passow, ed., *Education in Depressed Areas,* New York,

1963, pp. 24-45, and Havighurst, *The Public Schools of Chicago, A Survey*, Chicago, 1964, *passim*.

7. Robert J. Havighurst, "The Public Schools and Human Development in the Metropolitan Area," paper given at the Symposium of the Committee on Human Development, University of Chicago, June 5, 1965. The author recounts that in the 1920's the schools provided a variety of services to immigrant, non-English-speaking families and visiting teachers to work with maladjusted children and their families. Such programs were dropped in the Depression and have not returned.

8. The research has been conducted in collaboration with Morris Janowitz, supported by the Russell Sage Foundation, and based in the Center for Social Organization Studies, University of Chicago. Major findings will be reported in David Street, *Big City Schools: A Study of Organization and Change*, forthcoming.

9. For example, Jacob Landers of the New York City public schools worked hard just to compile a list of the titles of special projects for deprived children in his school system, produced several typed pages, and wound up feeling that his list was incomplete.

10. Philip Selznick, *Leadership in Administration*, Evanston, 1957.

11. For an interpretation of this pattern, see Robert L. Crain and David Street, "School Desegregation and School Decision-Making," *Urban Affairs Quarterly*, II (September 1966), 64-82. For the full results of study, see Crain, *School Desegregation in the North*, Chicago, 1966. A key finding of this study is that school boards are more likely to acquiesce to civil rights demands if they contain more high-prestige or civic leaders and fewer persons tied to the political party.

12. *The School Board Crisis*, Chicago, 1964.

13. Patricia Cayo Sexton, in *Education and Income*, New York, 1961, shows how inequalities in educational facilities and services in Detroit a few years ago extended even to free lunch programs, which were more often available in higher-income areas.

14. As Howard S. Becker showed years ago in a study of the Chicago schools ("Role and Career Problems of the Chicago Public School Teacher," unpublished Ph.D. dissertation, University of Chicago, 1951), the school system has few vertical rewards (promotion) to offer, but can provide horizontal rewards (movement to better schools or neighborhoods.)

15. This may come in large part because, as many studies showing low inter-judge reliability indicate, objective standards for judging teaching performance have not emerged.

16. Among numerous sources, this conclusion is documented in an experiment by Bruno Bettelheim carried on in connection with our Russell Sage project. He ran an intensive seminar for inner-city teachers dealing with the handling of "behavior problem" Negro pupils. The results indicate, first, that the problem is less one of racial prejudice than class attitudes which stigmatize the children as unteachable, and, second, that

the intensive seminar format can produce meaningful changes in attitude.

17. Bryan Roberts, "The Effect of College Experience and Social Background on Professional Orientations of Prospective Teachers," unpublished Ph.D. dissertation, University of Chicago, 1964.

18. Dan Lortie provides some reason for this when he analyzes the teacher's role as principally providing "craft" rewards, involving face-to-face relations with the pupils and reflecting no confidence in the ability of others to judge her performance. (In "Craftsman, Professional, and Bureaucrat: Current Innovations and Rewards in the Teacher's Role, paper given at AACTE Studies Committee Seminar, Lexington, Mass., 1962.)

19. I was told by the director of research of one large city system that even with unlimited funds he would not enlarge his activities beyond his present two-man bookkeeping operation. "Research is unnecessary," he said, "because we already know what should be done: we must lower class size."

20. An unpublished Master's paper by Gary Hendershot ("The Baby Boom and the Schools: The Social Organizational Consequences of a Demographic Event," University of Chicago, 1964), helps confirm this notion. He analyzed the relationship between size of the administrative staff and total size (number of pupils) over the period of the baby boom. He finds that, in contrast to previous findings of cross-sectional analysis, growth in pupil population is not accompanied by a proportionate increase in the size of the administrative staff. In fact, he discovered a correlation of —.59 between amount of growth and the size of the administrative staff at the final time period measured.

21. David Street, "Vocational Education in Change: A Policy Perspective," working paper, Center for Social Organization Studies, University of Chicago, 1966.

22. *The Rise of Meritocracy*, London, 1958. Of course, the various measures of merit used are subject to various socio-economic and other biases. This has led to a search for "culture-free" alternatives, but with little success. Recently the New York City schools abandoned the use of standardized intelligence tests both as a way to avoid biases and to avoid stigmatizing children by their merit, but it appears that reading tests are now being used as a basis for judgment and grouping of pupils. Because the reading tests have a very high correlation with intelligence tests, and are more dependent on verbal aptitude than most I.Q. tests, bias not only is not eliminated but may even be strengthened.

23. New York, 1960.

24. Roberta Ash, "Beyond Vocationalism: Aspirations of Urban College Students," unpublished Ph.D. dissertation, University of Chicago, 1966.

25. A dramatic example of the custodial requirements involved in operating inner-city schools has occurred in Chicago recently, as plainclothes policemen having teaching qualifications have been placed in the classrooms of disorderly schools.

26. Morris Janowitz and David Street, "Innovation in the Public School System of the Inner City: A Policy Perspective," working paper, Center for Social Organization Studies, University of Chicago, 1965.

27. Roberta Ash, "An Educational Experiment in the Inner City: A Participant-Observer Report," in David Street, ed., *Innovation in Mass Education*, forthcoming.

28. *Capitalism and Freedom*, Chicago, 1962, pp. 85-107.

II. COMMUNITY PROCESS
AND WELFARE GOALS

Elaine Cumming
Allocation of Care to the Mentally Ill, American Style

Introduction

The word allocation implies a shortage of something valued; volunteers for an unpleasant job may be scarce, or desired goods and services may be too few to go around. Psychiatric services must be allocated in the face of a complex combination of shortages, among them the scarcity of manpower, the shortage of patients who readily recover, and the dearth of enthusiasm with which the patients themselves view the services.

I am deeply indebted to many colleagues for making this essay possible —in particular, my associates Claire Rudolph and Laura Edell. Professor Nils Christie of the University of Oslo in Norway contributed many of the ideas put forward in the section on "openness" in American society. Edgar Pye of the Department of Mental Hygiene of the State of California and his colleagues patiently answered my questions about community organization. Kaspar Naegele, James A. Davis, Nils Christie, and John Cumming all read the manuscript and made incisive suggestions, some of which I have incorporated. Rhondda Cassetta has been a most helpful editor, and Beverly Martin has patiently typed and retyped the manuscript. The studies referred to in this essay were carried out in the Mental Health Research Unit, an agency of the New York State Department of Mental Hygiene located in Syracuse, New York. Some of them were supported by Grant M 4735 from the National Institutes of Mental Health.

We cannot, therefore, discuss the mechanisms for the allocation of psychiatric services without touching upon both the priorities of allocation and the values that underlie these priorities. In America we enjoy discussing our values, but we have not been much moved to confront directly the problem of priorities, partly because we have inherited from our earliest days the belief that we shall always have enough of everything for every deserving citizen. Thus, social planning, itself a way of making priorities explicit, has been slow to take hold.

In the time it has taken for social planning to arrive upon the scene, the mentally ill have been neglected, discovered, neglected again, and once more discovered. As our priorities have changed, so has our handling of the problems the mentally ill present. Therefore, this essay will start with a general discussion of what I feel to be the heart of the priorities, planning, and allocation problems—those American values and beliefs that seem to be most powerful in forming our attitudes about the mentally ill and the conditions of their treatment. Since de Tocqueville there have been many general observations on American values, and their usefulness has been as variable as the vision of the observers. Eventually, if we are to understand the relationship between our beliefs and our behavior, we must be able to design incisive ways of discovering both the ideological wellsprings of our priorities and the ways in which these ideologies shape the means by which we implement them.

After discussing the complex of ideas and beliefs that seem to shape our attitudes toward the care of the mentally ill, I shall consider—using examples, most of which will come from a group of studies of the helping system in a medium-sized city [1]—first, the assignment of the "mentally ill" label and the subsequent search for treatment; second, two mechanical models of the allocation of services in general and of psychiatric treatment in particular; and third, some apparent weaknesses and strengths of our own system of allocation.

Values and Anti-Values

In any complex society, firmly held values seem always to be accompanied by contrasting, and even inimical, latent values. Without a potential contrast, strong and unambiguous belief systems might lead to rigidity and extremism, hindering adaptation to changing circumstances. To use a frivolous example, the firm belief in the virtue of hard work, planning ahead, and achievement is accompanied by a latent but incompatible belief that we must live for today, because we shall be a long time dead. This contrasting value not only prevents us from working until we drop, but it is also available for conversion into a salient value if we are lucky enough to wake up one morning rich enough to join the leisured few. Conversely, it may be an inability to adapt that leads some of us to join sects and cults that have monolithic, unchanging values. It may be, indeed, that in a complex and often contradictory society, the more loudly we proclaim a value, the more accessible to us must be some contrasting value. Finally, the paradox of converse value-pairs seems to lie behind such essentially human productions as poetry, myths, humor, and ideology (Pareto; Lévi-Strauss).[2] The trouble with this idea of pairs or groups of values and contrast-values is that they tempt one to explain anything that doesn't fit with the value by the anti-value, which is a can't-lose game. For this reason I shall try to avoid all explanations in terms of anti-values and limit myself to suggesting where I think predictive studies couched in these terms might be useful.

Perhaps the best-known modern description of American values has been given by Robin Williams, and his work is my starting point. A less widely known monograph by Kaspar Naegele has provided a kind of "angle of vision" for the following section. With both these authors I shall take for granted that, with other Western cultures, we are an activist, achievement-oriented, freedom-loving, and humane people and limit myself to discussing certain aspects of individualism, equality, and openness. These values tend to "go together" and have areas in common, although, as I shall point out, there are issues that arise in the treatment of the mentally ill where one value seems to have to be disregarded because of the insistent strength of another.

INDIVIDUALISM

We are an intensely individualistic people, inasmuch as our reference point is neither our own lineage nor our own place in the social order but rather ourselves and our families here and now and separate from society (de Tocqueville). We take this individualism so for granted that it is hard for us to describe in what specific ways it affects our lives (Wilensky and LeBeaux). It is perhaps only when we come to know cultures with different solutions to the self-in-society problem that we become aware of our own bias. On the other hand, the amount we talk both for and against a contrasting value, conformity, suggests that individualism presents a problem to us, as does our rather low tolerance of dissent (Fromm). Indeed, a society that features individualism may require a strong latent value like conformity to promote social cohesion, and our ambivalence to conformity may only reflect our need of it. Of course, another contrasting value, group solidarity, is available to us, as it must be in any society, although it is not as highly developed here as in some other places, for example, Israel. We do feature "teamwork," but implicit in the team is the individual coordinating his particular skills with those of other individuals. Collectivism—a kind of legal, political, and economic expression of group solidarity and anti-individualism—we almost completely reject.

Our legal structures are designed to protect—and to accuse— the individual, not the group, and our politics emphasize individual rather than group rights. Anyone who has read Jane

Austen knows that the British were able, in the eighteenth century, to entail property so as to guarantee the integrity of a family name, complete with estates, and that this system often worked great hardships on daughters and younger sons. Our own tenderness toward individual welfare has made us unalterably opposed to such "alienation" laws. In spite of our emphasis upon "the family," we find it hard to understand that individuals would be willing to suffer, and others be willing to let them suffer, for the "family name." To us, families are concrete entities that do not transcend the sum of the individuals. Above all, our families and schools strive to develop individual self-reliance in every child.

Allied to our individualism and reinforcing it is an admiration of uniqueness. We take more naturally to the star system than to repertory, and the Japanese tea ceremony, with its perfectly stylized ritual, is unthinkable for the American hostess who strives to be "different" when she entertains. At the same time, we *are* organization men and dwellers in faceless suburbs; at the level of personal values, the most persistent conflict may be between conformity and uniqueness. At a more public level, we are suspicious of the *"überseele"* and the "state," and it is difficult for us to think of the welfare of the group—the school, the church, or the nation—as transcending the welfare of its individual members, except perhaps in time of war. A difficult abstract concept like "society" is hard for us to deal with, but we forget that the equally difficult and abstract concept of "personality," which we understand intuitively, would have been just as hard for our nameless medieval forebears who patiently contributed their anonymous lives to building those great cathedrals which ornament Europe.

Individualism and the emphasis on uniqueness have consequences for our attitudes toward the mentally ill; in the first place, we tend to locate all forms of illness and deviance inside the individual. To us, the inadequate, relapsing alcoholic is a sick man; the society in which he becomes sick does not concern us much. We are less interested in rates than in case histories. Thus casework is prescribed for the "hard-core" unemployed, although one wonders how casework can invent a job for a man of low ability and no training when there are too few jobs to go around.[3] But we reveal the fullness of our devotion to individualism by keeping it as a reward for full participation in society. For the prisoner, the chronically ill, the bedridden old, and the destitute we reserve the forced collective life.

Our individualistic values are acted out in a society deeply attached to egalitarian principles, and this has important consequences (de Tocqueville; Parsons, 1951, 1960; Lipset). Most of us would say that we believe only in equality under the law and an equal opportunity for each citizen, rather than in any literal or concrete equality; and yet, ironically, we *act* much of the time as if we believed more firmly in the latter than in the former definition. Perhaps for this reason we tend to be apathetic toward poverty and impatient with inadequacy. It is just not in our makeup to believe strongly enough in differential endowment to give us any sense of *noblesse oblige*. The very phrase is repugnant to most Americans, because status is a reward and therefore does not carry obligations. But we do evaluate one another in a way that suggests what one might call a "moral meritocracy." If a man is poor and ignorant then he must, at least in part, have chosen that way of life. The pride of place, for example, that makes a Scandinavian say, "I do not wish to represent a society that lets its poor live in rat-infested tenements," is unlikely to suffuse us. We are only beginning to entertain the idea that those who are not fit enough for the race should have a head start if the race is seriously to be run under egalitarian rules.

We have our reformers, but on the whole we tend not to be our brothers' keepers. This is, of course, to overstate the case—

we do provide services, but we believe that the fewer they are, the better for all concerned. Not all countries consider freedom of the individual from public services desirable; some of the welfare services in Norway, for example, would probably be considered actual harassment in America.

Nowhere is our belief in literal, concrete equality more evident than in our distrust of expertise, especially if it is allied with centralism, a fear which we have inherited from the French thinkers of the mid-eighteenth century. Hear de Jouvenel on Rousseau: "Rousseau offered no recipe for turning the government of a large and complex society into a democracy; on the contrary, he offered a demonstration that on the one hand great numbers, [and] on the other, the requirement of great activity in Government, inevitably led to the centralization of political authority in a few hands, which he regarded as the opposite of Democracy." This distrust is embedded in our Constitution in such a way that power is intended always to be centrifuged to the smallest possible unit, preferably from government to voluntary groups of citizens. In short, we do not trust large, expert-ridden governments; a member of a local government is just Everyman elected to office; a state government begins to be remote and probably venal; the federal government is a tyrant.[4]

The fear of centralism has consequences for the work of the world; a committee that meets to plan a service is likely to generate such themes as, "We must have coordination, but we must not have a superstructure." It is possible for such a committee to affirm and reaffirm for six months all those things that everyone knows and believes—and ultimately to make a decision that could have been made six months before, if all that had been necessary were facts and expertise—and then on top of that to ask, "Now why did we take six months to do that when we could have done it in two weeks?" The reason that the committee did not do it six months before is simple enough; if Americans do not trust experts and cannot have superstructures, some other kind of decision-making process is necessary, and for us it is consensus. Decision by consensus permeates many features of American life, and it militates against irreversible demagoguery and against monolithic power structures in city, town, or village. Arthur J. Vidich describes a meeting of a town government thus: "Decisions are delayed until it is apparent that unanimity is possible. A vote is not taken unless it is obvious that all will vote the same. All decisions are the unanimous decisions of the board, and all in attendance must indicate approval even though all do not possess the legal qualifications to vote on board matters." This author points out elsewhere, however, that the decisions have all been made by a small group of citizens *before* the meeting. In short, the combination of a value on grass-roots assent and the need to get things done to keep the system going has had two important consequences: first, covert grass-roots power structures have developed, and second, the art of persuasion has reached its zenith. Perhaps this is why people think Americans are other-directed. Unfortunately, we do not know *how many* people participate in so-called grass-roots decisions. Possibly a great many non-participating citizens are *represented* in them by the "community leadership," but it may be that, as Herbert J. Gans says of the New England town meeting, which is the model for such decisions, ". . . in many communities it was less an expression of direct democracy than a public forum in which the upper income townspeople gave orders to their fellow citizens."

In spite of our hypocrisy, or perhaps because of it, we do have a measure of genuine grass-roots involvement. For example, in California under certain enabling legislation, communities can organize a demand for a mental health clinic. In practice this often means that the technical staff of the State Department of Mental Hygiene arouses the initial "demand" for the service. In the end, however, not only the Mental Health Association but also such diverse groups as the League of Women Voters and the Kiwanis Club may become quite deeply involved. Their reasons for doing so may be idiosyncratic and unrelated to the general need for such a clinic, but having participated in getting it, they are likely to have an investment in seeing it prosper.

But is there any *other* democratic way of operating such a service? There is, but not given our values. As Irwin T. Sanders says, "In Western European countries . . . the . . . local governments are chiefly held responsible for the initiation and implementation of community improvement; in the United States, the stress is upon citizen involvement and the responsibility of the private, voluntary associations in cooperation with local, state, and national governments." In Britain, for example, welfare policy is made somewhat as follows: a political party— usually Labour in the case of welfare measures—asks a group of experts, often from the universities, to develop a plan. After this committee has studied the problem, discussed it with a variety of people, and made recommendations, the appropriate cabinet or shadow-cabinet member considers the proposal and discusses it with his colleagues. It may then be developed into some form of publication, perhaps a Fabian pamphlet, and eventually it will be considered, debated, and reworked at a party conference. At this point it becomes the official policy of that political party, and in the British political system the party is then committed to its implementation. The individual at the grass roots has a voice in the sequence only at the polls, but every individual, of course, has such a voice. In this British form of democracy (also typical of Canada) the individual has no automatic opportunity for influence at the planning level, let alone a veto, unless he is active in a political party. Furthermore, he has to vote on whole "packages" of plans and policies and cannot pick and choose among them. In America the involved individual can exert influence on program planning, but as I have said, we do not know exactly how many people actually do so. Our method certainly opens the door to more citizen participation, but it also tends to give rise to *ad hoc*

solutions to problems and to reduce the amount of experimentation and imagination that can infuse any planning that does
take place.[5] In contrast, while the British method may allow
more imagination to enter into social action, it can prove costly
when unacceptable social innovations atrophy from lack of use.
In Canada, for example, one mental health clinic staffed with
two psychiatrists had only eight new cases referred to it by
local physicians in one year.[6]

In order to make any use of expertise in our system, the
elected official must arrange to have the people at the grass
roots persuaded that, as individualists, they want the innovation that his advisers have suggested. Such a process is called
"community organization," and its success appears to rest on the
ability of the expert to persuade local power groupings that
they want what they ought to want. I am not detracting from
this method of carrying on the affairs of the world, because,
although the vision often gets lost among the grass roots, it has
the great strength that once a course of action is decided upon,
it has the support of those who must live with it. But unit
autonomy tends to fractionate society, and therefore a by-
product of our way of organizing ourselves seems to be our love
of reiterating the solidary values that bind us together—among
them the value of unit autonomy. Such reiterations help us to
avoid conflict-ridden issues and protect consensus, but they
stifle dissent and provide us with a self-congratulatory, moral-
izing community.

But even in our love of unit autonomy we harbor contrasting
values: in spite of our reluctance to put ourselves in the hands
of big government, we are tolerant of social security legislation,
and we really admire big industry.[7] In some part of our hearts
we admire the efficiency of the well-organized, well-run, centralized bureaucracy, and we are in awe of experts. Our admiration for strong, central leadership is also very near the surface
and can be quickly mobilized in war or disaster. In short, our
devotion to equality is sincere but not uncomplicated.

OPENNESS

American individualism is acted out in an open society: reflect on our preoccupation with "improving communication" and "getting feedback." We admire frankness; we believe that covert and secret acts are likely to be malignant; and we have many mechanisms for keeping one another in view.[8] In their schools, our children live under floodlights; if their behavior deviates from what is expected, the fact is soon communicated to the parents by one of a host of messengers: the teacher, the principal, the school nurse, or the "visiting teacher"—herself a social worker. The peer group, the arena for "learning to relate," also disseminates news of strange behavior.[9]

It is hard for Americans to visualize the European system in which events in the school are largely unknown by parents and children may insulate their various reputations. In a witty book about our child-centeredness, Martha Lear quotes an American school principal: "We had a visitor from the London school system who told me, 'In England, parents and dogs are not allowed in the schools.' Horrible attitude, isn't it? But sometimes . . . I wish—at least I *think* I wish—I worked there." [10]

Openness, like individualism, is thought of as "natural"; it is the contrasting value, privacy, that we declare ourselves to value. A certain minimum of privacy must surely be essential for individualism, and so a tension must always exist between these two values. The foreign observer sometimes fails to see how we suffer in reconciling openness and individualism. V. S. Pritchett, for example, says, "The attraction of the American social novel has been that it is about people who desire no privacy; this is a fact of American life and out of it comes these artists' distinctive opportunity," Indeed, for us "privacy" is often a synonym for "individual," as in "private enterprise," "private initiative," and "private philanthropy." Although such terms have nothing to do with privacy, there *is* a point where a genuine cry for privacy can be heard.[11] Maybe we like the *idea* of privacy, but we cannot seriously pursue it because the system will not work unless it is open. Thus the suburban housewife *anathematizes the Kaffeeklatsch* of which she is a member.

In America, after all, picture windows opening onto the street are funny only because there is no picture to view through them. And who would hamper the green sweep of a suburban street with fences and hedges? A Norwegian colleague on his first visit to America exclaims, "But all the office doors are open —how can you think or get any work done?"

A more serious aspect of our openness is our belief that everyone has a *right* to know everything that has a public side; hence we tolerate public tribunals of many kinds and believe that our newspapers should report all the details of any crime even if a miscarriage of justice might ensue.

Although we must have openness at least about public matters in order to run a consensual system, all things being equal, we prefer to be able to see upward rather than downward. For example, the machinations of government *ought* to be visible to us all, but our local affairs are not the concern of government. For the professionals who staff clinics in small communities, as well as for their patients, the asymmetrical openness may be hard to endure. Indeed, this may be the most important reason why we find it hard to recruit professionals to small communities.

For the mentally ill, the openness of our society has special meaning because it involves them in a cross-fire. On the one hand, they are told that mental illness is nothing to hide, it could happen to anyone, and that the stigma of mental illness is out of date. On the other hand, this very openness limits the degree of non-conforming behavior that is tolerable and thus imposes a sanction on acts that could go unnoticed in a more private system. In short, certain kinds of behavior must be hidden to be tolerated at all, but at the same time to hide them is intolerable.

To sum up this impressionistic account, I would say that on

the whole individualism and its contrasting value, conformity, and egalitarianism with its contrasting but perhaps more latent commitments to bigness, power, and leadership, are our most important beliefs. Openness is a value which, like individualism, is taken for granted. Its contrasting value, privacy, is more often a focus for discussion, perhaps because individualism thrives on privacy, while equality and openness are reasonably compatible. Assuming this pattern and striving to avoid ideological reductionism, I shall try to show how these values and the conflicts among them, as well as the social relationships under their control, shape the allocation of services to the mentally ill.

The Working of the System

THE PSYCHIATRIC LABEL

"Mental illness" is primarily a lay definition. By the time an affected person reaches the point of psychiatric treatment or diagnosis, he has often been ill for some time and is almost always under pressure from those around him either to seek treatment or to change his behavior. I am not here concerned with the limiting case of the analysand who feels no pain and creates no disturbance but is seeking insight for its own sake; the prototype I have in mind is the psychotic or severely neurotic patient who is almost always ejected from his social system because he cannot meet the expectation of its members. In our research, we have found (Cumming, 1962a) that by the time the average patient reaches a hospital, he has received advice or guidance from nine to ten people, four or five of whom are laymen, and he has usually been labeled mentally ill or socially undesirable somewhere near the beginning of his path to treatment.

There is a persistent belief that preventing mental illness is possible if "case-finding" is vigorous, that is, if a label is attached early enough.[12] This is an obvious *non sequitur* and need not concern us. But it *is* logical to believe that early labeling might lead to early treatment if we had confidence in the treatment. Whether or not early labeling is desirable in an open society where a label is a public affair is primarily a matter of clinical judgment. One price is paid if treatment is postponed and another if it is not. We should note, in passing, that while "case-finding" and early labeling are, on the whole, considered good, the imposition of services or treatment without the consent of the patient is considered a violation of privacy.

Because psychiatric illness is a diffuse disorder of the whole man, it is stigmatizing. Asking for any kind of public help is stigmatizing, and asking for help that is really needed is more stigmatizing than asking for help that can be done without in a pinch. Finally, it is more stigmatizing to ask for help for a diffuse problem such as unpredictability, helplessness, or loss of autonomy than for a specific problem such as an orthopedic operation or a summer camp for the kids. Outside of imprisonment for certain "loathsome" crimes, or perhaps for treason, psychosis is probably the most stigmatizing form of deviance in Western society. Furthermore, it seems that mental illness, unlike many crimes such as arson, desertion, and financial irresponsibility, is looked upon as deviant by *every* segment of society.

In cultures where group identity and group competence are valued more than they are here, the psychiatric label may not be as serious because the loss of a member's competence can be borne in part by the whole group. Individualism tends to make stigma a more solitary burden, shared, if at all, by family members. Perhaps for this reason lay people are reluctant to use the label "mentally ill" before it is necessary, whether it be self-labeling—"I went to the psychiatrist because I couldn't stand my nervousness any longer"—or labeling by others—"I took him to the psychiatrist because I couldn't stand his suspiciousness any longer." John Clausen and his co-workers, for example, have shown that wives of mentally ill men will deny the evidence of their senses rather than succumb to the stigma of defining their husbands as mentally ill. In a recent study, my colleagues and I found that family doctors are also unwilling to define a patient as mentally ill, a large majority of them preferring to treat their patients' emotional and mental distress until the illness either clears up or becomes unmanageable (Cumming and Ise). The doctors say that they do this because they know that the patient or his family will resent a psychiatric referral, and also because they themselves prefer to look upon emotional disturbances as transitory and therefore within the scope of their treatment. Finally, as Waxler and Mishler have pointed out, the family doctor tends to act in many of these cases as an agent of the family in the sense that he follows their wishes in his handling of the patient, and they are seldom in a hurry to have one of their members labeled mentally ill.

Studies of clergymen show that they, like laymen and physicians, are reluctant to apply the mentally ill label (Cumming and Harrington). Like physicians, clergymen will counsel with parishioners or, indeed, with anyone who approaches them for help until they can no longer manage the situation, and only then will they make referrals. We have also found that policemen (Cumming, Edell and Cumming) will give what help they can to grossly disturbed people and will withhold the label "psycho" except from the most irrational and combative of citizens. None of these agents like to give anyone an essentially stigmatizing label in a world where news travels fast.

It is only the psychiatrist, the social worker, and certain sophisticated lay people who are quick to see mental illness. This readiness seems to show faith in both the efficacy of psychiatric treatment and in the efforts to destigmatize mental illness. But such belief displays more wish than reality. There is no compelling evidence that early treatment of mental illness, especially psychotherapy, counseling, and casework, resolves the illness any better than time alone will do (Astin; Storrow), and there is no reason to believe that the stigma attached to labeled mental illness has in the recent past become less (Cumming and Cumming, 1965), although Paul Lemkau reports that the number of people able to identify the early stages of mental illness in others has greatly increased since early studies (Cumming and Cumming, 1957).

It appears, then, that those who are relatively distant from the specialized field of mental illness and relatively close to the patient are reluctant to use the label, whereas those who know more about the illness and are further from the patient are more eager to do so. Psychiatric specialists themselves are not often in a position to label the patient because they do not have access to him until after he has been labeled. In other words, services are unlikely to be allocated to the mentally ill, nor they to services, until this label has been attached. Accordingly, we shall first consider the point at which the labeling occurs and the allocation becomes possible.

THE SEARCH FOR TREATMENT

A growing body of evidence suggests that most people who encounter the kind of anguish that mental illness brings— whether it be their own or someone else's—turn first to those around them for help and guidance, and only when these informal sources fail, and when consensus has been reached about the seriousness of the case, do they approach someone more distant and more professional (Clausen; Hammer; Cumming, 1962a). After the efforts of kindred and friends have failed—and it is important to remember that no one knows how often they succeed—some of the more sophisticated may approach an acquaintance who knows a psychiatrist and so arrange for care. Many people go to a physician or to a clergyman (Gurin; Kadushin) unless they are very poor, in which case they may talk to a public health nurse, call the police, or perhaps find themselves in court. A few consult a lawyer. These are the social agents often called "gatekeepers" or "caretakers"

(Lindemann), and, whether they know it or not, they must do the allocating if patients are to receive specialized assistance at all.

The question now becomes, how do the gatekeepers know whom to send for specialized care and how do they determine the best place to send them? Do they ask themselves whether they can reasonably treat the patient, or do they instead ask themselves what would be the ideal treatment for him? To describe this allocation process, let me suggest two mechanical analogs or models. The perspective will be different: now we shall look at the process from the point of view of "the system," that is, the network of doctors, nurses, social workers, policemen, clergymen, lawyers, welfare workers, and probation officers who might conceivably ameliorate the patient's discomfort and bring him back under social control so that others could live with him and he with others.

Bear in mind throughout this essay that these analogs, and indeed this whole discussion, apply to the urban situation. In rural and semi-rural areas there is less specialization of professional role, more impact on the community as a whole from the loss of any member, and a different pattern of mobilization of a different range of resources. These formulations are also limited to routine, or at least non-cataclysmic, events. In sudden disaster, a latent and highly centralized system of social control is activated: the army, the Red Cross, Civil Defense, and so on.

The Dispatcher Analog or Model. This model for the allocation of services requires that once the label of mental illness is attached to the patient and he approaches or is taken to someone who might help him, the agent either treats him or sends him to a dispatcher whose role it is to see that the patient gets to the service most suitable to his condition. Such a model assumes that all agents in the dispatcher system are oriented primarily to the patient's treatment and only secondarily to their own reputations and incomes or to their agency's annual

statistics; they can neither compete for patients nor refuse to
see those brought to them by the dispatcher. More importantly,
it assumes an overall plan and policy which governs who shall
be treated and where, and which informs the dispatcher how to
allocate the available services. It postulates a central communi-
cations and planning center and perhaps a system of traffic
officers who help the dispatcher find and coordinate the facilities
and treatments needed for any particular client. In such a
model, all the agents or units are interdependent, have clearly
defined domains of action, and are subject to an overall centralized plan. They need not be especially visible to one another.
The terms of entrance to the agencies, that is, their boundary
conditions, are explicit in the laws and rules laid down by
central planners and policy-makers. The responsibility for the
agencies' functions lies jointly with the central authority and
the professionals themselves. Clients and patients have little
influence on practice.

Once the patient gets into the system, only his own volition
and perhaps a lack of skill or resources in the agencies themselves keeps him from the treatment ideally suited to his illness.

A system of service built on a dispatcher model sharply
restricts both the patients' and the agents' autonomy and is
much too centralized for Americans. Furthermore, given our
particular balance between openness and privacy, would a
central source of information about patients be supportable?
It is tempting to think that this is one reason why social service
exchanges have been difficult to maintain in this country, but
such does not seem to be the case. While we in America still
find it relatively easy to obtain lists of patients and clients from
both public and private agencies for research purposes, British
scientists in a more highly centralized system must develop
samples on a house-to-house basis because lists are never
released.

In spite of the dispatcher model's incompatibility with some
of our deeply held values, we seem to be moving toward it.

For example, although social security legislation was opposed by a large, articulate minority and a full generation was needed before attempts to hitch new services to it could be made, it represented a powerful thrust in the direction of centralism and hence coordination. But even now such a centralized service as social security [13] is provided only for those who are peripheral to the major institutions of society: the old, the orphaned, the disabled and the incompetent.[14] For the most part, funds made available through the federal government are still allocated through the familiar labyrinth from federal to state to county—as with the enormous program of Aid to Dependent Children. In other programs, especially in the eastern states, funds are often passed along to private agencies, in turn responsible to groups of citizens who meet and yearn for the utopia of coordination and communication without a superstructure.

There are almost no adequate studies of the workings of total integrative or helping systems,[15] so that we do not know whether or not the dispatcher ideal ever comes close to reality, although we do have subsystems of services that seem to approach the model. There are some hints of the kinds of problems that arise in systems more or less of this type, and I shall refer to them as I go along.

As I have suggested, some problems such as poverty in old age have become too big for the smaller governmental unit, the private agency, or the citizens' group, and the federal government's role is finally accepted in such areas. Eventually we can expect to see a range of services attached to social security and therefore centrally planned and perhaps administered. The Veterans Administration operates groups of services, but because it is a system of replicated units it does not have the interdependence demanded by the dispatcher model. The V.A. system is often resented because its services tend not only to replicate one another but also others in the community, and because it is a form of state medicine. But the system has solid support from those who cannot mobilize service anywhere else.

It is doubtful whether any but the most expensive services will become centralized in this way; there is no compelling reason why they should be, and centralization goes against our ideological grain. Nor can we assume that it would work. One description of a society in which almost all services, including the ameliorative, are operated in a somewhat ungainly way by a central government comes from New Zealand, where J. H. Robb reports:

> Influences from outside the family tend to impinge upon it from different parts of the network of services in a somewhat disconnected, unrelated and even contradictory fashion. It then becomes the task of the family to evolve a pattern of living which will permit these varied, external influences to be handled in such a way that adequate harmony and consistency is maintained . . .

Robb might be talking about the "multi-problem family" in our own system, but instead he is describing a dispatcher's system that does not work. He explains that there are reasons— professional exclusiveness, a strongly vertical administrative structure, and so on—why there is no coordination at the level of interaction between agent and client.

In Britain the observer can see a mixed picture of gratification and frustration among those concerned with the mentally ill. On the one hand, central planning has enabled the Ministries of Health and Labour to plan together a smoothly working dispatcher system of rehabilitation, retraining, job placement, and housing; but it is hard to achieve coordination of the ameliorative services: recreation, support, and guidance. One psychiatrist, noted for his creative work with chronic schizophrenics, says:

> One finds at the moment that the best laid plans either do not develop or else go awry for lack of some integrating force. Social workers don't seem to see themselves perform-

ing this function; they are willing to advise the patient where to go and what to do, but they don't see it as part of their job to see that he executes these plans. This means that for disabled patients nothing happens. In hospital wards it is done by the nurse who has to ensure that the doctors don't forget to see the patients and prescribe their medicines, the pharmacists don't forget to send their prescriptions and the patient doesn't forget to take them. There seems to be nobody performing this function in the community.[16]

It sounds as if this observer is in the middle of a dispatcher system without enough traffic officers. Nor is his experience unique; C. H. Rolph describes a similar breakdown of coordination among services available to children seen in London courts.

Coming back to the American scene, we can see a kind of dispatcher system in microcosm in the Roman Catholic system of charities. Here the ameliorative services are likely to be administered from the diocesan office, and many priests, as well as Catholic doctors, teachers, and social workers, send patients and clients to this service, from which they are allocated to various other agencies. But this is a centralism that is a part of a religious hierarchy already recognized and accepted by the people most likely to use it; its hierarchical features are apparently reconcilable with secular egalitarianism. Furthermore, like the English system, this one may serve best those people most able to approach the agency on their own.

These are a few sketchy examples of successes and failures in the allocation of resources in something approximating the dispatcher ideal. I conclude that a centrally planned system is feasible for dispensing psychiatric care, but certain pathologies afflict it. The planning is distant from the patient (Titmuss), coordination at the level of the patient can fail, and, in our own case, anxiety because of the contravention of some basic values,

equality and individualism, can make us timid. In summary, we
appear to make only a few exceptions; one is when the problem is too big, too dangerous, and involved with too many parts
of our pluralistic nation to be handled with any degree of
efficiency at the local level, as in social security. Another is
when the centralism is in the hands of those whom we consider
for other reasons to be above suspicion, such as the religious
charitable system.

Before considering the second model, I should make it clear
that I do not consider our frame of mind about centralism to
be necessarily immutable. Indeed, change is occasionally adum-
brated. Eugene V. Rostow, for example, asks a question that is
only half rhetorical: "Are we sure that the emotional development of the community wouldn't be better if there was more
delegation to bureaucrats, and less mass involvement in the details of the decisional process?" In general, as the nation has
become more urban, more differentiated, and more complex,
our eighteenth-century French ideals have been eroded. They
will suffer still more erosion, and we shall slowly evolve a way
of living with a strong central government that is compatible
with our ideological predilections, perhaps through the Norwegian formula of cooperation between government and citizen
groups.

The Pinball Machine Analog or Model. In the pinball analog,
a group of agencies and agents are coordinated not through a
plan or a central structure but through common commitment
to a body of values, and consensus about appropriate activities
for each agency and agent.

This manner of operating is both open and egalitarian. But
individualism, which leads to competitiveness, must be somewhat muted or the system will not work at all. The units of
the model can be overlapping and non-interdependent; their
boundaries are defined partly by laws and rules but also by
assumptions and norms developed in practice and in interaction

with agency boards. The agents' own standards or professionalization, as well as client behavior, can mold practice. When a client or patient is injected into a pinball type of system, he approaches or is taken to the agency seen as relevant, and the boundary conditions surrounding that agency determine his rebound to the next port of call. That is, the agency first contacted can either take him in, refer him, or turn him away so that he must start his search all over again; on the other hand, the patient himself may reject the service. For example, he may go through an "intake" procedure but never return to the agency.

In a perfectly operating system of this type, every unit is independent of every other unit and subject to no directives from a central body, but only to voluntary cooperation based on general agreement about what kind of client should receive service from what kind of agency. Thus the aggregate boundary condition serves the same function as a centralized policy in the dispatcher model and is the defining characteristic of the system. Put another way, the difference between the two systems is the difference between a division of labor based on a system of central planning, policy-making, and law, and a less complete division of labor based on consensus, competition, and law (Durkheim).

There seems little doubt that, given our beliefs, we are comfortable with the pinball way of organizing things. But if it does work for us, what about all the cries for coordination? Perhaps we are expressing in them our frustration with the inevitable errors and inefficiency in the system. After all, the same complaint is heard in the centralized New Zealand case. Inefficiency in our system arises, however, not only from ignorance and error but also from the fact that it is difficult to make any concerted assault on social conditions through a consensual system. Controversial action on behalf of groups of patients, for example, is inconceivable because no agency is powerful enough to act alone when consensus fails, and covert attempts to get outside help are difficult because the system is too open.

An example of these drawbacks in the pinball type of organization can best be seen in attempts to rehabilitate the chronically mentally ill, a process that requires carefully worked out programs and a high level of coordination among psychiatric, rehabilitative, educational, and employment agencies. In a relatively centralized system, this can be accomplished by careful planning; in a consensual system, where vested interests are easier to assert, the introduction of a new activity that cuts into the domain of other agencies can be filibustered. In Britain it was recognized about a decade ago that a large proportion of mental patients require occupational rehabilitation, and now the official plan provides that no community treatment center shall be set up without an accompanying rehabilitation facility. In this country rehabilitation for the chronically ill has been slow, partly because of difficulty in getting agreement upon who shall do it and partly because of difficulty in coordinating the necessary agencies once agreement is reached.

In spite of its awkwardness, a consensual system has no centralized control; it allows, indeed encourages, us to deal with misfortune on an individual basis, and it is a very open method of operation. Many meetings and much exchange of information underlies consensus. Inasmuch as it can be known at all, anyone can find out what goes on in our system, while in a dispatcher system, where much of what goes on is known only centrally, news does not get around and secrecy is possible.

A third model for the allocation of services should be considered briefly—a supermarket model (Dorothy Miller). In such an organization of services the agents are independent but visible operators in an open system, and the client has full choice to select what he needs. Such a model lies behind official medical policy for the distribution of medical services, and it probably comes close to describing the way in which our pinball system can sometimes be made to work for the well-to-do. I shall not discuss the supermarket model further, however, because it describes a system that requires of the user both knowledge and competence. Unfortunately, the earmark of the applicant for many services is that he is temporarily less than fully competent.

Given, then, that we like our own way of doing things, I think it is fair—on the ground that no choice is without its price —to consider what we have to pay for it. I shall turn now to a discussion of some of the ways in which, in the allocation of services, the pinball method seems to fall short of its purpose of returning people to autonomy with the least possible intervention, and after that I shall discuss some of the mechanisms that seem to expedite such return.

Failure of Purpose in the System

Certain kinds of failures of purpose seem to arise primarily in administrative frictions and discontinuities. Sometimes these are compounded by the structure of our major institutions. I have in mind the kind of problem that arises when two agencies who wish to tackle a local problem together find that they cannot because one, perhaps a V.A. mental hospital, receives its policy from a national body, while the other, perhaps a county clinic, has local autonomy.

The most important failures of this kind are probably those that arise in competition between units of government, particularly between levels of government. That local authorities should haggle over who shall have the responsibility for attending to the more hopeless patients seems preordained by our method of organizing our political lives. For example, Robert H. Connery points out that the metropolitan area of Philadelphia, which has 726 different governmental units, finds allocation extremely difficult. Upon reading his graphic account of the chaos caused by this fragmentation, we find ourselves asking how any kind of agreement is ever reached.

Competition among units at the same level of government is more serious and, on the whole, less rational. An example of such competition comes from a series of events in a middle-sized city, where training for boys who had dropped out of school was being planned by a large citizen group. When the federal government independently tried to promote a similar service to be carried out by the State Unemployment Service, the citizen group, instead of welcoming the help and trying to divide up this enormous task, made strong appeals to congressmen and senators to *stop* the money from being granted on the grounds that the state and federal governments were usurping local functions. One cannot help wondering who among all the people involved here is concerned about the youngsters who have dropped out of school. An analysis of this type of inter-agency conflict is given by Walter B. Miller. Our own researches have not made such frictions particularly manifest because our empirical focus has been on clients as they approach the boundaries of agencies. We have, as it were, studied the movement of the ants in order to infer the structure of the ant hill, and we have inevitably missed some aspects of it. Good discussions of failures of agency coordination from the administrative angle have been given by Sol Levine, E. Litwak, Harold Wilensky and Charles N. LeBeaux, and others.

In the following sections I shall discuss two key features of our particular system: the apparent scarcity of psychiatric personnel and the vagueness of the treatment process. Then I shall point out some unfortunate consequences of these features in the light of our pinball method of allocation and the values that underlie it.

TWO KEY FEATURES OF OUR SYSTEM

Scarcity. The first and perhaps most obvious features of the allocation of services is that there are not enough psychiatrists to go around if the mentally ill are to be treated on a one-to-one basis. Furthermore, as George Albee has pointed out in his report on manpower to the Joint Commission on Mental Illness and Health, there will never be enough psychiatrists because of the absolute shortage of medical doctors and even of college graduates from whom to recruit them. This shortage has inspired the invention of the milieu or environmental therapies that are carried out by paramedical personnel under the supervision of psychiatrists (Cumming and Cumming, 1962). Such new forms of treatment have theoretical rationale as well as making more use of the available personnel, but they are by no means universally accepted. Most psychiatrists like to deal with patients on an individual basis and to use paramedical personnel, not as central therapeutic agents but to do things they themselves do not want to do. Since psychiatrists usually have unlimited authority, whether it be in a hospital, clinic, or private practice, it is hard to get them to change.[17] Furthermore, psychoanalysis has found our individualistic soil fertile, and at least until the beginning of the 1960's it has been the aristocrat of psychiatric techniques. It should be noted, of course, that although it is commonly assumed that the one-to-one treatments are superior to either drug or environmental therapies, this has never been demonstrated to be so.[18] In spite of its unproven status, the best psychiatric residents are attracted to psychoanalysis because of its high prestige, its intellectual-artistic appeal, and its academic respectability. In choosing it they contribute further to the shortage because psychoanalysts treat so few patients (Cumming, 1962b).

The Vagueness of the Treatment and Its Outcome. Psychiatrists have never completely codified their therapeutics, although the more nearly their techniques have approached those of medicine and surgery, the more clearly they have been described and the more easily they have been replicated. Indeed, it was because of its replicability that lobotomy was shown to be ineffective and was discarded. Similarly, insulin therapy has failed to withstand clinical evaluation and has largely given way to treatment with pharmaceutical drugs, which in turn is undergoing intensive evaluation (Ødegard). The effectiveness of hospitalization in itself has been examined, and at least one study suggests that the longer the period of hospitalization, the greater the likelihood of relapse (Brill and Patton). But there seems little doubt that hospitals will survive this finding. Custody of the incompetent seems an inevitable social function for the measurable future.

When we leave the biological therapies and turn to psychotherapy and milieu therapy, we find that, although there are evaluative studies, the therapeutic processes themselves are hardly ever specified in any *systematic* detail, and there is no reason to believe that they are standard. It is doubtful, indeed, whether psychotherapy will ever be codified, because it is taught under a one-to-one apprenticeship system and is therefore intensely personal, individual, and variable. Things that cannot be specified can, of course, be evaluated, but attempts to evaluate psychotherapy have usually ended up showing "no effect" (Frank). Like the mental hospital, however, psychotherapy seems to survive. Indeed, the process is so individualistic in so many of its aspects that it has acquired a patina almost as sacred as that surrounding individual initiative, or even private enterprise.

As well as vagueness of method, all psychiatric practice seems to suffer from diffuseness of goals. It aims to restore the patient to mental health, or to restore his ego function, or to reconstitute his personality—terms that can be defined only in such generalities as "a sense of well-being," or "maturity," or, at best, "adequacy of performance." In other words, psychiatry is diffusely concerned with the whole man. Our studies suggest, however, that while the psychiatrist tends to see himself as the prototype of the physician to the whole man, so do a great many other helping agents, including everyone with any degree of training in any of the helping, supporting, or counseling activities. There is a kind of diffuse "professionally human" skill that is learned, formally or informally, by most of the people whose jobs are concerned with controlling deviant behavior. Social workers and family doctors all have it, and policemen are being urged to learn it, if indeed they do not already have it. Even people whose work does not bring them directly into contact with people have a stake in the whole man. Melvin Webber, a planner, seems to show a diffuse concern when he says, "As one of its paramount functions, then, planning in a democratic society is being seen as a process by which the community seeks to increase the individual's opportunities to choose for himself—including the freedom to consume the society's produce and the freedom to choose to be different." It is quite possible that all who work at integrative tasks must have a diffuse, holistic approach to the individual so that their more specific skills can be used in the context of his general welfare; but if the diffuse concern is not accompanied by specific skills, ambiguity, conflict, and competition can result.

COMPETITION, GAPS, AND REDUNDANCIES

Among all the agents who share the "professionally human" skill of ministering to the troubled, there seems to be competition for those clients most eager to be helped, those who are passing through a crisis of some kind that can be resolved more quickly with help, those who will return to their normal state of functioning fairly rapidly, and those who, no matter what their disorder, are genial and easy to work with. On the face of it, it seems perfectly natural that when the outcome of intervention is doubtful, intervention itself should be expected to provide professional satisfaction and that patients should be selected accordingly. I shall describe the misunderstandings and conflict that we have found in the relationship between family doctors and psychiatrists in the medium-sized community that we have studied, and then suggest, more briefly, some of the tensions and strains among other agents less centrally, but still importantly, concerned with the mentally ill.

The Family Doctor and the Psychiatrist. Somewhere in his search for treatment, often at the beginning, the mentally ill patient asks for guidance from a general practitioner or a family doctor. But this physician does not refer the patient for psychiatric attention immediately, especially if the afflicted person is already his patient. Among thirty-two family doctors in a study in our series, thirty said they would rather treat their own psychiatric cases than refer them, unless the patients were unmanageably psychotic. One physician said, "The psychiatrist listens to his patients and perhaps gives them a shock treatment or two, and after a while they get better; well, they get better when I treat them, too." On the whole, these doctors were quite explicit about their reasons for not making referrals—first, they believed it was good medical practice to treat a patient for *all* his problems; second, they feared the loss of patients, and psychiatric referrals can result in just that; and third, they were baffled by the attitude of psychiatrists. After all, the family doctor is accustomed to dealing with specialists who, like the surgeon, willingly accept a patient with an acute condition or who, like the obstetrician, expect to step in to handle a difficult delivery. The psychiatrist, in contrast, when presented with an acutely psychotic patient, complains about what he calls "a poor referral." Besides wanting to receive patients in the early stages of their illnesses, the psychiatrist is often recalcitrant about reporting the patient's progress to the family doctor, sometimes pleading "privileged communication." From other specialists the family doctor gets reports or at least phone calls, but psychiatrists—those arch individualists—not only pick and choose whom they will treat but also refuse to keep the system open. It is true that not all psychiatrists have these attitudes, and those manning emergency services certainly do not, but the doctors in our study group mentioned only two of the city's forty or more psychiatrists as being helpful to them when they lose control of the patient. Generally speaking, the more contact these doctors had had with psychiatric facilities, the more disaffected they were. They complained of the psychiatrists' refusals to accept referral, of the costliness of treatment by private psychiatrists, of their secretiveness, and of the length of clinic waiting lists.

On the other side of the coin, the handful of psychiatrists whom we interviewed agreed that the city's general practitioners needed education in making referrals (Rudolph and Cumming). This complaint also appears repeatedly in the report to the Joint Commission on Community Services. The clinics are said to be swamped with hopeless patients, the community does not know how to use the service, and so on (Robinson).

If we look at this *contretemps* between physicians and psychiatrists in terms of the whole system, we might describe it as part of a pinball allocating system that is dogged by ignorance and error. On the one hand, the physician would like to deal with the psychiatrist as he does with all other specialists, but when he tries, tension and conflict result. On the other hand, the psychiatrist, if he cannot train the doctor to make better referrals, would like to be in the physician's position himself, so that as a gatekeeper he could select from the flow of patients those who meet his individual specifications. As it is, he receives patients more to his liking from family agencies and perhaps through the lay referral system. Unfortunately, for two rather obvious reasons he is not, and probably never will be, a gatekeeper. First, as we have said, there are not enough psychiatrists to perform this function, and second, there is little likelihood that even our best efforts will succeed in destigmatizing the psychiatric illness for any but the most sophisticated. Stigma does not seem to result from ignorance; rather, it seems to occur because anyone who is diffusely impaired in mind or emotion is disqualified from responsible social interaction because of his unpredictability, and he is bound therefore to receive some kind of sanction—more particularly if he belongs to a society that believes in individual responsibility and initiative. It seems a better deployment of our scarce resources to try to improve treatment than to fight an uphill battle against a sanction so entrenched as stigma.

In summary, the psychiatrist-physician relationship is an example of a failure of consensus between agents with a rather high degree of unit autonomy, and this failure is then exacerbated by different standards of privacy. Since there is no central plan in our system, the relationship between these two will probably continue in much the same way until psychiatrists as a group either have a change of heart about whom they treat or develop a unique and successful technique of treatment that only they can perform, or until doctors repudiate the whole man and declare themselves interested only in his corporeal aspects—a prospect which seems unlikely.

Social Workers, Clergymen, Nurses, Policemen, and Welfare Officers. Social workers, especially caseworkers, are trained to counsel with clients, and some of them to do psychotherapy. They recognize psychiatrists as being like themselves, only more skilled, and they defer to them. The relationship between the two is something like that of nurses to doctors—they understand each other, it is clear who is legally responsible, and there is no feedback problem.

But between clergymen and caseworkers there is a permanent strain. Our studies suggest that caseworkers and clergymen counsel with almost exactly the same kind of people and refer them to physicians and psychiatrists at almost exactly the same point of difficulty. The result of this redundancy of function is intense competition and sometimes recrimination: the clergyman thinks the caseworker amoral and secretive; the caseworker thinks the clergyman judgmental—apparently failing to note that caseworkers exercise their own somewhat different canons of judgment. This tension is less frequent among Catholics, because Catholic caseworkers tend to respect the priest's moral and religious contribution to the case, and consensus is easier to reach.

Physicians take little note of social workers. When our study group of family doctors was asked if they used the special directory that the Council of Social Agencies had prepared for them, half of them had forgotten receiving it. Only one said he used an agency regularly for problems other than adoptions. Family doctors seem either to do their own social work or not to know it needs doing.

Many physicians are ambivalent about clergymen. They know that they ought to cooperate with them, but when asked if they make referrals, they grumble and say such things as, "I know I should send certain patients to their clergymen, but what good will it do?" On the whole, doctors cannot imagine anyone taking better care of the whole man than they do.

In contrast, clergymen and social workers are both glad to send patients to physicians for a technical service that nobody else is trained for or legally entitled to give. Our data gives no hint that either of these agents is aware of the family doctor's image of himself as the central, diffuse agent who takes care of all the patient's troubles, occasionally calling in a specialist. Both the clergyman and the social worker, however, see *themselves* in that role and, as far as I can tell, think that the doctor sees them this way also.[19] In general, this failure of consensus seems to be benign enough, for it engenders no great hostility. What might be best for the patient is so far unevaluated.

The policeman, the welfare worker (McCaffrey), and the parole officer are in somewhat different situations. Policemen act as everybody's emergency health service twenty-four hours a day, and, inasmuch as other helping agents are generally unavailable in the middle of the night when acute problems may arise, they look upon themselves as the agents who tackle tough problems alone. Furthermore, they stand to the very poor as the clergyman and family doctor stand to the middle and working class. Since their helping role is not recognized by the rest of the system, and since no one is competing for their clients, they tend to be an isolated agency trying to maintain a precarious and unstable balance of support and control in their dealings with difficult and disturbed people.

Welfare workers, like police, attend to people who are not good referrals: drunks, chronic psychotics, the inarticulate, the poor, and the ignorant. The problem is that they are defined as "social workers," on the one hand, but charged with defending the public purse from "chiselers" and "frauds" on the other. They find it hard to resist applying to their clients the stigma that the politicians have given them.[20] They have a conflict-ridden job with a difficult group and very little support in doing it. Parole officers also must deal with a high proportion of people with chronic mental illness (Cumming and Miller), and they too have difficult roles.

The Differential Allocation of Services. Besides the absolute shortage of psychiatrists, there is a differential distribution of the available talent. Generally speaking, there is ample psychiatric care in a few of the largest cities for those who can pay for it; there is less than enough elsewhere, with the supply getting shorter as the location gets more rural. There are usually enough psychiatrists to staff clinics but never enough to staff mental hospitals. There is enough service for the well-to-do and the well educated but very little for the poor and ignorant (Wootton, Cloward and Epstein).

Since Jerome K. Myers' and Leslie Schaffer's original statement, it has been confirmed many times that educated, articulate patients are treated individually by psychiatrists in one-to-one psychotherapeutic relationships, while less literate groups tend to receive biological treatment and custodial care (Forstenzer,

1961; Hollingshead and Redlich; Hunt; Rooney and Miller; Saenger; Winder and Hersko). This is because selection of the patient by the psychiatrist is so largely a matter of taste. As Erich Lindemann says, "Whether a patient is a good case for the doctor or a good case to treat, or whether he has a good illness rather than an uninteresting condition—*that depends upon the specific skill the given psychiatrist brings to his practice, to his style of communication, his likes and dislikes,* and to the unwitting determinants of his attitudes and goals which are derived from his own culture and class background." (Italics mine.) From another perspective, Hyman Forstenzer (1964) points out, "The Joint Commission on Mental Illness and Health recommended top priority for serious morbidity. Available data amply demonstrate that, except for public mental hospitals, psychiatric resources are occupied with caseloads that correspond to minor morbidity." Even within the public mental hospital the same kind of sorting takes place, with the better cases receiving individual treatment on the admission wards and the others being assigned to the part of the hospital known euphemistically as the "continued treatment service."

But this uneven distribution of psychiatric services is not the whole story. If the mentally ill could be counted on to be either ill and under treatment or else well and at work, some attempt at equalization of service might be made (John Cumming; Gruenberg). Evidence is accumulating, however, that perhaps only as much as half of mental illness is treated in its acute, disorganized phase by some form of psychiatric care—usually in a state hospital—while its chronic, inadequate phase is usually treated by some agent who does not even know he is concerned with a clinical problem (McCaffrey).

There is, for example, a consensus (so general that it hardly requires comment) that the policeman will take care of a wild family row in the slums even if one of the parties is clearly mentally ill, while the wife of a businessman, who, upon discovering her husband's infidelity, takes an overdose of sleeping pills, will first be cared for by either her clergyman or her physician. Both people may reach psychiatric treatment fairly rapidly, but the path they take and the type of service they get will be different.

Not only psychiatric care is allocated on a status basis. The physician of the working-class family is a general practitioner, but the physician of the middle-class family is likely to be an internist. Besides such parallel streams of service, there are special agencies to which only the inadequate can appeal, such as the Salvation Army and the rescue mission, while there are others to which only the "motivated" need apply, such as the private casework agencies and many psychiatric and child guidance clinics.

In a study of 275 men over the age of twenty-five years who approached various agencies for assistance, we found 16 percent who had a previous history of hospitalization—a large number by any standard. Among this group, the most severely affected were men who had a long-standing history of job failure, just short of a quarter of them having been in mental hospitals.

When we look at the kinds of agencies that serve these people, we find that the highest rate of previous hospitalization (about 20 percent) is among the applicants to two religious charitable organizations operating sheltered workshops and charitable services for transients and those temporarily down on their luck.

The rate of prior hospitalization for the applicants to the Department of Public Welfare is somewhat lower, around 15 percent, and the rate is lowest of all for a medical clinic and two family agencies—about 6 percent. It appears that the psychotic, who is not at the moment defined as such, is allocated, or allocates himself, to the community services whose workers have the lowest level of training for helping the mentally ill. On the whole, therefore, the psychologically impaired man or woman who is showing only the social symptoms of his illness will be allocated to the custodial rather than the therapeutic and counseling services in the same way as the patient showing clinical symptoms. Richard Cloward calls the process whereby the family agencies select the least troubled clients, "disengagement from the poor," and Richard Titmuss has shown that the "welfare state" benefits most the well-to-do and competent segment of the population. In all, a principle of allocation on which all agents appear to have a relatively high level of consensus is that the poorer, the more ignorant, and the sicker the patient, the more eligible he is for treatment by the less well-trained and less professionalized practitioner (Rudolph and Cumming). This is the apotheosis of our egalitarianism. We all have an equal start in the race for the analytic couch; if some of us end up in a back ward, we have only ourselves to blame.[21]

The discovery that many formerly mentally ill patients are to be found in the care of non-psychiatric community agents raises some vexing questions about the system itself. Although it is true that the agents who have contact with these patients are usually indifferent to and ignorant of the patients' contacts with other parts of the system, I am not sure this is altogether an undesirable thing, given the present unwillingness of psychiatric personnel to treat this group. Should such people be treated with the openness that characterizes, for example, the handling of a school child who has been labeled "disturbed," there might be a real danger of creating a permanently stigmatized pariah class. I am not sure that those who bear such labels as "hard-core family," "multi-problem family," "ADC family," and so on, are not that already. There seems no point in adding the label "chronic mental case" if we are not prepared to do something about it.

The Problem of Quality Control. The increasing evidence that psychiatric care is allocated more as if it were a market commodity than a restitutive service suggests that the private goals of psychiatrists and the public goal of restoring deviant members to full autonomy are at odds. This conflict may arise because our pattern of allocation is harmonious with our individualistic beliefs but disturbing to our egalitarian impulses. Historically, psychiatry has run a zig-zag course, shifting between enlightened and enthusiastic treatment for all patients to apathy and custodialism for most of them. Such shifts may reflect our inability to satisfy all of our basic values at one time. In dispatcher systems where there is central planning, it is possible to direct resources to the treatment of the less attractive patients, and this has been successfully accomplished in England where the therapeutic community, the open hospital, and the rehabilitation programs were initiated, and where viable standards of care in mental hospitals are being developed. For us, such directed change is impossible, and we must look to a quality control arising within the profession itself.

Professionalization in itself seems to lead to increased investment in method. The highly trained surgeon cannot help being elated at the chance to perform a rare operation, and it is perhaps for this reason that in America safeguards such as tissue committees and medical audits are being incorporated into hospital practice. No such safeguard is built into psychiatry (Cumming and Rudolph). For psychoanalysts, on the one hand, who have but one skill—and that one learned in a highly individual apprenticeship situation—it seems improbable that there will be. On the other hand, although a psychiatrist can use electric shock on all his patients if he so chooses, this use *could* be controlled because the technique is standardized and the outcome is moderately predictable. Nevertheless, while in America rising levels of professionalization in physical medicine have been accompanied by self-administered quality control through techniques of inspection that would probably be alien to less open societies, nothing like it has happened in psychiatry, which remains a mystery locked inside hospital doors or psychiatrists' heads and labeled "privileged."

Some Successful Mechanisms of Coordination

If I have made our pinball type of system sound ill put together, it is because in many ways it is. Nevertheless, it does work, so I shall conclude by discussing three features that seem to keep it from chaos. I shall not attempt to exhaust the strengths of the system, nor shall I talk about such obvious integrative functions as common beliefs and values and common legal mandates. I shall omit, too, administrative mechanisms such as domain consensus (Levine and White), overlapping board memberships, and well-known routine practices like referrals and staff conferences.

PATIENTS AS MESSENGERS

Several times in the course of our studies, when the system has appeared to be hopelessly recalcitrant, we have seen an agent tell a client or a patient how to present himself to another agency so as to maximize his chances of receiving service. For example, a social worker who feels that a client is in serious need of psychiatric care but fears that he is not sufficiently interesting or attractive for the clinic, may suggest to him desirable ways of discussing and describing his symptoms. Only in a *very* open, egalitarian system could there occur this inclusion of the client in the world of guild secrets.

Occasionally, agents use clients to express their dissatisfaction with available services. For example, a clergyman who was concerned about the welfare of the children of a woman in a mental hospital could find no source of home care for them, and so he sent the husband to a family agency to ask for the homemaker services that he knew the agency could not provide. He explained to us that a bombardment of the agency, seemingly from different and unrelated sources, might in the end provoke a service. Patients, it seems, must integrate not only the several services they receive but the system that dispenses them as well!

Clients and patients often train each other to use the system. In crowded waiting rooms of welfare departments and medical and psychiatric clinics, a friendly culture can develop, and no one yet knows how much information is passed back and forth there. Our studies show that many clients and patients present themselves to sources of help because they have heard about them from others who have used them through what Eliot Freidson calls the "lay referral system." This kind of messenger activity must go on in every society, but it perhaps plays a particularly important part in an open, egalitarian one. It is hard to imagine a British suburban housewife telling even her close friend, much less her neighbor, where she has gone for psychiatric help.

ROLE BLURRING AMONG AGENTS

A tendency toward role blurring makes a general contribution to the coordination of our system, even though, as I have noted earlier, it also leads to competition. Role blurring coordinates the system both by allowing consensus to cut across professional domains and by allowing emergency substitution of roles. For example, although the psychiatrist is a medical doctor, he is peripheral to the medical profession because he has moved so far from those issues of life and death that are the core concern of medicine and surgery. In doing so, he has moved toward other professions—psychology, theology, social work—whose core concerns are the patient's psychological, moral, and social well-being. This peripherality of psychiatry to medicine has resulted in strains, but at the same time it has brought the psychiatrist into contact with a range of other agents in a way that has allowed him to appreciate their activities and, if necessary, to achieve quick consensus with them about a wide range of issues.

This overlapping of the "edges" of professions is probably integrative in any society (Goode). In ours it allows for substitution of one role holder for another without the intrusion of disrupting status problems. Thus a psychologist and a psychiatric social worker can, and often do, replace a psychiatrist, and a public health nurse can replace a social worker. Samuel Z. Klausner has analyzed in some detail the overlap between psychiatry and religion.[22]

The public health nurse may potentially be the most important agent for the mentally ill patient because the particular type of role blurring that she has experienced may provide, in the end, the best coordination among medical doctors, psychiatrists, and social workers—the three groups most able to provide care to, and coordinate other services around, the mentally ill patient. Family doctors like to deal with public health nurses better than with any other agent because the nurses both understand their purposes and feed back necessary information. On the other hand, while these nurses relate in a more or less traditional way to the family doctor, they are now trained to be increasingly sensitive to the mental and emotional components in illness. At times some have gone overboard in their enthusiasm for this more diffuse approach to patients and have almost repudiated their nursing skills in their zeal for "interpersonal relations." Nevertheless, nurses are perhaps the strongest link that the family doctor has with the rest of the system, and, although social workers and psychiatrists tend to look down upon them, their entry into the "professionally human" integrative group may strengthen the network of support around the mentally ill patient. A similar role might well be developed by the welfare worker and the parole officer in order to coordinate training, employment, and treatment services for the patient with a chronic mental illness.

In general, role blurring is congenial to us because it tends to diminish status differences and so to cut down on inegalitarian practices. It also tends to maintain openness in the system and to spread news of changing professional norms. It might be profitable to consider how this feature of our system could be used to maximize coordination without at the same time creating competition among different specialties, and, what is worse, leading to reduced standards of specialty performance.

PLANNING AND CONSULTATION

Planning as a separate and distinct discipline or profession is quite old, but until recently the American variety has been concerned only with the physical background of our lives. Now social planning has become popular, and there has been a tendency to play down physical aspects.[23] As a general activity it seems to be an important integrative mechanism.

The development of planning as an active discipline has raised a problem, however, because it is difficult to do much social planning without sinning against grass-roots decision-making. Planners such as Melvin Webber who are attempting to develop theories of planning can be expected to precipitate the conflict between this new tendency toward central policy-making and our heritage of unit autonomy. But on the whole this conflict seems to be remote, because the major tendency among planners is to reiterate the dangers of centralization and at the same time to develop a rather vague and abstract approach to planning itself. John R. Seeley, for example, says:

> The definition [of planning] must not be too clear. Whatever definition is arrived at, or whatever definitions are adopted, must be of such a strategic nature that they truly allow room for strategy without making space for lack of principle.

R. C. Hoover, concluding a long article on the relation of ethics to planning, says:

The planner then, is the one who is given the good grace to be a servant who lives and suffers uncalculatingly with the family of urban specialists, but who, through love, helps others to transcend specialization in their own best ways. This prepares the terrain for the advent of integrative grace in the fullness of time.

These writers seem to be saying that they do not so much make plans as reaffirm the norms, integrate, coordinate, and carry messages. They are domestic diplomats. They fill roles that have no core of technical expertise. The planner-diplomat is in a strong position to help the development of consensus because he is outside of all of the subsystems that must be coordinated. In this way he can act as facilitator, can keep the system open, or, if necessary, keep secrets for a while. At the same time he can carry suggestions about reallocations, knowing that, since his sponsorship is from outside, it will not give rise to competitiveness. Because this type of planner is a value-reaffirmer, he can be invoked as an expert, but because he cannot be a tyrant he has only influence and no authority. In short, the planner may be a professional achiever of consensus. The rather startling lack of content in some of the planning literature, together with the retreat from a narrower but more concrete and therefore controversial urban planning, may suggest that the planner has found a key function as a professional expediter of consensus in a complex pluralistic society devoted to individualism, equality, and unit autonomy—which is, nevertheless, creeping ineluctably toward a welfare state. His advent seems to raise real possibilities for the efficiency of the system, even though there is some evidence from our study that, especially at the local level, planning can degenerate into a reaffirmation of the status quo. For example, after many meetings of a planning committee considering a county-based system of services, it is agreed that much needs to be done for the mentally ill and that the best way to proceed is for people to continue to do what they are now doing, perhaps under a new name. As Robert Weaver puts it, "In the broadest sense, the urban planning process represents the self-conscious attempt by men to order their environment so as to realize certain common goals and values. As such, it is concerned not merely with the rational allocation of resources, but more importantly, with the selection of goals and values toward which those resources should be directed. As a result, urban planning is an important part of the process by which consensus is achieved in a democratic society."

Re-examination

In the final analysis there is no real reason to believe that the restitutive purpose which I have attributed to the system exists in anyone's mind but my own. Both the pinball and the dispatcher analogs rest on the premise that we want to restore each deviant member to an acceptable level of functioning. But this assumption may simply arise in a mistaken belief that everyone values the integrity of our social system for its own sake. Why, after all, should we make such an assumption? It is certainly true that the *imminent* disruption of a social system calls into play certain well-known patterns of adaptation, as disaster studies have shown. But such behavior is surely parallel to our cry for the doctor when we feel that we are gravely ill and may die. When there is no imminent danger to our lives, do we take precautions against dying prematurely? Do we give up smoking? Do we fasten our seat belts? And if we do not, does that mean that we lack a sense of survival? In a parallel way, do we really care what happens to the members of the groups we belong to, except when we fear the disruption of the group itself? There are psychoses, for example, that are preventable but which we do not prevent. Pellagra is caused by a vitamin deficiency, but we do not try to stamp it out as efficiently as we have tried to stamp out syphilis (which, after all, is catching and hence always imminent). It may be that our concern for a well-integrated society, from which few people are permanently lost by preventable or curable illness, can never be the bona fide concern of many of the members of any society, because all-inclusive perspectives tend to be paralyzing. It may also be that in American society integration has a low priority compared with achievement of material goals (Galbraith).

Both our allocation of services to the mentally ill and our mechanism for delivering them, then, are generated through a series of major and minor choices—at the interpersonal, social, and political levels—which reflect our hierarchy of values. These values are hard to study, especially by those who espouse them, and especially because they are always changing. Nevertheless, because the allocation of an enormous share of scarce resources to the less competent members of society is at once a moral, ethical, and intensely practical pursuit, it deserves our continued critical concern.

Notes

1. A volume reporting the results of this group of studies is in preparation.

2. References to authors throughout are to works listed in the Bibliography following these notes.

3. For an account of some of the absurdities that can result from ignoring the situation and trying to treat delinquency and mental illness on a person-by-person basis, see Barbara Wootton.

4. This in spite of the fact that for every citizen in any way victimized by the federal government, hundreds are intimidated by local governments, local police, and lower court judges. For a fine analysis of such "yahoo justice" see John P. Roche.

5. It is remarkable how often an ad hoc patchwork of services is described in such terms as ". . . there has been a healthy pragmatism in the development of action programs . . ."

6. An interesting alternative to both American and British forms of decision-making is the Norwegian, in which much planning and execution is deputized to citizen boards.

7. We also apparently fear it. In the *New York Times* of March 29, 1964, a news story detailed the difference in prices of drugs in America and abroad. It described the federal govenment's practice of buying tetracycline in Italy while New York City's Department of Health paid eight times as much for the same product because of its fear that if it imported its supplies the American drug houses would sue.

8. Openness has many more implications than can be examined here. For example, Americans traditionally feel that control by such impersonal agents as policemen should be resisted. Freedom tends to mean just that— freedom *from* control. Since society requires a certain minimum of constraint, some other kinds of control must then be part of the system. If police, highway signs, and government are anathematized, openness and visibility can be one of the ways of increasing informal control.

9. It is not commonly realized that our belief that children need to be able to "relate to their peers" is unknown in some Western cultures. In France, for example, peer groups are looked upon as semi-delinquent; a child's legitimate memberships are home and school (Pitts).

10. A relatively small number of American private schools are modeled on the British pattern and discourage a close collaboration between parents and school. That they train an elite minority is of consequence but cannot be investigated here.

11. For example, in a city in Arizona in 1962 a group of parents hired a lawyer and demanded that the school officials stop asking probing questions of the children about their home lives. The school's inquiries were designated "tests," but there seems no doubt that they were designed to learn intimate details of the children's family backgrounds.

12. For a good discussion of the implications of the labeling problem for psychiatrists and their patients, see Thomas J. Scheff.

13. I am leaving unemployment insurance out of this discussion since I regard it as essentially an instrumental rather than as an integrative feature of society.

14. It is worth noting that even in such an eloquent appeal for central intervention as *The Other America,* Michael Harrington is careful to record his belief that programs should be locally controlled.

15. Margot Jefferys of the London School of Hygiene and Tropical Medicine is making a careful study of the social and medical agencies in Buckinghamshire, England, but this is still incomplete. A Ph.D. thesis by Annett Lawrence in the London School of Economics has categorized the descriptive axes along which people appear to have been allocated for service, but she does not attack the mechanics of this allocation. The Social Planning Council of Metropolitan Toronto has made an interesting study of the "best pattern" of service.

16. Douglas Bennett, Maudsley Hospital, London. Personal communication.

17. Ironically, the policy-making groups in bureaucracies and funding groups can ardently desire changes in psychiatric practice but be power-

less to bring them about because of their own deep belief in unit autonomy.

18. It is interesting to speculate on why this secretive, elitist form of treatment was so fashionable for so long. My guess is that it is one expression of the intense, retreatist individualism of the fifties that seems to have been a backlash from the sacrifices demanded in the name of the nation during the war (Cumming and Cumming, 1959).

19. It takes only one or two doctors using a family agency for adoptions to give that agency the feeling that they are receiving a lot of medical referrals. Similarly, the clergyman who receives patients for pastoral counseling from a physician friend has the same impression, because he gets so few referrals from anywhere else.

20. The worker himself is stigmatized just by working with incompetent people. It is an ironic by-product of our egalitarian system that people can be judged as equals through propinquity alone!

21. Since this has been written, it has been called to my attention that as there is a scarcity of services, and some allocation is necessary, it is not unreasonable to expect that there will be a principle of allocation. What is not made explicit in the above discussion is that the principle appears to be a simple market one—whoever can afford it gets the best treatment. But medical ethics demand, at least in theory, that the patient most needing care should get it, although those unable to pay may get it under uncomfortable or even humiliating conditions.

22. The openness of our society has caused these relationships among professionals to be visible to at least some of the laity. Peter de Vries has satirized the religion and psychiatry relationship in a tale of a split-level church in the suburbs with a psychiatric clinic in the basement. The clergyman is a non-judgmental, permissive fellow, but the psychiatrist doles out moral admonitions to his patients. There was a grain of prophecy in this spoof, because during the two decades in which the clergymen took up non-directive counseling, psychiatrists were beginning to emphasize ego psychology which, with its emphasis upon competent performance, easily translates into a call for individual responsibility.

23. For a good clear summary of the history of city planning in America, see Herbert J. Gans.

Bibliography

Albee, George W., *Mental Health Manpower Trends*, New York, 1959.

Astin, Alexander, "The Functional Autonomy of Psychotherapy," *American Psychologist*, XVI, 2 (1961).

Brill, Henry, and Robert E. Patton, "Clinical-Statistical Analysis of Population Changes in New York State Mental Hospitals Since Introduction of Psychotropic Drugs," *American Journal of Psychiatry,* CXIX, 1 (1962).

Clausen, John, and Marian Yarrow, "The Impact of Mental Illness on the Family," *The Journal of Social Issues,* XI, 4 (1955).

Cloward, Richard A., and Irwin Epstein, "Private Family Agencies and the Poor," mimeographed paper, 1963.

Connery, Robert H., "Mental Health in Metropolitan Areas," in Leonard Duhl, ed., *The Urban Condition,* New York, 1963.

Cumming, Elaine, "Phase Movement in the Support and Control of the Psychiatric Patient," *Journal of Health and Human Behavior,* III, Winter (1962a).

Cumming, Elaine, "A Review Article—The Reports of the Joint Commission on Mental Illness and Health," *Social Problems,* IX, 4 (1962b).

Cumming, Elaine, and John Cumming, "Two Views of Public Attitudes toward Mental Illness," *Mental Hygiene,* XLIII, 2 (1959).

Cumming, Elaine, Laura Edell, and Ian M. Cumming, "Policeman as Philosopher, Guide, and Friend," *Social Problems,* XII, 3 (1964).

Cumming, Elaine, and Charles Harrington, "Clergyman as Counselor," *American Journal of Sociology,* LXIX, 3 (1963).

Cumming, Elaine, and John Cumming, *Closed Ranks,* Cambridge, Mass., 1957.

Cumming, Elaine, and Momoyo Ise, "The Family Doctor as Part of a System of Support and Control," *Trans-action,* April/May 1965.

Cumming, John, "The Inadequacy Syndrome," *Psychiatric Quarterly Supplement,* Fall 1963.

Cumming, John, and Elaine Cumming, *Ego and Milieu,* New York, 1962(a).

Cumming, John, and Elaine Cumming, "On the Stigma of Mental Illness," *The Community Mental Health Journal,* I, 2 (1965).

Cumming, John, and Leo Miller, "Isolation, Family Structure and Schizophrenia," in *Proceedings of the Third World Congress of Psychiatry,* Toronto, 1962.

Cumming, John, and Lionel Rudolph, "Trends in Medical Care and the Future of Psychiatry," *American Journal of Orthopsychiatry,* XXXV, 1 (1965).

DeJouvenel, Bertrand, "Jean-Jacques Rousseau," *Encounter,* December 1962.

DeTocqueville, Alexis, *Democracy in America,* New York, 1956.

DeVries, Peter, *Mackerel Plaza,* Boston, 1958.

Durkheim, Emile, *The Division of Labor in Society,* Glencoe, Ill., 1953.

Forstenzer, Hyman, "Problems in Relating Community Programs to State Hospitals," *The American Journal of Public Health,* LI, August (1961).

Forstenzer, Hyman, "Planning and Evaluation of Community Health Programs," *Forum,* XXXII, March (1964).

Frank, Jerome, *Persuasion and Healing,* Baltimore, 1961.

Freidson, Eliot, *Patients' Views of Medical Practice,* New York, 1961.

Fromm, Erich, *The Sane Society*, New York, 1955.

Galbraith, J. K., "Quality of Life," *Encounter*, January 1965.

Gans, Herbert J., "The Relationship of Social, Economic, and Physical Planning within a Goal-Oriented Approach to Planning," mimeographed paper, 1958.

Goode, William J., "A Theory of Role Strain," *American Sociological Review*, XXV, 4 (1960).

Gruenberg, E. M., *Mental Disorders—A Guide to Control Methods*, New York, 1962.

Gurin, Gerald, Joseph Veroff, and Sheila Feld, *Americans View Their Mental Health*, New York, 1960.

Hammer, Muriel, "Influence of Small Social Networks as Factors on Mental Hospital Admission," *Human Organization*, XXII, 4 (1963-64).

Harrington, Michael, *The Other America*, New York, 1962.

Hollingshead, A. B., and F. C. Redlich, *Social Class and Mental Illness*, New York, 1958.

Hoover, R. C., "A View of Ethics and Planning," *Journal of the American Institute of Planners*, XXVII, 4 (1961).

Hunt, Raymond G., "Occupational Status and the Disposition of Cases in a Child Guidance Clinic," *International Journal of Social Psychiatry*, VIII, 3 (1962).

Kadushin, Charles, "Steps on the Way to a Psychiatric Clinic," Bureau of Applied Social Research, mimeographed paper, 1962.

Klausner, Samuel Z., *Psychiatry and Religion*, New York, 1964.

Lear, Martha Weinman, *The Child Worshipers*, New York, 1963.

Lemkau, Paul V., and Guido M. Crocetti, "An Urban Population's Opinions and Knowledge about Mental Illness," *The American Journal of Psychiatry*, CXVIII, 8 (1962).

Levine, Sol, and Paul E. White, "Exchange as a Conceptual Framework for the Study of Interorganizational Relationships," *Administrative Science Quarterly*, V, 4 (1961).

Lévi-Strauss, Claude, *Structural Anthropology*, New York, 1963.

Lindemann, Erich, "Mental Health and the Environment," in Leonard Duhl, ed., *The Urban Condition*, New York, 1963.

Lipset, Seymour M., "The Value Patterns of Democracy: A Case Study In Comparative Analysis," *American Sociological Review*, XXVIII, 4 (1963).

Litwak, E., and Lydia Hylton, "Interorganizational Analysis: A Hypothesis on Co-ordinating Agencies," *Administrative Science Quarterly*, VI, 4 (1962).

McCaffrey, Isabel, E. Cumming, and C. Rudolph, "Mental Disorders in Socially Defined Populations," *American Journal of Public Health*, LIII, 7 (1963).

Miller, Dorothy Hillyer, "Alternates to Mental Patient Rehospitalization," paper presented to the American Public Health Association, October 1963.

Miller, Walter B., "Inter-Institutional Conflict as a Major Impediment to Delinquency Prevention," *Human Organization*, XVII, 3 (1958).

Myers, Jerome K., and Leslie Schaffer, "Social Stratification and Psychiatric Practice: A Study of an Out-Patient Clinic," *American Sociological Review*, XIX, 3 (1954).

Naegele, Kaspar, "From de Tocqueville to Myrdal: A Research Memorandum on Selected Studies of American Values," Working Paper No. 1, *Comparative Study of American Values*, Harvard University Laboratory of Social Relations, 1949.

Ødegard, Ornulv, "Pattern of Discharge from Norwegian Psychiatric Hospitals Before and After the Introduction of Psychotropic Drugs," *American Journal of Psychiatry*, CXX, 8 (1964).

Pareto, Vilfredo, *The Mind and Society*, New York, 1963.

Parsons, Talcott, *The Social System*, Glencoe, Ill., 1951.

Parsons, Talcott, "Toward a Healthy Maturity," *Journal of Health and Human Behavior*, I, 3 (1960).

Pitts, Jesse, "The Family and Peer Group," in N. Bell and E. Vogel, eds., *Modern Introduction to the Family*, Glencoe, Ill., 1960.

Pritchett, V. S., "The Hiawatha Complex," *New Statesman*, March 13, 1964.

Robb, J. H., "Decentralization and the Citizen," in J. L. Roberts, ed., *The Decentralization of Government Administration in New Zealand*, Wellington, N. Z., 1960.

Robinson, R., D. F. DeMarche, and N. K. Wagle, *Community Resources in Mental Health*, New York, 1960.

Roche, John P., *The Quest for the Dream*, New York, 1963.

Rolph, C. H., "The Family Court," *New Statesman*, March 6, 1964.

Rooney, Herbert, and Alan D. Miller, "A Mental Health Clinic Intake-Policy Project," *Mental Hygiene*, XXXIX, 3 (1955).

Rostow, Eugene V., "Social Mechanisms and the Law," in Leonard Duhl, ed., *The Urban Condition*, New York, 1963.

Rudolph, Claire, and John Cumming, "Where Are Additional Psychiatric Services Most Needed?" *Social Work*, VII, 3 (1962).

Saenger, Gerhart, "Factors Influencing the Institutionalization of Mentally Retarded Individuals in New York City," a report to the New York State Interdepartmental Health Resources Board, January 1960.

Sanders, Irwin T., "Community Development Programs in Sociological Perspective," in James Copp, ed., *Our Changing Rural Society: Perspectives and Trends*, Ames, Iowa, 1964.

Scheff, Thomas J., "Decision Rules, Types of Error, and Their Consequences in Medical Diagnosis," *Behavioral Science*, VIII, 2 (1963).

Seeley, John R., "What Is Planning? Definition and Strategy," *Journal of the American Institute of Planners*, XXVIII, 2 (1962).

Social Planning Council of Metropolitan Toronto, *The Best Pattern of Services for a Metropolitan Area*, Toronto, 1960.

Storrow, Hugh A., "The Measurement of Outcome in Psychotherapy," *A.M.A. Archives of General Psychiatry*, II, 2 (1960).

Titmuss, Richard, *Essays on the Welfare State,* New Haven, 1959.

Vidich, Arthur J., and Joseph Bensman, *Small Town in Mass Society,* Princeton, 1958.

Waxler, Nancy E., and Elliott G. Mishler, "Hospitalization of Psychiatric Patients: Physician-Centered and Family-Centered Influence Patterns," *Journal of Health and Human Behavior,* IV, 4 (1963).

Weaver, Robert C., "Urban Planning Problems," in Leonard Duhl, Ed., *The Urban Condition,* New York, 1963.

Webber, Melvin, "Comprehensive Planning and Social Responsibility," *Journal of the American Institute of Planners,* XXIX, 4 (1963).

Wilensky, Harold, and Charles N. Lebeaux, *Industrial Society and Social Welfare,* New York, 1958.

Williams, Robin, *American Society,* New York, 1960.

Winder, Alvin E., and Marvin Hersko, "The Effect of Social Class and Type of Psychotherapy in a Veterans' Administration Mental Hygiene Clinic," *Journal of Clinical Psychology,* XI, 1 (1955).

Wootton, Barbara, *Social Science and Social Pathology,* London, 1959.

Martin Rein and S. M. Miller
The Demonstration Project
as a Strategy of Change

The "demonstration" or "demonstration-research" project is the current "in" phrase of the social services. It is becoming a favored way for foundations and government, especially at the federal level, to induce or facilitate changes in social services. In a variety of guises it appears in the war on poverty, manpower retraining, welfare programs, public health, vocational rehabilitation, public housing, education, and area redevelopment.[1] In 1964 the cost of demonstration projects probably ran above $50 million. Obviously, we are dealing with a major form of social innovation in contemporary society.

Investments in demonstration projects are popular because they create a sense of activity, are highly visible, and yet require only a relatively small financial outlay. Galbraith has described pilot projects (an older name for a type of demonstration project) as "the modern device for stimulating action without spending money."

The dialectic between a willingness to experiment and a reluctance to be committed to a firm course of action and direction is one indication of a policy vacuum in the present social welfare scene. A genuine uncertainty prevails: how best to fashion social policies which will both achieve their aims and avoid unanticipated costs? Institutions must change, yet the direction of change is unclear. For example, should emphasis be placed on integrated schools or quality schools in inner cities? In dealing with poverty, should we concentrate on youth who are the unfortunate victims of limited life chances, or on those who have been displaced from jobs and are least likely to be reabsorbed into the labor force? The demonstration project permits experimentation among these policy alternatives without commitment to choice. In the absence of a national social welfare policy, the demonstration project as a mechanism of change and experimentation becomes especially attractive.

Of course, demonstrations can also be a way to avoid action or postpone major change.[2] Big, political, recalcitrant issues can be transformed into small-scale, professionalized activities to reduce unrest and the loss of votes. Social service institutions can accommodate pressure for change by setting up a highly visible, insulated demonstration project with only a surface intention of changing practices, no matter what the outcome of the project.

Social Service Innovation

The demonstration-research project is a strategy to promote performance (quality of service offered) and spread (adoption of the program in new, expanded, or permanent circumstances) by the appeal of "tested" results of small-scale innovative programs. Experimenting to produce new approaches for more effective service intervention is a time-honored tradition. What is new is subjecting these newly designed approaches to rigorous testing in order to build confidence in their validity. It is an attempt to wed purpose to science in the hope of replacing the rhetoric of the social services with the rigor of social science. The bond of this union is the discontent with traditional services, which have failed to curb and often even to engage the complex problems of urban communities. The research emphasis bathes in the glamour and prestige of science in a space age and in the hope that social science can accomplish as much in the realm of social problems.

Although research plays an important role in demonstration-research projects, it should not be overemphasized. The rationale underpinning the demonstration is not so much the testing of ideas for their own sake as it is a commitment to enhance the quality of services rendered by established social welfare institutions through systematic inquiry. It is research in the service of action and social reform, in which emphasis is placed on policy modification through social innovation and experimentation. Presumably, demonstrations can have impact by developing an arsenal of techniques and strategies, by showing which actions can be effective, by mobilizing frequently competing resources, and by energizing professionals, organizations, and communities.

By approaching policy modification through social innovation and experimentation, the demonstration may gain a time dispensation during which judgment of the value of the program and the need for change is deferred. The cost of failure is less severe than it would be if a project did not carry the experimental title of a "demonstration."

The demonstration project is well adapted to gradual institutional change. Its very existence establishes and legitimizes a need for change. At the same time, because it is only an experiment, it does not severely threaten established institutions by demanding an immediate modification in their programs. Peter Marris observes that demonstrations steer to "the middle ground between conforming social service programs (which accept the limitations of institutional resources) and uncompromising reform (which is willing to accept temporary setbacks in the welfare of those it champions in order to promote more immediate institutional modification.)" [3] He feels that the demonstration project is an attempt "to professionalize social reform."

The Liabilities of the Demonstration

Are we justified in placing so much hope in the demonstration project? Does professional control of discontent obscure the dramatization of issues that is often necessary for significant change? Demonstrations are caught in a compulsive tension between pragmatic visible success and innovative changes in policies and strategies. Their characteristic weaknesses are pre-promotion of an inequitable distribution of resources, distraction from national policy formulation, and overemphasis on success.

Demonstrations by their very nature favor some people, some organizations, and some communities over others. Some slum children get to go to well-organized nursery schools, while those a few blocks away do not even have kindergartens; the poor young residents of the lower East Side of Manhattan receive aid from Mobilization for Youth which is not available to similar groups in the rest of Manhattan.

Generally, this differentiation is defined as a social good. Some help, somewhere, is better than none, anywhere. Furthermore, it is only by contrast with a control group that the worth of an experimental program can be established. Whether people in similar situations in the nation get the help they need depends on local initiative and willingness to invest resources, skill, and effort in securing demonstration funds. The social services flourish in those cities willing and able to experiment; they languish in other cities. Regional differences in the distribution of resources are thus further aggravated, with the result that inequalities grow in the quality of treatment citizens receive. A new source of social injustice emerges; its origins are based on whatever factors determine differential community willingness to experiment.

Since demonstrations emphasize local initiative, they work against the establishment of national standards and direct intervention below the national level. Entrenched local interests often vigorously oppose liberal welfare benefits—many of the important changes in public policy have come about because it was necessary deliberately to overcome local interests which preferred low taxes to adequate benefits.

In addition, some critics have argued that small-scale demonstration projects are essentially misplaced do-goodism, detracting from the major tasks to be done. They foster local tinkering and activity as permanent substitutes for national mass interventions. For example, demonstrations are now being used to train unemployed youths to qualify for jobs. But any retraining program with national meaning requires a major reform of public vocational high schools. Research-demonstration projects cannot be a substitute for this kind of policy.

It is unfortunate that a good idea does not always supersede a bad idea or lead in turn to another good idea. It may, instead, prevent the use and adoption of an even better and more important set of actions which happens not to have been tested yet. It is important to recognize this, otherwise we shall support any good idea because it is "better than what we have," without any attention to the unintended consequences of such action. We do not want to rush into all programs because they offer some advantage over what we have, if the price we pay is being turned away from more important actions. (In fact, improvement should never stop at any terminal goal, no matter how good. The ideal is open-ended adaptability—*continuing* improvement to meet changing circumstances.)

Since demonstrations are by definition small-scale interventions, they may be too small in scope to discover and bring about the major changes that need to be made. For example, such programs as public assistance carry external stigma, a repressive means test, and low standards of subsistence. To test the impact of public assistance on some dependent variable like rehabilitation, it may be necessary to change the whole operation of welfare systems, rather than to create partial changes in selected variables within the system, such as client-worker interaction, quality of worker training, or worker-client ratios. The demonstration may fail because experimentation must modify the whole rather than a fragment. The relevance and importance of selected variables may become visible only after large-scale changes in the organization of the program are initiated.

How Are Demonstrations Designed to Influence Policy?

The implicit assumption underlying all demonstrations is that marginal programs funded over short periods of time for selected small populations will promote change, improvement, and greater effectiveness for major institutions. Yet the process by which this transformation is to occur remains surprisingly obscure. In some unstated way it is hoped that these projects may constitute the first link in the process of social change.

Three questions are fundamental to the strategy of the demonstration. What kind of influence do the promoters of demonstrations seek? Whom do they hope to influence? How will they exert that influence?

Demonstration of What?

What is the demonstration demonstrating? Is the aim to have an exact duplicate of the demonstration program adopted more widely in this community or another community, a concern which we call *spread?*

Or is it rather that the sponsoring institution wants to secure additional funds for *continuity* and program expansion? Continuity is often regarded as a first stage, to be followed, hopefully, by spread. Where more money is available for demonstrations than for program expansion, many administrators learn the art of "grantsmanship," applying for new demonstrations and the continuity of old ones as a means of expansion.

Or is the purpose of the demonstration simply to attract attention to a problem—delinquency, youth job training, and so forth—to show something must be done about it (the solution not necessarily the same as developed in the demonstration)? [4] This is the concept of *spillover*, in which a spirit of reform and experimentation is created. The demonstration serves as a catalyst, stimulating a spirit of innovation and flexibility without attention to specific reforms.

Target of Change

Those responsible for demonstration projects are often uncertain about *who* must be influenced to do *what*. The President's Committee on Juvenile Delinquency and Youth Crime, for example, tried on the one hand to impress a national audience with the necessity of learning and doing something about delinquency, and on the other hand to select projects which could invite the greatest local change. The demonstration program was oriented to both a national and a local audience.

Demonstrations in each community can be seen as part of a national demonstration to convince Congress or state legislatures that direct federal and state aid to localities are needed to solve local problems and expand social services. Or the demonstrations can be aimed at convincing local authorities that it is the community's responsibility to adapt and expand the demonstration programs, and that it must modify its own tax structure or secure revenue from other local sources. An improved school program for all inner-city children can be achieved by expanding the local tax base or by securing federal aid for education. In the first instance, the demonstration is oriented to a local and state audience. In the latter case the demonstrations are oriented to a national audience. It is difficult to see how different audiences can be satisfied simultaneously without developing some priorities.

Most demonstrations rely heavily on rationality as a major tactic in promoting change: if it is a good project, and if it works, it will "naturally" be accepted by rational men pursuing rational policies. But the definition of "good" depends on who is to be influenced. It makes a great deal of difference whether the demonstration is directed at elites—political and business— or professional groups which manage the institutions, or the public at large. The definition of "good" results depends on the value biases of the observer. In a given demonstration in an urban school, are the more crucial variables school performance, pupil adjustment, or reduced costs? Teachers, parents, social workers, administrators, and business elites will be influenced by different standards. Thus the critical question is, who is the demonstration audience?

Strategies to Promote Spread, Continuity, and Spillover

We now consider a number of approaches to bring about the continued life of a demonstration, after the period of initial funding has ended. Questions of strategy must be answered, because the pervasive failure to implement successful demonstrations is strong. Established institutions have a vested interest in their own survival and a built-in resistance to serious change. To get institutions to recognize and incorporate reforms, demonstrations must first be successful. But a successful program is one that is accepted—and established institutions will not readily accept anything threatening. They favor change in small doses—regular, logical steps, built firmly on the foundations of existing programs. Planning organizations and professionally inspired reform must often settle for those programs likely to win financial support from those with local influence. In the resultant political maneuvering and mutual accommodation, innovations and problems that need solving may come out second best. The necessity for the project to survive usually results in abandoning strategies for promoting spread and spillover and concentrating on strategies to bring about continuity.

Nevertheless, in practice, spread often occurs because national funders implement their own policy before the results of demonstrations are available. The 1962 amendments to the Social Security Act are a case in point—the policy of rehabilitation to reduce dependency was inaugurated despite only scattered evidence to support its validity; demonstrations were then promoted to prove its worth. Pre-school programs for the poor followed a similar pattern. The federal government has rescued these demonstrations by serving as a mechanism—through Operation Head Start—for encouraging spread, despite our limited knowledge of the long-term effectiveness of such ventures. The Community Action program of the Economic Opportunities Act has absorbed the major reforms promoted by the Ford Foundation and the President's Committee on Juvenile Delinquency. In an unusual period of national expansiveness, the federal government has unexpectedly provided the mechanism for encouraging spread. Frequently the pressure for spread undermines the very purposes of the demonstration: to implement policies already tested.

The funders have not left the fate of their demonstrations to chance. They have placed their faith in three interrelated strategies designed to promote continuity—the power of participation, the power of money, and the power of knowledge. These are the crucial ingredients in the recipe of social change.

PARTICIPATION

Some projects attempt to develop a local board with "clout"— power and influence. Presumably this board will accept the findings of the demonstration project and will then actively seek to promote their widespread implementation. The assumption underpinning this approach is that if the elites are convinced of the correctness of a particular position, they have both the influence and the power to bring it about. The task then becomes one of educating elites, and the demonstration is seen as a strategy for elite education. But people with power and influence are often reluctant to push programs which call for fiscal expansion. In the area of social welfare they operate under a broad philosophy of "fiscal containment." While recognizing that voluntary philanthropy has limited resources and consequently cannot do the job, they also are reluctant to see a major expansion of public services which would mean, in the end, increased taxation. So they often tend to think in terms of a substitution rather than an expansion of funds, a notion alien to their philosophy.[5]

Why would a power board vigorously promote continuity and spillover? It is assumed that acceptance by the board will grow out of its involvement in the conduct of the study. This orientation is based on the widely held assumption of small-group theory and social work practice that the most effective way to win commitment is through participation and involvement in the decision process. But the mechanism for involvement of board personnel is seldom specified. Formal representation on a board by, say, the city's mayor, is by itself no sure measure of involvement. Nor is dutiful attendance at formal monthly meetings, at which highly selective agendas screen out the most controversial items or reserve "hot" issues for brief consideration at the end of long, late meetings—a tactic designed to reduce involvement. The assumption of a realistic relationship between involvement and commitment is infrequently borne out in practice. Often the principle of involvement is more rhetoric than reality. Moreover, much participation is defensive, designed to protect organizational or personal stakes. This type of involvement inhibits the development of commitment. One of the most common myths in promoting planned changes is that participation leads to commitment.

MONEY

Fiscal participation is a second strategy for assuring demonstration continuity and spread. This approach assumes that demonstrations that are joint financial ventures—involving matching of funds between the sponsor of the demonstration and the participating agency—assure a built-in commitment for continuity by the participating agency. The participating agency has a financial investment in the demonstration and therefore will act as "economic man"—protecting its investment and trying to make it yield dividends. Many national funding bodies, like the Ford Foundation and the President's Committee on Juvenile Delinquency and Youth Crime, require some matching fund participation as evidence of community interest in making permanent those programs which have proved themselves effective during the demonstration period.

In practice, however, the participating agency or community is able to reduce its fiscal involvement by committing funds already allocated for on-going services as credit toward meeting its matching funds obligations. The concept of fiscal partnership thus tends to be undermined. A city may argue that parts of its regular budget outlays for vocational schools or playgrounds are "matching funds" for a retraining or delinquency project, and the funder may accept this—although in fact the city has spent nothing more. The President's Committee on Juvenile Delinquency has accepted a Ford Foundation grant as a community's matching fund; and the Ford Foundation has in turn accepted the committee's grant to meet its requirement. Demonstrations have neglected the difficult question of developing a strategy for accommodating the costs which spread must imply. Urban centers with limited tax bases are confronted with the task of expanding consumer demand for services and amenities. The demonstration, by its very nature, is committed to an ideology of fiscal expansion. Invariably, this end conflicts with the fiscal realities of urban communities as well as with the contrasting ideology of fiscal containment—the concern with saving funds or substituting relatively inexpensive programs for more costly ones.

Closely related to the strategy of fiscal participation is that of fiscal seduction. Here it is assumed that the piper can call the tune if enough money is offered to participating agencies, especially voluntary agencies which are desperately searching for funds for expansion and survival. Such a strategy may lead to some accountability to the sponsoring organization for the conduct and management of the project by the participating agency, but by itself it provides no basis for project continuity. The funding source, after all, may only fund the project during the life of the demonstration. At issue here is maintaining continuity beyond the life of the demonstration, and fiscal seduction cannot perform this function.

Clarity of aims and strategies in demonstration will help solve the problem of how to influence whom to do what. If ambiguity is not resolved, these experiments may be largely ineffective; they may create the illusion of change through motion, rather than serve as the spearhead for operating innovations.

KNOWLEDGE

We have suggested that vigorous research has been intended as the crucial ingredient in the demonstration policy. Research was to provide not only the basis for program development but also the means of evaluation. The proof that a program had succeeded was to be, perhaps, the most powerful of all influences to assure the implementation of the experimental innovation. The results of demonstrations would be so clear-cut, dramatic, and definite that organizations would be impelled to find the resources to apply the innovations on a large scale.

Surely the hope for such self-evident findings in programs for social intervention is like a search for the philosopher's stone. In practice, demonstration findings are usually non-dramatic and inconclusive. Most projects fail to probe real issues. Their sponsors simply assume that good ideas will inevitably be adopted and accepted by existing institutions.

Consider the early experience of the President's Committee on Juvenile Delinquency, which put great emphasis on research. Often the two research functions—policy formulation and evaluation—were confused. The former task included the gathering of data relevant to the demonstration policy and the formulation of a theoretical rationale ("the overview") for the demonstration project. The research scope was often too ambitious. Moreover, the time needed for gathering and analyzing data, then developing programs, was dramatically underestimated. The inevitable result was that frequently programs were first developed, then research served as a *post hoc* rationalization for decisions already made by the action group. Overviews tended to be empty, very similar to each other, unrelated to local conditions, and unconnected to the specific ingredients of the demonstration package.

Not only was the idea that long-range comprehensive planning could be based on short-term research misdirected, but the very effort by researchers to conduct base-line studies had the unintended consequence of contributing to goal displacement. The planning organizations, supported by the President's Committee, hired researchers to conduct studies to help confirm or reject the basic underlying rationale of the funding organization—that social institutions throw up barriers to achievement and thereby bring about the very alienation and delinquency they deplore. But the demands for rigor in social science technology have led researchers to favor the more traditional and tested approaches, such as surveys of individual attitudes, self perceptions, role models, and so on. They have avoided inquiries which would examine how institutional behavior bars low-income youth from achievement.[6] They have neglected institutional analysis in favor of a more individualistic approach and have been unwilling to engage in what Peter Marris calls "speculative evaluation." [7] They often sacrificed relevance to the search for rigor.

The second task for which research has been called upon is the evaluation of demonstration results. This calls for firmly identifying the input variables expected to be the major cause of change and agreeing on output variables which can serve as measures of project effectiveness. Efforts to find answers to these questions have posed formidable problems. Input variables are broad and global, and they often change as continued knowledge evolves. In addition, many variables are introduced simultaneously, thus making it difficult to sort out the variables affecting outcomes. Control groups are important, but complexities of community life make it difficult to create and keep significant controls.

The job of deciding output variables is equally difficult, for it requires probing the basic purpose of the demonstration. But goals are seldom made very explicit. Each evaluator knows that the most intractable problem he faces is to get a clear statement of the goals of action. But even if goals can be specified, the problems of evaluative research are distressingly complex. For example, if we establish an innovative nursery school program on the assumption that it will reduce delinquency or poverty, then a valid test requires that we follow these youngsters through their school careers to adolescence, or even to young adulthood. Even if we ask a more limited question about whether nursery school programs make later school adjustment easier, we would need to wait at least five years for reliable answers.

As a result of these difficulties, evaluation research alone can seldom serve as the primary justification for continuing a project. Perhaps this is for the best, because it is unlikely that research findings will provide the positive results that are hoped for. Research findings are more likely to show that demonstrations hold unrealistic expectations about the impact of services on the lives of people. For example, a decade of research and more than a million dollars have gone into an evaluation of the effectiveness of casework practice. Yet the Hunt Movement Scale showed that on a seven-point movement scale the average case is likely to move only a half a point. But statements regarding the failure or the limitations of casework cannot be made with confidence, because no control groups were used, and it is impossible to know what might have happened to the families in the absence of treatment. The best inference to be drawn from this long-range and costly study is that further research is needed.

Barbara Wootton has observed that the positive achievements of the social sciences have largely been negative: "Up until now the chief effect of precise investigation into questions of social pathology has been to undermine the creditability of virtually all the current myths." In summary, present-day research methodology is simply inadequate for measuring the impact of programs.

Turning now from the strategies which the funders have used to promote continuity, we consider three other approaches by which demonstrations may produce institutional change. All of these strategies—infiltration from within, duplication from without, and pressure from without—are not equally appropriate to the various aims of the demonstration—spread, continuity, and spillover. Selecting a strategy designed to achieve the objectives of the demonstration is obviously one way of strengthening it as an instrument of change.

INFILTRATION FROM WITHIN

Sometimes a small demonstration is set up within an established institution (the experimental pre-school program within an existing school system) in the hope that the rest of the institution will in time come to adopt this or some other appropriate innovation. How this will come about is not clear, but presumably the force of good example is operative. Here again, if the power of knowledge is to create change, results must be dramatic and unambiguous to be effective. Unfortunately, they seldom are.

The demonstration project has to fit into the established institution as well as try to change it. Sometimes this is a difficult task. Some demonstration projects are supporting pre-kindergarten programs in school systems in which all schools do not yet have kindergartens. The likelihood of the pre-kindergarten program having much impact on the school as an institution is low, because the rest of the school is isolated from the innovations of the early years programs.

In utilizing existing institutions as vehicles of innovation, the problem of quality is often important. Since direct operating control is usually in the hands of established institutions with competing needs and interest groups, innovations usually get watered down.

Even assuming that a particular program works well, it may become an enclave within the institution that operates it. The other programs operate much as before; in one area there is change, but with no assurance of spillover into other programs of the institution. As we mentioned earlier, most institutions are not likely to accept programs that require structural changes in their operation. They are, on the contrary, likely to support projects which require only modest organizational change and produce visibly "successful" outcomes.

Demonstrations chiefly oriented to maximizing spread and continuity must consider their projects in terms of their acceptability to established institutions: acceptance is equated with success. Consequently, new programs cluster about remediation, for such activities need not penetrate or disturb institutional realignments. Confrontation on deep-seated change is avoided, and only a token change in program may occur.

In short, as long as the host organization has control, significant change can be resisted. If sponsoring or funding organizations wish to achieve their project goals, they should retain some control over the program's activities, but the more control they exercise, the more alien the project becomes to the host.

Under some circumstances, however, infiltration from within can produce demonstrable change. In one city, former Peace Corps volunteers were introduced into a school system. The energy, commitment, and enthusiasm of these young people disturbed the old equilibrium and shook up the permanent teaching staff. At the same time, resentment against these intruders developed, and in the end it undermined the changes they wanted to bring about. Planners acting as chemists of social change must somehow find the proper mixture to release great energy and innovation while avoiding explosion.

DUPLICATION FROM WITHOUT

The difficulties of affecting established institutional structures make attractive the strategy of duplication: attempts to develop a parallel institutional structure. A new structure unencumbered by the resistance of entrenched institutions to change and innovation is developed to show the established institution how to function more effectively. In Philadelphia, for example, "Opportunities Industralization," an organization led by neighborhood Negroes, is attempting, with support from the mayor, the Ford Foundation, and the Office of Economic Opportunity, to create a vocational school system separate from and parallel to the public vocational schools.

But a parallel structure, in effect, carries the message that the major educational and social service institutions are not working well and cannot be truly innovative. Implicit public indictment may incur swift retaliation from the established institutions. Cooperation must then be superficial as antagonism between the old and new institutions develops. The old institutions usually have superior resources and greater experience. The new institutions are likely to be subject to constant and pitiless criticism, exposure, and examination. Established institutions can raise difficult and embarrassing questions about the reasons for the duplication of structures.

The virtue of newness also bears the vice of expense. To set up a separate school system, for example, is enormously expensive, especially when the aim is high quality. Nevertheless, the virtues of the approach should not be overlooked. Charles Frankel calls for "deliberate planning to provide alternatives"— a model which permits comparison and provides a standard against which to measure not so much excellence as other possibilities: "We need to invigorate existing agencies, to create new ones whose function is to be a thorn in the side of existing bureaucracies—agencies that bear witness to what might be, that animate, enlarge, and discipline the public imagination. Such agencies could give the public a better chance to choose what it wants and, indeed, to discover what it wants." [8] But if the strategy for promoting spread and spillover is not effective and only continuity is achieved, then duplication can further reduce the coherence of an already fragmented local system for delivering services to people.

PRESSURES FROM WITHOUT

Another way to assume the implementation of demonstration findings is to organize citizen groups—especially those with a personal stake in improving service—to put pressure on local officials and institutions. Those affected usually know whether they have been getting the services they need, and they can, if organized, be useful in seeing that they get them. Saul Alinsky's Industrial Areas Foundation has been using such tactics for some time, and it has inspired others, like the Syracuse Community Development Association, to use them. Started with OEO financing, the Syracuse project is an anti-poverty demonstration program to develop techniques for organizing the poor. Organizers have " 'provoked' the poor to take action in their self-interest . . . they have helped organize sit-ins, pickets, and campaigns to protest everything from garbage collections to welfare procedures." [9]

How can a citizen reform group best be organized—as representing all segments of the neighborhood, as a partisan interest group representing one segment of the community, or as a citywide political action group? Organization of pressure from without does not avoid the decision to infiltrate or circumvent established institutions. It is a way of promoting involvement from these institutions or building pressures to bypass them.

Partly because of growing difficulties in bringing about institutional change, social action through citizen participation has become increasingly necessary and important. It has many advantages; but it has the great disadvantage that it may quickly build a backlash of resentment which can make almost any cooperation or alternative strategy impossible. This happened to Mobilization for Youth when it organized and encouraged mothers to put pressure directly on school administrators for better conditions for children. The principals, enraged, counterattacked MFY, accusing it of irresponsible agitation. Future cooperation obviously became very difficult. The Syracuse project lost its OEO funds because of the mayor's pressure.

Program Goals of the Demonstration Projects

Up to this point we have considered the demonstration project as a strategy of change. Another facet of the demonstration is the substantive nature of its goals. Although the goals of demonstrations are as varied and as vague as the goals of social welfare itself, three major goal sets can be identified. Some projects seek to reduce individual pathology by improving the social skills of individuals so that they can more adequately cope with their life situations. Here, the primary emphasis is on *changing people*—their adjustment and capacity to use community resources. It is assumed that if enough individuals can be helped, the scope of pathology in a given community will be reduced. Some school drop-out programs attempt to help individuals acquire the social skills that would enable them to apply for and hold a job more effectively. Other demonstrations direct their efforts toward increased citizen involvement in social action in order to reduce the people's sense of *powerlessness*. The problem of limiting social alienation and disengagement from dominant norms is another dimension of this goal.

A few demonstrations have the third aim of producing *institutional change*. The goal is to modify the social conditions under which people live by changing the major institutions which impinge on their lives. At times a specific change is called for, either in a single organization or in arrangements among organizations. For example, Higher Horizon programs were presumably aimed at changing school-community relations and the school climate.

GOAL ATTRITION AND GOAL DISPLACEMENT

If we consider only two goals of demonstrations—changing people's adjustment and capacity to use community resources, and changing the societal institutions which provide such service —we recognize that each goal has encountered some difficulties.

Demonstrations aimed at helping individuals to adapt to their community conditions originally worked with those individuals who were most vulnerable. In its policy guide to communities engaged in planning demonstration projects for the prevention and control of juvenile delinquency, the President's Committee on Juvenile Delinquency and Youth Crime made this goal explicit. Changes in social arrangement were sought "so that our most vulnerable youth have the opportunity for behavior which conforms to the expectations of the larger society." But the definition of "vulnerable" is obscure; it might include at least four different populations. The problem population consists of those individuals who participate only marginally in the services of the institution and pose a problem for the institution. In a school situation this might include truants, or students with behavior or learning problems. A second group includes youngsters who are not involved in institutional services. For example, some youngsters fail to use settlement houses or other recreational facilities. A third group is composed of those who are already deeply disturbing to society—youngsters who have committed delinquent acts or have high recidivist rates from correctional institutions. Finally, a vulnerable population might include young people who are likely to become delinquent: they may or may not be unengaged, disadvantaged, or problems to agencies.

Given these varying meanings of vulnerability, it is not surprising that communities which sought guidance from these national standards found them ambiguous. Diverse approaches may be thus encouraged, but ambiguous standards almost in-variably contribute to the selection by local projects of the least marginal population, as a focus on "prevention" comes to dis-place work with "the hard core." For example, Mobilization for Youth's work program has tended to exclude the toughest prob-lem youngsters. To accept work with the hard core would leave the demonstration with a permanently difficult caseload in which a small number of individuals would receive service over a long period of time. A commitment to serve the largest possible number was one among many factors that displaced the original aim of experimentation with those in greatest need.

The second goal deals with change in social arrangements. The policy guide developed by the President's Committee wishes to "support those actions aimed primarily at changes in social arrangements affecting target area youth rather than changes in the personality of the individual delinquent." [10] Clearly, it is far harder to change institutions than to change people. As a result, this goal was slowly watered down in prac-tice. The projects shifted from institutional change to a preoccu-pation with program development and citizen involvement.

Almost none of the research studies, for example, accepted as their prime target the failure of institutions to perform their functions for disadvantaged youth. Although some school fail-ures, especially in reading retardation, have been documented, no project viewed all the social services as an integrated pattern, and inquired into major defects in the overall pattern. This is surprising, since the demonstrations sought to avoid a frag-mented approach in favor of comprehensive programs of action. Since many demonstrations have only a partial grasp of the forces that influence institutional behavior, they can offer few specific suggestions about the direction institutional change might take.

THE MANAGEMENT OF CONFLICT

As we discussed earlier, demonstrations are frequently subverted from their goals because they are engaged in a power
conflict with the institutions they seek to modify. They lack
the power to influence long-entrenched interests. The resources
they command are simply not large enough to provide the kind
of bureaucratic muscle necessary to assure demonstration
spread, spillover, and continuity.

Planning organizations encounter conflict when they simultaneously sponsor demonstration programs to promote institutional change and citizen action groups. Institutions fight when
they see their domains challenged by planning bodies or "by
indigenous social movements which frequently produce effects
that reorder or challenge the existing structure of power . . ." [11]
These attacks on established interests, and the implied bid for
a broader sharing of power, cannot help but produce conflict.

We have already given the example of conflict in the Mobilization for Youth program. In contrast was the response of New
Haven's Community Progress, Inc., when it was faced with a
crisis. A Negro youth was accused of raping a white girl. CPI's
neighborhood lawyer learned about it from the family; she uncovered new evidence to support the claim that the accused
youth and the girl had been seen together before the alleged
rape incident. The lawyer became convinced that the public de-
fender, who did not want to use the information, was mishan-
dling the case, but she could not become actively involved in the
case in court because an open fight on this issue might have
weakened CPI's wide community support and embarrassed the
mayor who was a strong CPI supporter. Was the cost of containing conflict too high? Could Negroes now count on CPI's
support when their interests conflicted with those of the politicians who backed CPI?

More often, the conflicts engendered by planning organizations are closed conflicts, but bitterness and tension can be even more destructive in a closed conflict among vested organizational interests to which the public is not privy. In one city an active citizen's group, supported by some lower-echelon staff members in the planning organization, found itself in conflict with the organization's executive and board of directors. As a result, a proposal submitted to the President's Committee was not accepted, partly because of lack of unity in the project.

The role of citizen action groups, the conflict with community agencies, and the general tension created by the activities of the planning organization pose sensitive questions of how best to manage conflict—achieving survival without losing purpose.

CITIZEN ACTION PROGRAMS

The involvement of citizens poses two critical questions of neutralization and embarrassment. On the one hand, involvement can become a device for coopting and neutralizing potential opposition. The "mark"—the discontented—are "cooled out," made less angry, by giving them token increments of attention, power, and service. This strategy attempts to dampen agitation for deep change. The danger is that the aggrieved will be tranquilized and will give up the struggle for basic changes. At the other extreme, there is the danger that citizen groups will embarrass the sponsoring group, thus producing institutional crises. Lloyd Ohlin asks, "How can a [planning] board promote indigenous movements which will demand change in the agencies controlled by board members?" Professionals who are trained to promote cooperation feel uncomfortable about contributing to community conflict and seek devices to avoid controversy. As Ohlin says, overriding "interests of the sponsoring organization tend to affect the selection of members, the form of organization, the specification of objectives, and the determination and control of the implementing activities." [12]

Vagueness about the goals of citizen action programs serves

to intensify the conflict and confusion. There are many different types of social action programs, although they have not been adequately conceptualized.[13] One type is directed toward social criticism. It is so organized as to raise questions about the functioning of institutions. Another type is concerned with giving political power to inarticulate groups to counterbalance elite power groups. The task is to organize new centers of power in the urban setting. A third type of social action program focuses on changing people. The hope is that as people try to change their world, they themselves also change in the process, as self-esteem replaces social stigma. The main emphasis is not on changing the community as a result of social action but on changing the mental health of the people involved, although it is assumed these aims are mutually reinforcing. A fourth type of social action calls for community involvement and participation to reduce the problem of social alienation in the urban setting. Community action becomes a goal in itself. A fifth variant is self-help, in which the stress is on the people of a block improving their particular conditions by sweeping the sidewalks or holding a festival; action toward political and social service caretakers is not involved.

These various motives and goals are fused in citizen action programs so that there is a blurring of purpose. The failure to develop an adequate typology of citizen action programs masks the different and potentially conflicting roles that such groups perform.

Regardless of the etiology of conflict, demonstrations must find some way of responding to it. They might, for example, seek to avoid social action programs altogether and thereby avoid the possibility of any controversy. Some health and welfare councils have withdrawn from area or district subcouncils because they often serve as sources of embarrassment.

A second road is for demonstration projects to accept fully a commitment to social action. In so doing they must be ready to bear the costs in the form of tensions and conflicts which are likely to develop as a result of the actions of citizen groups.

A third choice is to accept the principle of social action but be willing to abide counterpressure and attacks only within pre-determined limits. If the limits are drawn too sharply, the very vitality of the citizen group may be destroyed rather than reduced, and the problems of apathy and disengagement aggravated. The community problems to which social action groups address themselves have both local and national dimensions. Neighborhood-based groups are frequently grappling with problems that require national action. There is a conflict between immediately accessible local sources of power and less visible but important national decision-makers. Although neighborhood-based social action can influence local power groups and effectively reduce feelings of powerlessness, it is limited in affecting large-scale national decisions. The very attractiveness of programs for neighborhood residents—their concern with immediate and concrete problems—is also a major limitation. Crucial problems are not always immediate and concrete. Even on the city level, a neighborhood view may be inadequate. The social action programs have an allegiance both to the pressing and personal interests of neighborhood residents and to effective courses of action which may require broader support. While these commitments overlap, they also compete.

Suggestions for Strengthening Demonstration Projects

This essay is not a full-scale assessment of demonstration projects. We have concentrated on issues in the conduct of these projects and have ignored their contribution in stirring interest in problems, in trying out innovations, in delineating goals and plans before action, in attempting a systematic estimate of results, in mobilizing resources, and in integrating and coordinating facilities. Although we believe more attention should be given to alternative means for achieving action goals, we recognize that demonstration projects can contribute to the development of effective modes of action by testing various kinds of policies and programs. The following suggestions may help strengthen small-scale innovations as a strategy of change:

1. Funders have traditionally insisted that the demonstration they support be relevant to the social problem involved. But funders should also demand the answers to questions of broader social policy. Few things are more subversive than a good question. Who supports the innovation? What evidence is there of real innovation? Policy questions confront more directly than do social problem questions the politics of reform. For example, how do local committees plan to reorganize the employment or retraining program in the community? Policy questions are more sensitive to the question of feasibility—can the resources at hand overcome organizational resistance and push the program through?

2. Greater clarity of purpose would propel demonstration projects more effectively into the strategy of developing effective, coordinated, and implemented social policies. Part of the research problem is not technology but ideology—what is the goal? Is the demonstration project intended to achieve spread, continuity, or spillover? When purposes are not clear, not only is direction and momentum lost, but outcomes are difficult to evaluate. How can "results" be judged unless the demonstrator knows whether he is (a) planning to provide choice, (b) planning for coordination, (c) planning for accountability, (d) planning for innovation, or (e) making a master plan, to be used as a model?

3. Funders have a responsibility to stay with their projects and not pull out because of hardships and difficulties encountered. To begin several activities without providing some assurance of their continuing life can be very damaging. Constant rumors of the end of funding are not conducive to effective program innovation. The best available evidence suggests that large-scale community planning takes at least seven to ten

years—we have not found ways of expediting this process. Funders who succumb too readily to fads, impatience, or politics cannot provide the necessary leadership.[14]

4. Funders must be more concerned with ways of getting and maintaining well-directed, quality programs. Of course, it is difficult to tread the line between monitoring and meddling, but funders have underplayed their on-going monitoring functions to insure quality and the maintenance of direction.

A public review board for a demonstration project is one way of building in accountability, a central concept for improving social service activities today. A blue-ribbon panel of experts, chosen for knowledge, perspective, and integrity, might issue public reports on how well the projects are meeting their objectives.

5. New modes of reporting and accountability would be useful. Ernest Gruenberg relates an illuminating incident about a state department of mental hospitals which was concerned about the number of patients kept in straitjackets. To provide a basis for policy, the department added a question to the monthly report expected from each hospital, asking for the number of patients kept in restraint. The department discovered that as a result of asking the question, the number of patients kept in restraint was reduced each month. Similarly, Peter Blau, in his study of bureaucracy in an employment service, observed that when interviewers were required to report how many Negroes got job referrals, the rate immediately went up.[15]

In both cases, reporting brought immediate reform. These incidents suggest that projects should be asked to make reports which provide accountability. For example, having to describe and break down the number and kinds of youths contacted, served, and rejected in a delinquency or training program might give administrators a clear idea of how effective they were, and would tell those who shape policy whether the tough cases were being rejected. A simple but accurate recording of the number of youths rejected, referred, and trained in a training program, and

the fate of each group in terms of later employment, could be
the housekeeping statistics of a planning organization concerned
with the lives of youths, rather than a specialized agency function. If knowledge of these facts were made public, they could
contribute substantially to making all partners in the service
system more accountable for performance. If funders have a
clear perspective of what they wish to accomplish, they might
program in the kind of reporting that scans operations for
specific kinds of desired results.

6. Choices must be made. A program cannot promise or
achieve everything. Demonstrations must select specific goals
and means. As Selznick has pointed out, the adoption of a
policy—TVA's decision to work with particular farm groups—
is a commitment which itself shapes the development of an
organization.[16] Multiplicity and alteration of goals often substitute for effective action.

7. Demonstrations should call for continuous change. While
a goal should be definite it should indicate a direction, a focus,
and not a terminus. An experiment should yield feedback information which can be used to provide for continuous modification. Even though there is danger in change for change's sake,
and the illusion of change is also likely, the greatest danger is
the rapid shrinking up of change into stale custom. Mechanisms
must be built which are continually sensitive and adaptive to
new problems and new weaknesses.

8. Funders, staffs, and boards of demonstration projects must
be prepared for and learn to live with conflict.[17] They should
not seek it out; they should try to minimize it; but they cannot
do their job without at times challenging existing practices and
stirring up resistance. Too little conflict may very well be proof of
failure rather than success. Since they must work and contend
with established institutions, they should have some sophisticated knowledge about the internal nature of organizations and
professions. Organizations are not monolithic; even when they
seem to be "consensus establishments," there is almost always a

restless underground willing to go in another direction; progress and cooperation depend on finding and strengthening those who support the demonstration policies or can suggest new directions.[18]

There is no sure way of getting desirable results—each action provokes reaction and involves risk. But the primary talent in running a successful demonstration is not technical but administrative and political. It is not enough to know what is best to do—the administrator must be able to organize forces to get things done.

9. Research perspectives should be broadened so as to be relevant to all social needs and to all social services. The important issue is an understanding not of the operation of a single service but of the overall pattern. The research inspired by Richard Titmuss of the London School of Economics, for example, is designed to discover the shortcomings in the operation of present social institutions in serving disadvantaged groups so as to highlight social policy issues. Research can play a vital role in probing the consequences that flow from the present organization of social services. And since much of what we are doing is attempting to learn what is useful, research can help in the search for relevant goals. This effort requires new kinds of links and tensions between programs and research. Non-success oriented demonstrations are needed which can probe basic policy issues, ask tough questions, and regard skeptically the accepted decisions of established institutions. The demonstration project can serve as, in Peter Marris' phrase, "moral witness" to accepted social and welfare services.

Notes

1. See Elizabeth Wickenden, "Collaborating with the Government," prepared for the National Social Welfare Assembly, February 1964; and Charles Schottland, "Federal Planning for Health and Welfare," in *Social Welfare Forum*, New York, 1963.

2. Robert K. Merton, "The Role of Applied Social Science in the Formation of Policy: A Research Memorandum," *Philosophy of Science,* XVI (July 1949).

3. Peter Marris, "Experimenting in Social Reform," paper given at the annual meeting of the American Orthopsychiatric Association, Chicago, March 19, 1964. The parenthetical material is ours.

4. Cf. S. Miller, "The Strategy of the Demonstration Project," Syracuse University Youth Development Center, 1963.

5. The underlying element in this assumption is that ignorance or stupidity rather than interests of various kinds are involved in resistances to needed social programs. We have called this the "stupidity argument." See S. M. Miller, "Stupidity and Power," *Trans-action,* I (May 1964), 7.

6. Cf. Martin Rein, "The Social Service Crisis," *Trans-action,* I (May 1964), 3-7, 31-32.

7. This issue is discussed in S. M. Miller, "The Prospects of Applied Sociology," in Alvin W. Gouldner and S. M. Miller, eds., *Applied Sociology: Opportunities and Problems,* New York, 1965.

8. Charles Frankel, *The Democratic Prospect,* New York, 1962, p. 161.

9. *New York Times,* December 3, 1965.

10. Brager has put it neatly: "In designing programs . . . it is necessary to pay attention to both parties to the interaction: the served and the service system." George Brager, "Some Assumptions in the Strategies of the Mobilization for Youth Program," mimeographed paper, Mobilization for Youth, September 1962.

11. Lloyd E. Ohlin, "Urban Community Development," paper presented at the Conference on Socially Handicapped Families, UNESCO, Paris, February 1964.

12. *Ibid.*

13. Discussions of social action have been too polemical and have interfered with penetrating analysis of the field. There has been a failure to depict the various types of social action, their roles at different times and in different places, the degree of effectiveness of the types of social action with different groups and neighborhoods, and so on. Many adherents of social action have had as their frame of reference the severe critics of social action, and have consequently not developed an analytical frame for thinking about the development of their approach. See S. M. Miller, "Social Action Programs: Some Questions," mimeographed paper, Syracuse University Youth Development Center, 1962.

14. It is one thing to cut off funds because a demonstration project is of low quality or is not meeting its objectives. It is quite another matter to cease the funding because that type of activity is no longer "in" or has become "controversial." The latter cause of discontinuation has a deeply demoralizing effect on projects and communities.

15. Peter Blau, *The Dynamics of Bureaucracy,* Chicago, 1965, pp. 74-80. See also Louis Schneider, "The Category of Ignorance in Sociological Theory," *American Sociological Review,* XXVII (1962), 492-508; and S. M. Miller, "On Changing Lower-Class People and Communities,"

mimeographed paper, Syracuse University Youth Development Center, September 1962.

16. Philip Selznick, *TVA and the Grass Roots*, Berkeley, 1949.

17. Lewis Coser, *The Functions of Social Conflict*, Glencoe, 1956.

18. Michel Crozier discusses this issue in his stimulating *The Bureaucratic Phenomenon*, Chicago, 1964. The interview with Arthur M. Schlesinger, Jr. (*Harper's* magazine, June 1964), on his White House experiences is illuminating on the Chief Executive's selective support of and reliance on those officials and civil servants who supported his policies.

III. SOCIAL PROBLEMS:
      DEFINITION AND CHANGE

Edwin J. Thomas and Robert D. Carter
Social Psychological Factors in Poverty

Introduction

The now voluminous literature on poverty reflects the contributions of economists, psychologists, political scientists, sociologists, and anthropologists as well as the work of social workers, public health specialists, physicians, public administrators, and educators. The highly diverse problems of poverty rightly deserve an interdisciplinary attack. But at this writing, the contributions of social psychology have been underrepresented. Consequently, policy implications that might be drawn from a social psychological analysis have yet to be evolved, and insights for social psychology deriving from work on poverty have not been articulated.

Social psychology contributes to the poverty question a mode of analysis as well as the application of a specialized body of knowledge. The mode of analysis is perhaps the most important, for it entails a distinct amalgamation of diverse psychological and social phenomena—and, in this case, related economic factors as well. It synthesizes much, but certainly not all, of what is often separate and disparate in other approaches. And the social psychological body of knowledge offers concepts, hypotheses, theories, and research findings which help illuminate critical and sometimes neglected aspects of poverty.

The guiding theme of this analysis is the supposition that

the poor are a distinct social category embedded in a more general social-structural context, and the individuals and families are differentially assigned membership in this category. Contained in this very general statement are three sets of problems. Viewed social psychologically, an integral feature of poverty is the existence of a social category of the "poor" or, in more contemporary terms, the "economically deprived." As a distinct social category, the poor are a social position. This is the first set of considerations analyzed here and will be referred to as the *positional problem*. The second focus of analysis will be addressed to the differential allocation of individuals and families to the category of the poor, this being referred to as *differential assignment*. A third focus of attention will be upon the social context in which the social category of the poor is embedded. The social and economic factors attending the social position of the poor we shall call the *structural context*. Implications for policy deriving from the details of the analysis will be considered mainly in the final section.[1]

The "Poor" as a Social Category

As a socially differentiated aggregate of persons, the social category of the poor may be viewed as a social position. A position may be conceived as a collectively recognized category of persons differentiated from other categories on the basis of the common attributes or behavior of its members, or by the common reactions of others toward its members.[2] We shall elaborate each component feature of the poor considered as a social position and, in so doing, indicate the ways in which the existence of the position is independent from its membership. We shall try to demonstrate that much more sustains this social position than the common attributes and behaviors of the people involved.

GENERIC FEATURES

The position of the poor shares generic similarities with all other positions, and, as we shall see, even these have practical implications.

Collective Recognition. The poor are unquestionably a collectively recognized category of persons and have long been so identified in our nation's history and in the history of other countries.[3] The poor have probably always been visible to those segments of the population closest to them. But visibility to those less closely related to them appears to be periodic. Just before the War on Poverty, collective recognition of the poor in this country was made more secure by greatly increased national attention to the problems of poverty.[4] While in many ways the visibility of the poor is the least important factor we shall discuss, one economist has stated that in his view the increased sensitivity to poverty is the most outstanding contemporary fact about it.[5] Dwight Macdonald, after earlier having written in the *New Yorker* an influential book review of Michael Harrington's *The Other America,* entitled "Our Invisible Poor," has now written an article called "The Now Visible Poor." [6]

Visual salience of the poor is sustained less today by distinctive dress, speech, and manner—although these are still detectable—than by residential segregation in rural or urban ghettos, by telling publicity in the mass media, and by the large proportion of non-whites who are poor.[7] Offenses to the middle-class conscience brought about by periodic welfare exposés and by the protests and insurrections of militant Negroes in urban slums receive generous attention in the mass media. The very programs of the War on Poverty are themselves constant reminders to all that the poor are still with us. The civil rights movement nurtures collective recognition of the poor perhaps as effectively as anything else because, increasingly, appeals are made for equality of condition as well as of opportunity.[8]

Less obviously related to visibility but nonetheless important is the fact that, unlike the problems of poverty in certain European countries where administrative action in the context of an existing program is routinized as the means to solution, similar problems in this country more clearly involve the free market, politics, and legislation [9]—all matters catalyzing opinion, dialogue, and controversy. Automation and cybernetics, and the attending displacement and creation of jobs, force to consciousness the implications for unemployment and poverty. The missions of foreign aid designed to benefit the poor of other lands, and the increasing affluence of most Americans at home, press to mind inequities in our own society. Visible inequality at least fosters attention to the poor as a distinct social group.

As with most social positions, collective recognition is not by itself the only basis for category differentiation. But collective recognition catalyzes reactions of others and of the position members themselves. In the case of the poor, their greatly increased visibility has served in part to speed additional welfare legislation, to energize protests and action on the part of the poor themselves as well as of their defenders, and to direct long-needed academic and professional attention to poverty. Much of this is commonplace. Perhaps less well known is the fact that in recent decades the composition of those designated as poor has changed very little, if at all, and that by refined criteria the proportion of the population called poor has, if anything, decreased slightly.[10] This contrast appears ironic only if one fails to distinguish the factors affecting the existence of a social position, in this case its collective recognition, from those relating to membership in that position.

Common Attributes and Behavior. The single most common attribute of the poor and, indeed, the main defining condition for membership in the category is the lack of economic resources—income, capital assets, or even anticipated future income.[11] The poor also tend to lack power [12] and prestige,[13] for in the American class structure these criteria for class placement are often interrelated at the extreme socio-economic status levels.[14]

Demographically, the economically deprived are more likely to be aged, disabled, a female single parent with children, poorly educated, Southern, rural farmers, and non-white individuals, among others. But this is only a composite profile, and it incorrectly suggests that these poverty-linked characteristics are highly interrelated. Actually, in one analysis of the convergence of selected poverty-related characteristics, Oscar Ornati found that the vast majority falling at or below three different levels of low income had only one poverty related characteristic (e.g., being aged, female, rural-farm, non-white).[15] But the risk of poverty increased with the number of characteristics that appeared in combination. When each characteristic was examined separately for its independent association with low income, non-whiteness was the single most damaging characteristic.

The fact that most of the poor are members of the lower class has inspired numerous analyses of the behavior of members of the lower class in an attempt to demonstrate that the poor behave and live as they do because they have been socialized in the lower class. The presumed cultural features of poverty have been engagingly sloganized with the phrase "the culture of poverty," and some analysts allege that the poor are as they are partly because of a distinctive culture. Studies of racial factors have taken a similar tack, and psychological inquiries have disclosed selected psychological correlates of poverty.

Surely there are demonstrable relationships (to be discussed more fully later) between poverty and selected class, cultural, and psychological factors. But the point here is that the search for common attributes and behavior of the poor, other than the economic and the demographic, has failed to reveal any basic sociological, cultural, or psychological homogeneity. The relationships simply have not been that strong. Behaviorally, the poor are not homogeneous, and this relative behavioral heterogeneity looms large when considering the poor as a social position, for many social positions contain members whose behavior would appear to display much more homogeneity. Behavioral heterogeneity of position members makes it difficult for others outside the position to react uniformly and unequivocally to its members. In the case of the poor, behavioral heterogeneity combines with heterogeneity of causal conditions, with the result that diverse and complex solutions to poverty are needed.

One of the solutions to the behavioral heterogeneity of the poor has been to distinguish subtypes. Perhaps the oldest such distinction has been between the "deserving" and "undeserving" poor. The dichotomy has typically been a blend of moral and motivational criteria, the moral elements having been weighted more heavily in the past and the motivational being most emphasized today. One historian of welfare, Robert H. Bremner, has observed that legislation for the poor in various historical periods has clearly reflected this conception of the deserving vs. the undeserving.[16] Many of our existing welfare programs (e.g., the categorical assistances) and policies (e.g., suitability of the home[17]) mirror this distinction all too well today. As long as the poor are significantly heterogeneous, the societal mechanisms, including the welfare programs, will be constrained to react differentially.

Morality aside, the significant task, in view of the heterogeneity of the poor, might appear to be to develop relevant subtypes. David Matza, a sociologist, has distinguished three categories, each differing in degree of inclusiveness.[18] The most inclusive group consists of all the poor, and this group for Matza coincides roughly with the lowest fifth of the income distribution. The next group, intermediate, includes the poor on welfare assistance. Here Matza quotes the research of James N. Morgan and his associates who found that during 1959 less than one-fourth of the poor families they studied received public assistance.[19] The most restricted group Matza calls the "disreputable" poor. Estimated to be from one-quarter to about two-fifths of the families on AFDC, this group consists of the poor associated with whom there is criminality, illegitimacy, unknown occupations, or long-term dependency.[20] As distinct subtypes among the disreputable poor, Matza also isolates "dregs," "newcomers," "skidders," and the "infirm."

One of the most basic typologies suggested in the literature distinguishes those poor in the labor market, or marginal to it, for whom market solutions might be relevant, from those (like the aged and disabled) who are basically "involuntarily" poor and essentially out of the labor market. About half of those classified as poor are of the latter type, and therefore solutions involving a manipulation of employment and the economics of the labor market are for these people mainly irrelevant.[21] This is an important distinction, and attending to even such gross bases of heterogeneity as these has major implications for the development of policy and programs. But there is more to the problem, as we shall see.

Reactions of Others. Attitudes of others toward receiving economic assistance would appear to be mainly negative. The range of viewpoint is large, however, for at one extreme is unequivocal condemnation and at the other is the liberal's compassion for the suffering of the downtrodden and unfortunate. But the liberal typically does not accept the form of assistance given to the poor, because his point of view constrains him to see the dysfunctions of welfare assistance, given, as it is, in modest amounts under apparently degrading conditions and serving perhaps more to sustain poverty than to overcome it. Thus the status of the poor appears to evoke negative reactions, the conservatives reacting more to the attributed shortcomings of the poor themselves, and the liberals objecting to the amounts and forms of assistance provided.

In a 1964 Gallup Poll a cross-section of the country was asked: "In your opinion, which is more often to blame if a person is poor—lack of effort on his part, or circumstances beyond his control?" [22] Thirty-three percent endorsed lack of effort, 29 percent circumstances, 32 percent said that both were equal, and 6 percent had no opinion. Eliminating the last two responses, 54 percent said lack of effort and 46 percent said circumstances. Republicans and independent voters, as well as those with incomes over $10,000, more often said lack of effort—these groups generally being those most removed from the risks of poverty and contact with the poor.

We are not aware of adequate studies bearing directly upon the question of how the poor are viewed. But casual observation of reactions suggests that there is widespread ignorance of the actual conditions of the poor, especially of the impersonal and social factors associated with poverty. The attribution of the causes of poverty on the part of large segments of those who are not themselves in poverty suggests oversimplified explanations, generally to the effect that the poor are as they are because of defective character, laziness, and lack of motivation. Even professional social workers, especially in earlier days, have tended to associate with at least some economic deprivation a cluster of negative character traits.[23] Many—but significantly not all—relevant contemporary research does little to dispel this view. But because most persons are not familiar with this research, the tendency to see the poor in terms of a cluster of essentially negative character traits must be explained, if it can be explained at all, in terms of the observer's perceptual tendencies.

Studies in the psychology of perception show that when people are ignorant of affairs, they tend to simplify causes. One way to achieve cognitive balance, given a negative evaluation of the poor and the knowledge that a person is poor, is to attribute negative character traits consistent with this negative evaluation.[24] In keeping with this tendency, one can assume that both selective perception and retention of the diverse characteristics of the poor, when these do become known, will tend to favor negative over positive characteristics. Furthermore, persons in a lower status tend to be viewed as less purposive and self-directed, compared with those in a higher status.[25] Also, individuals are assigned greater responsibility for their actions to the extent that the consequences are judged to be serious or negative.[26]

Perhaps the single most important fact about the perception of the poor is that despite the greater current concern with poverty, the conditions of the poor have generally not been considered a problem of material inequality. The data on the distribution of income reveal clear-cut material inequities: the lowest quintile of the population receives 5 percent of the total family income, whereas the highest quintile receives 42 percent.[27] These percentages have remained about the same for the last two decades. Even informed observers, with only a few exceptions,[28] do not define the problems of the poor in terms of inequality of condition and all that this implies.

One of the reasons why the undeniable material inequality of the poor has not been seen by the poor and others as an equivalent inequality psychologically is that psychological inequality is only partly dependent upon material inequality. To explicate this point and the more general problem, let us apply to poverty J. Stacy Adams' penetrating analysis of the psychology of inequality.[29] According to this approach, psychological equality or inequality is based upon a relationship of "inputs" and "outcomes" for at least two persons or groups. "Inputs" are such contributions to exchange as effort, work, or even money, whereas "outcomes" are all reinforcements such as income, fringe benefits, prestige, and so on. Examine this definition of psychological inequity: "Inequity exists for Person whenever job inputs and/or outcomes stand psychologically in an obverse relation to what he perceives are the inputs and/or outcomes of Other."[30] Thus, equal outcomes for Person and Other, if their inputs are perceived as different, are not likely to be perceived as psychologically equitable by either individual, whereas unequal outcomes, if the inputs are appropriately different, may be perceived as entailing psychological equity.

Consider what is required for a hypothetical middle-class American to perceive the status of the poor as involving psychological equity. In keeping with Adams' approach, objective material inequality, based largely on income differences, must be translated into middle-class perceptions of outcomes. According to this theory, if a middle-class American who works hard and receives ample outcomes sees the poor as investing little input in return for no outcome, this middle-class person will see little or no inequality in the comparison. In this example, the poor were depicted as receiving no return. But often the poor, if they receive welfare assistance, are perceived as gaining a relatively large outcome for the investment of little input. In this event, if the middle-class observer views his own input as high and his outcome as low, then psychological inequity will prevail. In our view these are the two basic ways in which the facts of material inequality between the poor and their more fortunate higher-income counterparts have been handled by the latter, by those who are not poor.

We may extrapolate from research on psychological inequality to infer some of the conditions necessary to perceiving psychological inequality for the poor.[31] Our hypothetical middle-class American is more likely to perceive inequality for the poor when the outcomes of the poor are judged to be low relative to those of the middle-class and the input of effort of both groups is judged to be similar. Inequality would also be a likely perception even if the poor were judged to invest less effort than others, providing that the outcomes for the poor were viewed as disproportionately less than the outcomes for the non-poor. The first condition requires recognition that the poor invest effort on their own behalf roughly equal to that of others and the second, that the payoff relative to effort is less for the poor than for others. Unfortunately, the perceptual tendencies mentioned earlier—and others, too—conspire against these perceptions for most persons who are not poor. We surmise, however, that the increased visibility of the poor and the attending legislation to reduce poverty have crystallized a more widespread perception of inequality for the poor by causing more Americans to acknowledge that the poor do indeed invest effort on their own behalf, or that, relative to their effort, their share of economic returns is less than that of others.

In the above comments we have emphasized the comparative independence of objective inequality (i.e., outcome differences) and psychological inequality,[32] using existing conditions of material inequality as the point of reference. But the full significance of the distinction between these two types of equity is not fully plumbed without using material equality as the other point of reference. Consider the extreme case of complete equality of income. If such a condition is accompanied by differential inputs—amount of work, educational preparation, skill—then those whose inputs are perceived as large will experience psychological inequality *vis-à-vis* the others judged to invest less. Dissatisfaction and malcontent are likely to follow from the perception of inequality.[33] For example, if income were guaranteed as equal for a segment of the population, and there were no other outcomes at issue, and if some persons had higher education than others receiving the same income, the former would tend to perceive their inputs as higher. This would result in an experience of psychological inequity along with some dissatisfaction.

This brief sketch of the operation of psychological inequality has implications for policy. If remedies for poverty are proposed and implemented in a context of an essentially unchanged and continuing material inequality—as most current programs appear to be—then a significant segment of the population must perceive a condition of inequality for the poor in order to sustain support for the programs. But if remedies for poverty are introduced which reduce material inequality in favor of the poor, there will inevitably be a significant portion of the poor who, by virtue of such factors as disability or old age, will be unable to invest input in return for their increased income; and others, who invest more for their income, will consequently tend to see a condition of psychological inequality for themselves. This contains an ironic conclusion: whereas at least some psychological inequality would appear to be necessary to sustain poverty efforts under conditions of material inequality, psychological inequality would very likely not disappear under conditions of material equality. The problems of psychological equity are real, and in remedies for poverty they must be addressed along with matters of material equity.

A significant aspect of the reactions of others involves the formal and informal assistance systems for the poor. Because such assistance systems so clearly implicate more general structural conditions as well, however, we will discuss such systems in the section on "structural context."

PARTICULAR FEATURES

There are at least three relatively distinct features of the social position of the poor.

The Poor as Deviant. By most standards of deviance, the social category of the poor qualifies as a deviant position. We have already mentioned the usually negative evaluation of poor persons. More generally, a stigma typically attaches to poverty which is not unlike that associated with most deviant positions.[34] In the preceding analysis we have mentioned other features which index deviance for the poor. They have low incomes; they tend to be demographically distinct; selected features of their behavior are somewhat atypical; and in general the reactions of others are definably different.

But the poor are deviant in a more fundamental sense, for their behavior and attributes depart from a culturally established ideal. In our society the model of the self-sufficient individual, at any given age level, is expected to display appropriate emotional behavior, reliance upon others, and self-sustained achievement and task accomplishment. In adulthood, achievement is typically reckoned in terms of income. The poor generally depart from this ideal on one or more counts. Because of sporadic or continued unemployment and low income, the poor are judged to display less self-sustained achievement; and because they must rely for help upon assistance in its various forms, the poor are judged to be less self-reliant.

The cultural ideal of the relatively independent individual is sustained by social values which esteem achievement, success, activity and work, efficiency and practicality, mastery of the environment, material comfort, effort, optimism, and individualism.[35] The attributes and behavior of the poor, because they depart from the culturally established ideal of the relatively independent person, are judged as deviant in *relation* to the ideal. Deviance is thus relative to some standard of excellence, and without the standard there can be no judgment that there is a departure from it. The attributes and behavior of the poor may be altered so as to depart less from the ideal, but if the relationship between the ideal and the departure remains sufficiently large, deviance may still be judged to be present. In the extreme case, it is possible to have the attributes and behavior of the poor altered radically and still have deviance, providing that the cultural ideal is raised so it still retains a large discrepancy. For these reasons, successful efforts to alter the behavior and attributes of the poor will not necessarily eliminate the deviance, unless corrective attention is also paid to the cultural ideal which has defined such characteristics of the poor as deviant in the first place.

The Poor as a Relative Position. The poor are necessarily defined as economically impoverished in relationship to some criterion, and one of the best indicators of this standard is the "poverty line." Welfare specialists and economists have given considerable attention to the details of specifying this line in dollar terms.[36] According to most economic analyses, the line has been inching upward during the past few decades. Thus Herman Miller presents data to show that for the period 1947–59 the level of "modest but adequate income" in New York City rose 28 percent—a growth rate of 2 percent per year.[37] (In this and other calculations, proper adjustments are made for changes in real dollar value.)

Miller and others have argued that cultural conceptions of basic needs enter into establishing the poverty line and that these socially defined needs have increased through the years. Detailed analysis of factors entering into specifications of the poverty line by welfare departments at various points in time will sustain this point. More graphic, however, is Miller's observation about Tunica County, Mississippi.[38] There, where eight out of ten families are poor by national standards, 52 percent own television sets, 46 percent own automobiles, and 37 percent own washing machines. In her study of over one hundred welfare families in Philadelphia, Jane Kronick found that 52 percent had television, 28 percent telephones, and 84 percent washing machines.[39,40] More generally, a strong case can be made for the point that throughout most of history, the absolute level of impoverishment has been gradually decreasing, whereas, at least in recent decades in this country, the line that defines relative economic deprivation has been gradually rising.

But to contend that poverty is relative is not sufficient, and, indeed, the assertion can be very misleading. The problem is that the poverty line does not appear to rise as rapidly as general economic well-being. Thus Theodore Schultz has shown that since the mid-thirties, real per capita family income has doubled, while the poverty line, as measured in constant dollars, has risen only 75 percent.[41]

Granting the above, and that for this period the distribution of income has remained relatively unchanged,[42] it follows that for the general period in question there should be a steady decrease in the proportion of the population falling below the poverty line, and that the lot of those below the line should be relatively less adequate. Ruth Mack has presented data relevant to the first point.[43] For three categories of poverty, she demonstrates a steady decrease in the incidence of poverty for the period 1929–60. Eugene Smolensky, using somewhat different assumptions and measures, has shown this same downward trend: in 1935, 37 percent fell below his poverty line; in 1947, 27 percent fell below the line; and in 1959, 23 percent were below it.[44] The secondary corollary point is that those who are designated as poor now are poorer, by relative standards, than the poor of earlier years. Leon Keyserling has produced data to show that in recent decades there is a widening gap between the average income of the poor and the average income of all Americans.[45]

Available data on the poverty line in recent decades in this country suggest that neither a purely relativist nor absolutist model is fully adequate. An uncomplicated relativist model would predict that movements of the poverty line through time, allowing perhaps for some lag, would be relatively fixed percentages of indicators, such as per capita income, of general economic well-being. An absolute standard of poverty, in contrast, would not fluctuate greatly with indicators of overall economic well-being. Thus, if per capita income increased, the poverty line would remain the same, other factors equal. As was indicated, the poverty line has actually been responsive to increased standards of basic needs, and it has risen; but its elevation, through recent years at least, has been less rapid than increases in per capita income. Thus, to oversimplify, the actual state of affairs falls someplace between the pure relativist model and the pure absolutist model; a sort of "modified relativist model," as it were.

Although we have too little longitudinal information upon which to venture firm predictions for future poverty lines, we have nevertheless an adequate basis to reconsider the simple view that poverty may be eliminated, providing sufficient funds

are allocated to the poor. The reduction or even the elimination
of economic deprivation may simply result in redrawing a poverty line at a somewhat higher level. Such remedial efforts for
the poor might even result in a smaller proportion of persons
falling below the line, as has apparently happened in recent
years, but this is not the elimination of poverty as a social category. Under conditions of increasing affluence, combined with
raised conceptions of minimal sustenance needs, the division
between the poor and non-poor may gradually creep upward
while the absolute level of economic deprivation may actually
decrease. In these ways economic deprivation, by essentially
non-relative standards, may be reduced—indeed, even eliminated—and still leave a social category of the poor with a sizable proportion of the population.

Mixed Ascription and Achievement. A final distinct characteristic of the poor is that, as a social position, it is neither
fully achieved nor fully ascribed. All things considered, Linton's
familiar distinction between achieved and ascribed statuses
(positions) [46] pertains mainly to the conditions of acquiring
membership in a social position. He did not distinguish, as he
might have, between the conditions of acquisition and those of
maintenance and departure.[47] Actually, all positions have conditions of entry, maintenance, and departure, and achievement or
ascription may pertain at each juncture.

The condition of pure achievement, in all respects, is probably applicable to only a small segment of the poor. Consider
the poor who by volition become economically deprived, stay
that way by choice, and choose not to leave that status. (We
use "volition" and "choice" advisedly here, recognizing that
behaviorally these are subtle matters.) Similarly, the condition
of pure ascription is undoubtedly pertinent to only some of the
poor. These would be persons born to poverty, maintained in
it for reasons beyond their control (such as infirmity), and unable to leave poverty. Most of the poor display diverse profiles
of achievement and ascription in relation to position entry,

membership maintenance, and departure, respectively. "Skidders," whose fall from economic grace may involve choice and lack of effort and who are beset by illness that proscribes movement out of poverty, illustrate "volitional" entry and "nonvolitional" maintenance in the category of the poor. The individual born to poverty who postpones marriage, continues further in school, has few children once married, and thus achieves an income above the poverty line, is another mixed type. And there are others. Not many social positions contain such a mixture of diverse profiles of achievement and ascription as the poor.

Positions in which it is largely achievement that attends the individual's entry, membership, and exit are typically received by others very differently from those characterized mainly by ascription. The members of such achieved positions are treated as if they were responsible for their own fate. Thus the physician is held responsible in considerable measure for his professional behavior, and if he deviates significantly from established form, social pressures will generally be forthcoming; he will be expected to comply or suffer the consequences. The members of ascribed positions, in contrast, are not held responsible for their membership in the position, their failure to leave the position, or in extreme cases for their behavior while in the position. Thus males are generally not held responsible for their biological sex or for not having been biological females (although males and females are held responsible for their sex role behavior as males or females). Individuals are not held responsible for membership in age grades. When we treat members of such ascribed positions as being responsible for their position membership, we place the individuals in conflict.

Now, the problem with the position of the poor, composed as it is of such a variety of achievement and ascription profiles, is that there is no single complementary behavior for others which can possibly match the diversity of position profiles of those in the category. To treat the poor as an achieved position,

the members of which are considered responsible for all attending aspects of their condition, places undue pressure on the
many economically disadvantaged for whom poverty is partly
or fully ascribed. To minister to the poor as an ascribed position, the occupants of which bear no responsibility for their
plight, is to relieve from social influence those whose behavior may be subject to modification. The indignant and self-
righteous middle-class denizen generally errs on the side of
treating the poor as an achieved position, the naive do-gooder
on the side that emphasizes ascription. The informed citizen,
official, scholar, and practitioner has struggled more seriously
with this sociological dilemma, attempting to formulate compromise stances, in which modified or conditional responsibility
is applied, or pluralistic approaches, in which some of the poor
are absolved of responsibility and others are not.

The history of welfare programs is in part a record of how
the sociological dilemma has been translated into assistance
programs. From this perspective, assistance programs have
faced two problems. The first is that of matching assistance
programs to sub-categories of the poor. Much of the criticism
of past and current welfare programs by laymen and professionals alike centers on the match between the welfare programs
and the types and subtypes of the poor, as outlined above.
The second problem is whether or not responsibility should
be placed upon given subtypes and, if so, how much and for
what behavior.

Differential Assignment

We turn now to the second major topic of the analysis, namely,
the differential allocation of individuals and families to the
social position of the poor. It is characteristic of most all social
positions to have a circulating membership, i.e., at any moment

in time to have some individuals entering the position, to have some with short- or long-term tenure, and to have others leaving. The members of the position come and go, but there is always a member cohort. The particular factors associated with in-selection, out-selection, and sustained membership, however, are restricted in type and scope by whether the position is mainly achieved or ascribed. In the case of the poor, being a position containing diverse achieved and ascribed sub-types, an unusually large variety of factors is associated with the dynamics of the circulating membership. The objective of this section will be to order and analyze the "correlates of poverty" in the more general context of the allocation processes characteristic of all social positions.

It will not always be possible to distinguish antecedents from consequences. Most of the studies upon which the details of this analysis are based were not designated to disclose causal or quasi-causal relationships. Many of the findings on the correlates of poverty are just that—correlations between diverse factors and economic deprivation (i.e., co-variation of variables at one period in time). Thus the niceties of articulating a set of originating, sustaining, and precipitating conditions will only occasionally be afforded. But certain gross distinctions may be made nonetheless, and these will be essential for the level of analysis undertaken here.

We shall order correlates of poverty in terms of agents (personal, social, and impersonal) that influence selection into or out of a position of poverty.[48] Through *selection*, individuals (or families) are either selectively entered or selectively moved out of poverty. The first we call in-selection, the second, out-selection.[49] Socialization and recruitment into and out of the category of the poor serve to sustain the selection process. By *agent* we mean the apparent locus of determination, but not necessarily the originating causal condition. Thus we speak of an individual's intellectual ability as a *personal agent,* for ability is a variable having locus in the person. While numerous social factors may well have affected his level of ability, the person's behavorial tendencies which we call ability are uniquely associated with him; it is these, regardless of how they happened to have come into being, that may determine his fall into poverty or, if in it, his climb out. A *social agent* is analogously conceived for the determinants of behavior at the level of social subsystems or relationships in which the individual in question participates. Events transpiring in these subsystems may influence the selection process. Family events and conditions are especially important as social agents, as are peer-group influences and social class factors. *Impersonal agents* include age, the color of one's skin, disease and disability, and the workings of the economic marketplace—all those agents which ordinarily operate more or less apart from and usually beyond the control of role behaviors of particular social actors and the social subsystems in which these actors are involved. They are impersonal features of the social or natural order which affect the outcomes of individuals in significant ways.

In the discussion of poverty correlates that follows, we have had to follow an arbitrary format. In some instances it seemed justified to consider certain personal, social, or impersonal agents as separate and worthy of attention apart from others. In other instances, however, it was felt that categories indicating amalgams of agents that normally operate together was the best mode of presentation. For example, family events and conditions, while essentially social in nature, are discussed under the heading "Personal-Social Amalgam," for the reason that family factors interact with individual or personal factors and in turn are influenced by them as well.

Also, agents of in-selection and out-selection will be considered together, for generally factors conducive to in-selection, when reversed, are agents of out-selection. Thus, low academic ability appears to be related to dropping out of school and, through related consequences, to unemployment and poverty. Superior academic ability, on the other hand, usually contributes to higher educational achievement, regular employment, and the absence of poverty.

The references given here are mainly illustrative of pertinent research in this area.

PERSONAL AGENTS

Attitudes, motives, needs, traits, psychopathology, intelligence, cognitive capacities, skills, and knowledge are among the many factors that have been identified as personal agents entering into potential or actual poverty. But abundant speculation has not been tempered by enough careful research, and consequently the factors considered below, even though they have been based upon a sample of the stronger inquiries, must be viewed as most provisional.

Intelligence: Individuals who score very high on intellectual ability (e.g., the upper 2 percent) manage to go to college, irrespective of family income,[50] whereas those who score very low are more likely to be school drop-outs [51] and to come from economically deprived backgrounds.[52]

Knowledge: Studies and common sense indicate that lack of relevant job knowledge will reduce chances for employment.

Verbal, Cognitive, and Problem-Solving Capabilities: Evidence derived from the performance of lower-class youngsters suggests some underdevelopment of these capabilities relative to middle-class standards.[53]

Job Skills: Here again, the lack of job skills is a determinant of unemployment and low income.[54]

Psychological Dependency: Chronic welfare recipients display somewhat more psychological dependency than non-chronic cases; [55] welfare recipients similarly display more psychological dependency than a matched sample of non-recipients.[56]

Attitudes: Various studies suggest that attitudes of fatalism, apathy, hopelessness, and passivity, as well as a general sense of powerlessness, tend to be characteristic of at least some of the poor.[57]

Orientations Toward Public Support: Welfare recipients evaluate public support more positively than do most middle-class Americans.[58]

Values: Chronic welfare recipients, when compared with middle-class respondents, display preference for (1) subjecting oneself to, or living in harmony with, nature; (2) focusing on being rather than doing; and (3) being oriented toward the present rather than the future.[59]

PERSONAL-SOCIAL AMALGAM

Education: This amalgam as it applies to education can be viewed as a complex interaction between personal motives, attitudes, values, and abilities, and the interpersonal agents of change in the school system (chiefly teachers). Exposure to education presumably brings about significant preparatory changes in individuals. Most importantly, perhaps, it provides the individual with certain significant credentials for the job market.

In general, the less the education the greater the chances of unemployment or of only marginal employment.[60] Education is perhaps the main contemporary means for individual occupational advancement.[61]

Mating and Dating Behavior: Unmarried parenthood is associated with poverty by virtue of its relationship to subsequent problems, such as dropping out of school, marrying early, and family estrangement.[62]

Marriage Practices: Early marriage and factors relating to it are part of a series of actions culminating in a higher probability of poverty.[63]

Family Planning: Despite stated preferences for a modal-sized family, the poor tend to have more children.[64]

Family Structure: As is well known, a large proportion of poor families, especially families receiving AFDC aid, have only one parent.[65] Instances of desertion, separation, and divorce are much higher among the poor. The absence of a role model—generally the father—tends to centralize labor, authority, interaction, decision making, and affective relations within a smaller group of individuals, placing a proportionately greater burden on the remaining parent.[66] While not all of these correlates are necessarily deleterious, most of them tend to have generally adverse effects. Available evidence would suggest that it is not so much the mere absence of a sex-role model that is troublesome, for symbolic and actual sex-role models abundantly populate the child's social world. Rather, it is the complex of social psychological conditions (such as those mentioned above) associated with the single-parent family that may cause personal difficulties.[67]

Family Instability: This is generally indexed in terms of child neglect and abuse, family estrangement, prostitution, excessive drinking, and the like. The instability of families, to the extent that it is actually overrepresented among segments of the poor, may create problems for both children and adults. These problems, in turn, may produce or enhance personal limitations to moving out of poverty.

When considering family stability it is tempting to recite the long list of social and behavioral problems alleged to be found in poor families, and to highlight the adverse effects upon children which these problems presumably generate. To do this would be to reinforce a stereotype of the indignant press and a viewpoint that, unfortunately, even some informed observers have held. The problem is that despite ample statistics on the

behavior problems of welfare families—these serving allegedly
to sustain the case—more searching analysis reveals that there
are few behavior problems that can be convincingly demonstrated to characterize poor people as compared with the non-
poor. In one such analysis, Henry Miller compared various
characteristics of AFDC families (a group that Matza claims
is exemplary of what he calls the "disreputable poor" [68]) with
those of the general population.[69] Miller's verdict is surprising,
for he concludes that ". . . with the one exception of illegitimacy
and possibly of mental retardation, there is no convincing case
for the allegation that AFDC clients are more deviant in the
characteristics discussed than are people of the general population." [70] In addition to the problems of illegitimacy and retardation, Miller examined data on alcoholism, juvenile delinquency, and mental illness. The fact that for a very small segment of the poor these problems are clustered does not alter
the more general picture for the poor as a whole. At present
it would appear that the behavior difficulties attributed to the
poor are a slim reed upon which to build a case for their family
instability. But to say this is not to deny the possibility that
future inquiry will be more revealing of the impact of other
indicators, such as the problems of single-parent families, mentioned before.

   Child-Rearing Practices: Preliminary reports from research
that is apparently still in process give evidence that lower-
class Negro mothers, in their face-to-face communication with
their children, behave so as to develop in their children a passive, non-reflective orientation toward problem-solving tasks.[71]
Another study of child-rearing attitudes among lower-class
mothers suggests much the same thing.[72] Also, from these
studies and from what is known about the development of a
"need for achievement" in children,[73] it would appear that in
this connection as well, many lower-class parents fall short as
agents of socialization.

Incentives: Studies of incentives to work suggest generally fewer incentives of all relevant types—money, prestige, affiliation, achievement, and autonomy—for unskilled and semi-skilled workers as compared with higher-level jobs.[74]

SOCIAL AGENTS

Social Class: There would appear to be some agreement, despite the absence of fully adequate information, that lower-class values are generally different from those of the middle class. But the difference is not simply a reverse turnabout, yielding upside-down middle-class values. Walter Miller has emphasized the distinctive, long-term tradition of "lower-class culture." [75] In the context of discussing delinquency, he has noted six such distinctive "focal concerns," these being avoiding trouble, being tough (especially for males), smartness in manipulating the environment, periodic emotional excitement, belief in and concern with fate at the hands of external forces, and overt striving for autonomy combined with covert yearning for restricted environments.

Rodman speaks of the "value stretch," by which is meant that without abandoning values placed upon success, high income, and high educational and occupational attainment, the lower-class person "stretches" these values so that lesser degrees of success also become acceptable.[76] And "without abandoning the values of marriage and legitimate childbirth he [the lower-class person] stretches these values so that a non-legal union and legally illegitimate children are also desirable." [77] The result, Rodman says, is that "members of the lower class, in many areas, have a wider range of values than others within the society." [78] But combined with the greater range is a lower commitment to all of the values within the range. This view has much to recommend it because it reconciles a great deal of otherwise seemingly contradictory evidence.

Various experiments support the conclusion that children of the middle class have more autonomous and generalized success strivings, whereas achievement motivation of working-class children is more highly dependent on the manifest material reward of the present task.[79] There is also evidence that the *type* of reward makes a difference for individuals from middle and lower classes. For instance, in one experiment middle-class children learned to discriminate on a learning task much more rapidly when working for a non-material than a material reward, while lower-class children learned most rapidly in response to the material reward.[80] It was interesting, too, that in this study the learning speeds for the two groups, when working for the most differentially effective reward, were equally rapid.

Peer and Neighborhood Relations: Hylan Lewis has made reference to the early loss of the lower-class child to socializing agents outside the home, particularly peer groups.[81] Lewis speaks of this as "one of the most insidious and eroding processes affecting child-rearing." [82] Consider the slum in which mothers must compete with the street system for the control of young children and lose out early to these influences; in which prostitutes, thieves, hoods, alcoholics, drug addicts, junkies, and pimps may provide the role models (these often being exemplars of success) and compose the regular members of the role set in the street system; and in which the everyday manifestations of conventional, conforming, middle-class behavior are generally conspicuous by their absence.

Culture: Some anthropologists and sociologists have been active in attempting to explicate a "culture of poverty" as a main determinant of poverty. For example, Oscar Lewis, the anthropologist, has identified features of such a culture that he contends are characteristic of continuing poverty in different times and places.[83] But other informed observers have seriously questioned whether there is a distinct culture for the poor.[84] Jane

Kronick has contended that the urban AFDC families she studied were highly diverse and often residentially separated and that, if anything, defective socialization rather than a distinct culture accounted for many of their problems.[85] Lewis, in his case analysis of the poor in Washington, D.C., contends that it is simplistic and inaccurate to try to characterize the mosaic of determinants in terms of a "culture of poverty." [86] Everything considered, we believe that if there are distinct cultural factors in urban poverty, they have yet to be sufficiently explicated and distinguished from non cultural factors.

This is not to deny that cultural factors do enter into poverty, at least indirectly. Matza's analysis of the condition of poverty in Ireland before and during the large immigration of the Irish to this country suggests numerous cultural factors in the pauperization of this group.[87] There may be cultural correlates of poverty for many Negroes, especially those from the rural South. The most promising test case for the hypothesis of a culture of poverty today is afforded, we believe, by the highland poor of Appalachia. Some discussion in detail seems warranted.

In our analysis of poverty in Appalachia we have concluded that (1) numerous factors other than the cultural proper contribute to their continued poverty, and (2) the cultural component, to the extent that this can be readily identified, is more accurately to be characterized as a folk culture surviving from an earlier era and not a culture *of* poverty *per se*. This folk culture does indeed socialize members so that they frequently end up in poverty, but non-cultural factors operate as well.

Jack Weller, Thomas R. Ford, and others who have examined Appalachian poverty can serve as sources of information from which insights may be drawn concerning how cultural and other social factors contribute to poverty among these people.[88] Significant value emphases that have been uncovered include individualism, independence, and self-reliance. And yet it seems in general there is no reluctance in accepting relief. Also, the self-reliance apparently does not include a motivation to achieve, and it is combined with a failure to be rational and cooperative by more general standards. It is clear that self-reliance, which many mountain people have to a fault, is not enough to produce economic achievement. We infer that self-reliance combined with high motivation to achieve is more conducive to economic success. Studies of "need for achievement" would seem to support this view.[89]

Among other significant values of the Appalachian folk culture are: traditionalism (involving a "regressive, backward look," in which individuals are oriented toward existence more than improvement), fatalism (entailing passive and unquestioning acceptance of one's fate combined with a religious flavor typified by saying it is "God's will"), as well as the seeking of action, a psychology of fear, a personal orientation, equalitarianism, and allegiance to a reference group of same-sex peers.[90] The latter is very important, for in the social structure of the Appalachian Mountains the reference group of same-sex peers is the dominant primary group, more influential apparently than even the family. This reference group is the main source of sanctions. The norms demand a flattening equality, and no one can succeed in matters of money or work without fear of hurting the feelings of others.

There are other influential factors in the beliefs and behavioral patterns of the mountain people. Mention can be made of disinterest in and rejection of education, inability to save and budget, difficulty in manipulating the formal language of ideas and abstractions, little interest in careful or long-range planning, little recognition of outside expertness, minimal status seeking, the lack of skills to participate in community groups, low interest in job security or job satisfaction, and antagonism toward government and law.

Because the mountain people are poor and transmit from

one generation to the next much of the content indicated above, the resulting social patterns dramatically reveal socialization into a way of life in which people are poor. More than in any other group (except perhaps religious orders in which vows of poverty are sworn) we find here in Appalachia a socio-cultural complex that actively socializes *against* success, achievement, accumulation of economic assets, and material acquisition.

But the cultural factors are integral to a folk culture of long-standing duration and function, originating at a time when the level of economic well-being relating thereto was neither pauperism nor poverty. While much of the early folk culture has persisted, at least three events—none of which is patently cultural—highlight the economic deprivation of these people. One is the inability of the primitive farming technology, combined with poorer ratios of farmers to available land, to sustain prior levels of well-being. While the technology has thus flagged, the economy in rural areas has simultaneously been converting to monetary exchange rather than trade in kind, further handicapping a people who have relied upon the trading of goods. The second is the extreme paucity of mining jobs as well as of other unskilled and semi-skilled jobs in which to employ these people. The third is the increasing affluence and higher poverty lines which contrast the lot of mountain people most unfavorably when their level of life is placed against even the economic well-being of the urban poor, let alone the middle classes. All in all, the case of Appalachia is not one that gives clear support to the "culture of poverty" hypothesis, although this discussion has identified folk-cultural and other social and impersonal agents that serve to sustain poverty in this region.

SOCIAL-IMPERSONAL AMALGAM

The Educational System: Education was mentioned also under "Personal-Social Amalgam," but here we wish to focus briefly on the "system" apart from the individuals (students) that it processes.

There seems little doubt that poor education may contribute to the further handicapping of the poor. The disgraceful level of education in many areas of Appalachia is well known. In urban areas John T. Dailey isolated four school characteristics out of over thirty potential characteristics that survived controlled analyses as the most significant correlates of such school outcomes as achievement, going to college, and staying in school.[91] These were teacher salaries, number of books in the school library, teacher experience, and per-pupil expenditures; all were low, or little, as the case may be. To the extent that these variables operate in schools serving mainly children from low-income parents, these children will obtain a less adequate education.

Racial Discrimination and Prejudice: With so much literature on and familiarity with this subject now, it is gratuitous to recite again the long list of blatant and subtle prejudicial and discriminatory practices which have conspired to keep so many Negroes impoverished for so long. The overrepresentation of Negroes—and other non-whites as well—among the poor is probably indicative of racial oppression.[92] In the analysis of poverty correlates done by Ornati, mentioned earlier, the reader will recall that of all such characteristics, non-whiteness was the single most damaging. For non-white Americans this is perhaps the single most potent factor in sustaining poverty.

Assistance Programs: Unfortunately, we must also include here many of the assistance programs avowedly established to aid the poor.[93] We shall emphasize their effect on sustaining economic deprivation. Consider such categorical aids as General Assistance and Aid to Families with Dependent Children as points of reference. The caseloads are exceedingly high, pressuring the worker and allowing little time for each recipient; few rehabilitative services are given, those given are provided by essentially untrained civil servants and, in any event, there is little firm evidence to suggest that such services produce any of the anticipated positive effects; [94] prejudice and discrimination, in the form of "suitable home" clauses, disadvantage some of the most impoverished of the assistance population—the Negroes; [95] the receipt of relief sometimes entails humiliation and debasement; [96] the assistance is given only *after* income and resources have reached a very low level, much too late to serve any preventive function; [97] recipients are not rewarded—and sometimes the incentives are actually less—for working part or full time; [98] and perhaps most significantly, the assistance is so low that there is essentially no "capital" with which to change one's behavior or improve one's condition to begin to reverse the self-perpetuating features of poverty. In all of these ways— by coming into poverty too late and providing too little—assistance programs may sustain poverty. To say that assistance programs do not reduce poverty is of course not to say that they make people poor in the first place—except in extreme and unusual cases.[99] But in general, assistance programs help sustain poverty by default of what they do not accomplish. All things considered, the fact that many of the poor would be much the worse for not having received assistance, while true, does not deny the contribution of assistance programs to keeping many persons in poverty.

PERSONAL-SOCIAL-IMPERSONAL AMALGAM

Consumer and Marketing Practices: David Caplovitz has provided evidence sufficient to document the claim that unsophisticated buying practices and exploitative marketing systems are conducive to becoming poor or to remaining in poverty.[100]

Marketing practices serve to limit seriously the accumulation of capital assets among the poor. High and exorbitant interest rates, "easy credit," installment buying, dishonest merchants,

outright swindles, garnisheeing of wages, and the repossession
of goods are among the marketing practices that cause the poor
ultimately to part with more of their money than they should
have to. This is to say nothing of deceptive advertising, inces-
sant bombardment by the mass media to buy for reasons of
prestige as well as of necessity, and a pervasive and inescapable
materialistic surrounding. With all this it is little wonder that
low-income families engage in what Caplovitz calls "compensatory consumption" and, in so doing, fall prey to the above-
mentioned marketing practices.

Social Mobility: Social mobility indexes a complex of personal, social, and impersonal agents, and, in a sense, the failure
of achieving mobility indirectly reflects factors that help sustain
poverty for those affected. According to recent reports, inter-
generational (occupational) mobility rates have not changed
appreciably over the last three decades. If anything, the data
suggest some "loosening up" of the overall occupational structure.
For example, Elton Jackson and Harry Crockett found that the
rate of occupational mobility in the United States had actually
increased somewhat over a period extending from the end of
World War II through 1957.[101] And Otis Duncan has recently
reported more "upward" mobility (chiefly into salaried professional and technical positions) and less "downward" mobility in
1962 than in 1932, 1942, or 1952.[102] While these findings should
be accepted only with caution, given the methodological problems involved in such research, the fact that two recent studies
seem to support each other indicates that in recent decades the
overall occupational structure has not become more rigid in
terms of opportunities. There is a good deal of evidence, however, that the supply of unskilled and semi-skilled jobs has
been steadily decreasing in recent years,[103] these being the types
of jobs the poor—when employed—are most likely to occupy.
And as Tom Kahn has demonstrated, this "blue-collar decline"
looks especially disadvantageous for lower- and working-class

Negroes.[104] So while the occupational structure as a whole offers no cause for immediate concern, that segment of the structure that relates directly to the poor seems most unfavorable in terms of prospects for out-selection or mobility upward.

Poverty Itself: In a recent article by Mollie Orshansky, in which she examined the effects of poverty on poor children, she concluded that poverty itself was the main factor sustaining poverty.[105] Catherine Chilman and Marvin Sussman have drawn the same conclusions.[106] It is almost impossible to appraise the truth of this assertion, and these writers probably overstated the point, but there is support for the main idea that the conditions of poverty for a family are conducive to continued economic deprivation for those involved. Elaine Burgess and Daniel Price, in their study of 5,517 closed ADC cases, were among the investigators who helped confirm the suspicion that some poverty was generationally repeated.[107] These researchers found that 40 percent of the mothers or fathers studied were themselves reared in homes in which public assistance (mostly ADC) was provided for some period of time. In attempting to stipulate exactly what the self-perpetuating features of poverty are, Robert E. Will and Harold G. Vatter identified poor education, high birth rates, alienation and apathy, and legal discrimination.[108] We add the following to the list: low-paying jobs,[109] family estrangement,[110] illegitimate pregnancy,[111] and low educational aspirations.[112] Others will no doubt be isolated.

Poverty may or may not be the main generating condition for economic deprivation, but clearly it indexes a relatively large battery of factors which, considered together, constitute an influential complex. It does not follow, however, that the complex will necessarily be broken up by simply substantially raising the economic well-being of the poor. For example, what really determines economic deprivation among those who have many children may well be, and indeed probably is, different from what causes poor people to have many children.

Change of Social Conditions: Philanthropies, legislatures, private and public agencies, unions, and action groups have all achieved important changes in this context, although their effects—with the possible exception of legislation—are often subtle and difficult to demonstrate. In any event, this is more the task of the historian of welfare. Without denying the significance of these agencies of change, we wish to discuss briefly social action on behalf of the poor by the poor and others—specifically the civil rights movement and community groups of the poor. The significance of such groups is that they seek power to control their own fate and, increasingly, in civil rights groups, equality of condition as well as of opportunity.[113] It has always been embarrassing to Marxism that class consciousness and militant action did not emerge in the lower classes in this country. Recent studies indicate that economic deprivation is decidedly not a determinant of political militancy.[114] The surge of action that has occurred has apparently been stimulated largely by problems of race, and poverty itself has rarely been the issue.[115] The coupling of civil rights with action for equality brings in the issues of poverty more directly, and such action may gradually begin to counter the numerous factors outlined in the above sections which index the selective processes associated with poverty.

IMPERSONAL AGENTS

The Job Market: The availability of jobs is directly related to rates of unemployment and to low income.[116]

Health and Disability: Disease and disability are directly related to earning capacity.[117]

Age: The aged [118] and the very young [119] are disadvantaged in the job market.

THE INTERPLAY OF AGENTS

The numerous factors identified above indicate clearly that a complex of diverse agents affects the selection of individuals into and out of poverty and, once in poverty, serves to sustain or relieve economic deprivation. Recognition of an on-going, intricate interplay, however, raises the question of the relative potency of the variables and of how they function in full concert. There is virtually no evidence which speaks directly to this question. The research design required to provide even moderately informative results for this question staggers the imagination. Until long-term longitudinal studies of large samples of relevant persons, including the poor and the non-poor, are conducted, and until all important variables are measured and analyzed properly, we shall have to be content with relatively imprecise and limited information.

There is one general fact that helps place the subsequent discussion in context: the catalog of agents developed in the previous section underestimates the true potency of social and impersonal determinants. This is because the so-called personal agents, while being variables having locus in individuals, have their origins largely in an environment of numerous social and impersonal influences. For instance, defective language skills may have great impact on a person's life, but these skills were determined significantly by formative social experiences.

Given available information, there are at least two significant issues to which attention should be addressed. The first is the relative weighting of the numerous poverty-related variables. Only a handful of studies have included a sufficiently large battery of variables which were analyzed systematically for their relative potency. Ornati's study of the differential impact of diverse demographic variables, the reader will recall, disclosed that non-whiteness was the single most adverse characteristic.[120] Burgess and Price, in their detailed analysis of assisted ADC families, have come to a similar conclusion.[121] Considering non-white persons, it is probable that the group of determinants indexed by skin color is the single most important factor in their economic deprivation.

For white persons, it is probable, as Burgess and Price suggest,[122] that psychological factors weigh more heavily in their poverty than in the economic deprivation of non-whites. But in general, available evidence concerning how psychological variables compete with social and impersonal variables suggests that psychological variables are relatively weak. In his review of research on the relationship between psychological dependency and economic deprivation, Thomas concluded that: "Impersonal and social factors account for most of economic deprivation and that, altogether, psychological factors, including those of psychological dependency, are minor determinants." [123]

The national survey of income and welfare in the United States, done by James N. Morgan, Martin H. David, Wilbur J. Cohen, and Harvey E. Brazer, included all three classes of predictor—personal, social, and impersonal.[124] The multivariable regression analyses of the predictors of participation of spending unit heads in the labor force is illustrative of how classes of variables function in competition. It is pertinent to quote from the review just mentioned:

> These researchers found that the impersonal factors of old age and disability were the main factors in keeping family heads from working. Only two motivation factors were predictors, the first being an educational difference between the man and the wife (in favor of the wife) and the second, plans requiring future income. The need to achieve . . . was not a predictor here. As I read the intricate results of this study for the predictors of other economically relevant factors, this same type of pattern

emerges time and again: the impersonal factors, either singly or combined with social predictors, are the most potent, and motivational factors run a poor second. This no doubt confirms what many of us have begun to suspect as we have perused the now voluminous reports on the demographic and economic correlates of poverty. In these reports, even though they virtually never include direct indicators of psychological factors, the impersonal and social factors appear fairly well to account for the lion's share of poverty.

But, still, there is one haunting exception in their results which cautions against overstating the above point. Morgan and his associates combined such predictors of income as age, education, skill, urban vs. rural residence, disability and female headed families isolated in their prior analyses as predictors of income and, when applied to the actual predictive characteristics of the spending units having inadequate incomes, estimated an income of $2,204. But the heads of these families actually earned only slightly more than $900! This is a relatively large discrepancy. Although error of prediction and an underlying variability of income may be operating here, as the authors acknowledge, differences in ability, motivation, or in other characteristics not measured may have caused the difference between the actual and expected earnings.[125]

The recent study by Robert Stone and Frederic Schlamp is pertinent to the present issue.[126] These researchers contrasted a sample of unemployed AFDC recipients with a matched group of non-recipients. Because this method of matching groups holds relatively equal a large number of poverty-related variables, the design affords a rare opportunity to highlight more subtle differences. A long-term assistance group differed from the group not receiving assistance as follows: in the assistance group, health was poorer, there was greater psychological dependency, and, as mentioned earlier, there were fewer contacts with friends and less mutual aid given by them. These are revealing and, aside from the disability correlate, indicate indeed that the differences are subtle. But most significantly, there were relatively few large differences between the groups, and many similarities. In drawing policy conclusions from the findings of the study, the sponsor, the State of California Department of Social Welfare, concluded in the annual report to its board that because the differences between the two groups were so small, the groups were "interchangeable parts of *one* high-risk, dependency-prone group," and that prevention should be addressed to the entire high-risk category rather than to those who happen to be receiving assistance.[127]

The variable of income is particularly significant. In addition to being virtually the defining condition for poverty, low income is associated with a cluster of factors which themselves serve to perpetuate economic deprivation. Although it does not follow that raising income will necessarily reverse the self-perpetuating factors for the poor, it may alter many and, in addition, provide the "capital" with which to begin to change in other ways. Thus simply raising the income of the poor in substantial amounts may well be one of the single most effective corrective means of reducing poverty.

The second issue requiring attention may now be stated: it is the problem of the order in which poverty variables are operative. Some variables are present from birth, some are most influential in childhood, and others later in life; and given any age grade, variables often occur in an order, some being more potent than others. Obviously this is relevant to prevention.

Alvin Schorr's analysis of the "choice points" in the family cycle and how the "choices" affect the likelihood of subsequent poverty is exemplary.[128] As we understand his analysis, one of the most costly actions for a poor boy or girl—especially a girl

—is to participate in unwed parenthood. Consider the girl. If she becomes pregnant at fifteen, her chances are very high of (1) dropping out of school, (2) marrying early rather than later, (3) marrying a boy who has little education and few job skills, (4) having more rather than fewer children (the transition from four to five being most penalizing), and (5) having a family broken through desertion, separation, or divorce. Each factor increases the likelihood of the next and each, in turn, increases the chances of being poor in later years. Viewed as points of potential intervention, it is clear that earlier rather than later interventions would be preferable, and that at any point in the sequence before the last, intervention may be pinpointed. We need similar analyses of the order of occurrence of poverty-related variables, attaching to each variable an estimate of poverty risk.

The attention given to the multi-problem family deserves brief commentary here, for one still finds authorities advocating an attack upon such families as a promising way to reduce poverty. We do not think this approach offers much promise. As we have indicated at various points in the previous analyses, the poverty variables do not cluster together that strongly for most of the poor. Only a very small percentage of the poor are "multi-problem" families; the majority have only a few poverty correlates apparently accounting for their economic deprivation.

A much more promising mode of attack on poverty, we believe, is to focus on the potent variables, acting on these at the crucial stages when reversal of their effects would most reduce the risks of poverty, and doing so on a mass basis. The present analysis of such poverty-related factors has necessarily been incomplete but, hopefully, it reveals some of the more influential variables and indicates the scope and diversity of factors apparently operative in poverty.

Structural Context

The social category of the poor and the differential allocation of
individuals and families to this category occur in a socio-cultural
context and are very much influenced by it. We shall first consider the structural factors pertaining to the social category
itself and then take up the conditions relating to differential
allocation.

POSITIONAL FACTORS

In the previous analysis of the social category of the poor, six
distinguishing features were identified. For each of these there
are more general social conditions, some of which were mentioned in the earlier analysis. Here we shall highlight and
elaborate these social conditions as among the underlying conditions sustaining the category of the poor.

The visibility of a social position is in many ways not unlike
the visibility of any object. The salience of an object and its
perception in general depend upon the properties of the stimu-
lus object, as well as upon the properties of the perceivers. In
the case of the poor, considered as objects of perception, they
are visible to large segments of the population and undoubtedly
more so now than in years past. As was observed, however, the
increased visibility cannot be attributed to an increased size of
their lot, for their number has not increased proportionately in
recent decades. (During periods of mass unemployment, the
sheer size of the cohort designated as poor undoubtedly contributes to visibility.) The current visibility of the poor is really
more a matter of an increase in the number of those who recognize that the nation has a problem of poverty. In recent years
the new frame of reference of those who are not poor has made

this recognition possible. Missions of foreign aid addressed to the poor of other lands call to mind the poor at home; and the increasing affluence of most Americans at home contrasts the lot of our own poor adversely. Underlying all this is the relative economic strength of the United States.

The basic common attribute of the poor is the lack of economic resources. But in the American class structure it appears that economic deprivation, power, and prestige tend to crystallize at the two extremes of the class hierarchy, so that individuals (and families) at the very top and very bottom rank on all three about the same—very high or very low, respectively.[129] The diverse means by which power, prestige, and income have been interlinked are not as important here as the fact of their interrelationship. The main sociological consequence of binding together economic resources with power and prestige at the lowest level of our society is that inequality extends over all three. In this sense there is likely to be a triple penalty for economic deprivation: economic impoverishment itself, as well as low power and prestige.

The reactions of others to the poor—generally negative—derive largely from the fact that the category of the poor is a deviant position. Standards of achievement, industriousness, and success serve as reference points from which the poor depart and, as mentioned before, there can be no deviance without such criteria of desirable behavior. The value complex which includes achievement and success as central has been a characteristic of most modern, industrialized societies—capitalistic as well as non-capitalistic. This value system, while generally functional in such societies, sets a relatively demanding standard of excellence, considering the entire populations of individuals upon which it is imposed and the many constraining conditions that prohibit some members in these societies from achieving the standard.

But the reactions of all individuals to the poor has obviously not been entirely negative. Many of the non-poor experience psychological inequality when they contrast their condition to that of the poor, and such perceptions are sustained in part by values of equality and humanitarianism.[130] Equality of opportunity has long been a part of American ideology, and although this has rarely meant equality of condition for most Americans, we surmise that there has been an increasing adherence to this more liberal conception of equality. Humanitarianism, which in a sense is a partial outgrowth of the discrepancy between actual inequality and values of equality, also has a long tradition in this country. Humanitarian values temper negative reactions to the poor, on the one hand, and help support concern for the poor and their increased visibility, on the other.

In the discussion of the poor as a relative position, we observed that in recent decades the poverty line has gradually risen, this occurring largely because the standard of what constitutes basic sustenance needs has crept upward. In a way, this increase in sustenance standards merely reflects a more affluent way of life. But if equalitarian and humanitarian values were not part of the American value system, the fact of increased affluence for most persons would not necessarily imply any increase in standards of basic sustenance needs for the poor. But, of course, if egalitarian and humanitarian values were dominant rather than relatively secondary features of the ideology, there would be much higher standards of basic sustenance needs, given the same affluence. Holding affluence constant and high, the degree of departure of economic well-being from that of most of the population which is required for the departure to be defined as poverty would appear to depend in part upon the extent to which egalitarian and humanitarian values are espoused.

The fact that the social category of the poor contains mixed profiles of achieved and ascribed positional features creates a sociological dilemma, as was observed earlier. The poor cannot be treated as if the position were entirely achieved or fully ascribed. Underlying this dilemma is the tendency for society to attach individual respcnsibility to the actions of members of achieved positions, for those factors pertaining to entry, membership, or departure; and society tends to reduce or to eliminate responsibility for these factors as they apply to ascribed positions.

Because the poor cannot be viewed satisfactorily as in either an ascribed or an achieved position, societies and the assistance systems they evolve have been forced to develop criteria by which differential reactions may be justified. Until very recent decades, most societies have labored over decisions regarding such criteria within a context of an ideology that reflects a strange blend of politics, economics, and homemade moral psychology. These ideological conflicts have only recently been informed by data—political, economic, sociological, and psychological—by which more accurate subtypes of the poor may be distinguished, so that specific remedial action might be taken. As accurate social science information is amassed about the poor, the problem is increasingly less that of not having factual guidelines for creating workable remedies for poverty, and increasingly an ideological issue—whether or not the society should divert to poverty the funds and social reconstruction required to eliminate it.

ALLOCATIVE FACTORS

Richard Titmuss has distinguished between two types of dependency: natural and man-made.[131] (The economic dependence of the old and infirm would illustrate the former and technological unemployment the latter.) Man-made dependency, Titmuss contends, is generated fundamentally by a societal interdependence which is manifested in a complex division of labor having numerous positions into which and out of which individuals are selected. A highly differentiated system of roles is indeed an underlying factor, but to explicate more clearly its relationship to poverty it is necessary to emphasize additional factors. Titmuss' social differentiation is really characterized by a plethora of positions involving achievement rather than ascription, as well as specific levels of role performance required to enter such achieved positions. The processes of selection and rejection have become highly refined in our time and, on the basis of such processes, individuals are selected into very particular achieved positions and rejected from others. If the specialized niches are frequently in flux, with new ones being created and others eliminated (as is the case for jobs) and if individuals are not being fully socialized in advance for given position possibilities, then some persons will inevitably be unable to find suitable positions. The problem is compounded by having achieved positions which require high standards of accomplishment.

Implicit in the above is the supposition that income is the main return for successful achievement. More generally, as Titmuss has observed in another context,[132] the distribution of resources in many modern societies, and especially the United States, is based upon success or failure in what is fundamentally economic competition. Stated as a contingency of return, success in achieved positions is generally directly related to income, either in terms of whether or not the income is provided or in terms of how much. No work, no pay, in other words.

Now, in a complex division of labor, where income is made contingent upon achievement and where this is generally occupational achievement, misfits and rejects will receive no income, or very little. Furthermore, because low income tends to be accompanied by low prestige and power, misfits and rejects will be additionally penalized. In all of these ways the social differentiation and complex division of labor in modern society serve as a structural condition without which there would be no man-made poverty.

The impersonal and social agents of selection detailed in the preceding section, as they relate to man-made poverty, will operate here. They reflect the means by which, in a complex division of labor, positions are created or eliminated, on the one hand, or the selection and rejection of position members are brought about, on the other. All this in a sense serves as the structural backdrop—the props and script, as it were—for the play of poverty. The characters in the play also come and go on the social stage as a function of individual differences. Such differences arise from innate dispositions, as illustrated by the inborn factors of ability and temperament, and from social experience. The numerous personal and social agents discussed earlier index the individual differences of which we speak here.

Now, given the complex social differentiation and allocative processes by which some individuals avoid poverty and others do not, the question is how the poor have been treated by societies. The assistance programs for the poor in most societies have not eliminated poverty and, everything considered, this is perhaps the major irony in attempts by societies to cope with poverty.[133] In earlier eras there was generally a lack of resources and factual knowledge which placed genuine constraints on efforts to eliminate poverty. Increasingly, at least in relatively affluent societies, these are less limiting. Now the most serious problems of poverty are mainly ideological, not technical or scientific. The ideological battle concerns not only whether or not poverty is to be reduced or eliminated but also, if it is to be reduced or eliminated, by what means. Unfortunately, ideology infuses the technical details as well as the general issue.

There are at least three different principles upon which informal and formal assistance systems have been based, and each involves ideological factors as well as contingencies of exchange. The first, which we call *exchange justice*, asserts that individuals

obtain outcomes (generally income in monetary economies) in
some direct proportion to their investments (generally work or
merit of contribution). (This is not unlike George Caspar
Homans' principle of distributive justice, except that Homans'
principle is a detailed refinement which also includes compari-
sons between and among persons.[134]) Exchange justice is essentially the principle of market exchange and, of course, derives
from a contingency system in which money is the main reinforcer employed to sustain work and achievement. *Positive
exchange justice* involves returns provided in some direct proportion to the amount and types of investments of work or
effort people make; in general, high outcomes are provided in
exchange for high input, medium for medium, low for low. The
extreme instance of "no effort, no return" is merely a special
case. In contrast, *negative exchange justice* asserts that in
exchange for an individual's aversion to the social system, a
like amount of aversion is given in return. This is *lex talionis*,
"an eye for an eye and a tooth for a tooth," as the bible says.

Those poor in our society who work for low incomes, either
regularly or irregularly, and who receive no assistance are provided with small return for what society has deemed little input.
This is the operation of positive exchange justice outside of an
assistance system. If such persons are compensated for work on
a work-relief program, we have an example of positive exchange
justice in a formal assistance system. If an individual makes contributions to social security during his working years and
receives payments in old age based in part upon the amount of
his contributions, this also illustrates the principle of positive
exchange justice. In this case, it is as mediated by an insurance
system which intervenes between the contributions and the outcome payment. (All the insurance system does is recalculate
the relationship between input and output so as to distribute
risks over a large population.) If the poor fail to meet financial
obligations (e.g., to support a wife or to repay a loan) and are

consequently put in jail, this illustrates negative exchange justice. In past eras the poor were sometimes simply put in jail as
punishment for their poverty—negative exchange justice in an
even more aversive form.

Clearly, exchange justice is still with us in diverse forms. Positive exchange justice is the main type; there is less negative
justice prevailing today than in past eras. The main shortcoming
of exchange justice, even in its positive form, is that not everyone who is poor can contribute the input necessary to obtain a
satisfactory outcome. This problem has been recognized in social
security regulations which allow individuals to receive some
benefits for very few quarters of contribution. But even so,
these persons, while benefiting proportionately more than others
who have contributed much longer, receive relatively little considering what is needed to avoid economic impoverishment. We
believe that one of the reasons for the relative popularity of
social insurance systems in this country is that they are a particular form of the main prevailing method of work reinforcement—namely, exchange justice.

The second principle of assistance is *reciprocity*, in which,
according to Alvin Gouldner's seminal discussion, "people should
help those who have helped them, and people should not
injure those who have helped them." [135] Informal mutual aid
among families and friends illustrates generally the operation of
this principle. In formal assistance systems we find this well
illustrated in many of the veterans' programs, especially those
which provide disability compensation benefits for service-
connected injuries. This is an example of heteromorphic reciprocity, the exchange of unlike resources to meet reciprocal
obligations. Homomorphic reciprocity, in which like resources
are exchanged, is illustrated by one neighbor loaning money to a
friend in need, who had earlier loaned the first money under
similar conditions. These types of reciprocity, which come from
Gouldner also, are mentioned here because we believe that the

most common type in both formal and informal assistance systems is the heteromorphic.

The reciprocity principle is different from the exchange principle primarily on the basis of the degree to which indebtedness
and gratitude prevail over the more impersonal give and take
of the marketplace, where one provides inputs in order to
receive outputs. As Gouldner suggests, these principles may and
often do work conjointly. But with regard to assistance systems,
it seems that some programs (such as those for veterans) are
based more solidly on collective gratitude and the desire to
compensate for losses experienced in the provision of special
services to society.

The main difficulty with the principle of reciprocity is that it
presupposes the ability of each party to help the other. Many
of the poor, especially the involuntary poor, obviously cannot
invest the effort to merit help in return; stated otherwise, if
helped by another they cannot always reciprocate. The norm of
reciprocity, which Gouldner claims is universal in some form in
all societies, cannot be sustained for those who fail to reciprocate. The principle of reciprocity, then, while functional for
most persons, is mainly inapplicable to large segments of the
poor, simply because they cannot properly honor the obligations
to help in return. Furthermore, the principle of reciprocity,
while a long-standing mainstay of most informal assistance systems, is difficult to translate into state responsibility and individual responsibility in a complex modern society.

The third main principle of assistance systems is that of
responsibility,[136] by which is meant that one unit has an obliga-
tion to help the other on a non-contingent basis. There are
three distinct forms. The first is *full responsibility* in which all
help is provided by one unit; the second is *partial responsibility*
by one unit; the third, *no responsibility*. The amount of help
provided is another question, however, and this may vary
from much to little.

Most of the assistance programs in this country that involve the responsibility principle involve partial responsibility, in which only limited help is given altogether. Consider the categorical assistances. The federal and state governments jointly contribute and, in some cases, relatives may contribute as well; and the responsibility is limited, i.e., only a modest amount is contributed, considering what recipients get. This fact of low welfare grants has been acknowledged time and again and needs no documentation. The low grants are not just due to the apparent limitation of resources and the penny-pinching proclivities of fund-granting bodies. A recent study calls the phenomenon "the law of the Constant Welfare-Grant Gap." According to this law, "no matter how high a welfare grant gets, income from jobs on the labor market are either (a) higher than the grant, or (b) lower than the subsistence budget of the family." [137] This may be stated as a generalization in terms of our assistance principles: *the limit of assistance under the principle of responsibility tends to yield outcomes for those assisted which are less than the outcomes that would be yielded by positive exchange justice in the employment market (or which are below the poverty line).*

Now, to return to the question of ideology. Exchange justice is clearly the principle of assistance that is most consistent with the economics of the marketplace, with an achievement-oriented society, and with a reinforcement-contingency system in which income is the main reinforcer for work and effort. Many of our assistance programs are merely a form of exchange justice in another guise (e.g., social security). Furthermore, exchange justice takes precedence over the other principles of assistance in at least two ways: responsibility systems would appear to be resorted to only after exchange justice, in its various forms, has been shown not to work; and the limits of assistance under the responsibility principle, when instituted, are fixed at generally *less* than equivalent outcomes that exchange justice would provide were this principle of exchange employed to yield outcomes.

Implications for Policy

In some ways the analysis provides support for most specialized professional and disciplinary solutions. There *are* class-related factors in poverty for which an opening up of the opportunity structure and resocialization of the poor would be relevant; there *are* cultural factors for which mass acculturation would be pertinent; there *are* personal defects among the poor for which education, training, and behavior change would be suitable remedies; there *is* relatively low power of the poor for which increased autonomy and control would be relevant; there *is* racial inequality for which extraordinary programs would be desirable; and there *is* economic impoverishment and a clustering of self-perpetuating features of poverty for which much higher income would be beneficial.

This analysis also confirms many of the main emphases in current policy and programs in the poverty area. Despite a still vocal coterie who propose simple and sovereign approaches, poverty is widely acknowledged to be determined by many factors. This analysis of the various "agents" in poverty, we believe, corroborates the multi-factor view. Indeed, if anything, the analysis of "agents" presented herein discloses perhaps an even more diverse and complex battery of factors than have heretofore been catalogued. We found that some "agents" or "agent amalgams" appeared to be more potent than others. The variables we identified as apparently more potent in poverty may help to specify relevant points of intervention. Informed observers have been thinking along related lines. The notion of "strategic entry" suggested by selected findings on the temporal and "causal" ordering of poverty variables is not really new either, although we believe that because of insufficient evidence of this type on all the poverty variables, it has not been possible to inform policy and programs adequately in these matters.

By considering the poor as a social position, and by indicating some of the structural factors relating to economic deprivation, we have seen that there is much more to poverty than a cohort of low-income people. The analysis emphasized the numerous ways in which the position of the poor is partly or largely independent of the particular persons who happen to be called poor. Some of the points made in the analysis are more directly pertinent to understanding the broader social and psychological context of poverty than to possible action to eliminate poverty. But there are some general implications for policy.

If one wishes to eliminate the social position of the poor and not merely to reduce economic deprivation, this analysis suggests a number of factors to be kept in mind.

1. The social position of the poor is a relative position sustained by numerous psychological, social, and economic conditions. Changing the behavior, attributes, or condition of the poor may simply redefine the boundaries of the category differently, so that some segment of the population will remain in the category. This will be likely especially if the standards from which the poor depart are themselves increasing while the poor are changing. Thus, increasing the income of the poor while general affluence and conceptions of basic sustenance needs are also rising may very well result simply in redrawing the poverty line at a somewhat higher level; increasing the educational level of the poor while the general level required for most jobs is also increasing may retain the relative educational handicap; increasing the achievement of those poor who are able to work while general achievement standards simultaneously inch upward may simply redefine higher minimal achievement levels.

2. The social category of the poor is mixed in its composition in terms of the degree of achievement and ascription character-

izing the positional profiles of the members. Those whose poverty is in part or fully ascribed, i.e., largely "involuntary," will obviously not respond to social influence and efforts to modify their behavior. Solutions involving employment and the free market and their assistance counterpart—the type of assistance here called exchange justice—will be largely irrelevant. The assistance principle here called responsibility will have to be applied for such persons, involving assistance, preferably in ample amounts, on a non-contingent basis.

3. Assistance programs have been dominated by the principle of exchange justice, this principle prevailing generally over the principles of responsibility and reciprocity. Exchange justice is relevant only for those poor who can make an investment of effort and work so as to justify the provision of outcomes for them in return. (In a somewhat different way, the same limitation obtains for reciprocity-based formal assistance systems, but these systems are relatively minor.) In order to have adequate assistance systems based upon the principle of responsibility, a general norm of responsibility must prevail over those of achievement-success; and the related contingency system that makes the sustenance essentials of life dependent upon income, and income in turn upon work, will have to be altered.

4. If assistance systems are to operate more effectively in the reduction or elimination of poverty of a non-ascribed type, it will be necessary to modify the relationship between inputs and outcomes now built into the operation of exchange. In assistance systems, exchange does not often raise the income of persons above the poverty line. (For example, maximal social security benefits for an old person would not be enough by themselves to bring his income above most poverty lines.) In the free market, exchange justice for individuals working for low incomes does not ordinarily assure freedom from poverty. Thus, in both the assistance and market contexts, much larger outcomes for inputs should be provided. This of course means

higher wages for low-income people and higher social security benefits. The above discussion was based on the premise that a principle of exchange justice should govern the outcomes that enable individuals and families to obtain the basic essentials to live. This is a debatable assumption, because the principle of exchange justice has never eliminated low incomes, to our knowledge, and the principle itself is based upon dubious assumptions beclouded by an elaborate ideology.

5. The substitution of the principle of responsibility for that of exchange justice for *all* forms of poverty might well undercut numerous props which now sustain the social position of the poor, provided that more than limited responsibility were assumed by the state. Because this may seem surprising, let us elaborate, remembering that our discourse involves considerations of the possible elimination of the social category of the poor.

As we have tried to show, the basic contingency system in our society has made the essentials of life largely dependent upon income, and the latter in turn upon productive work. We surmise that once in the earlier history of man, brute strength and physical superiority in general were needed to obtain the bare essentials of life—a natural as contrasted with a man-made contingency. At various points in history, selfishness, guile, and deceit were probably also requisites to survival. Now, by making the essentials of life contingent upon income, we have penalized large segments of the population: their health suffers; they live shorter lives; they live under conditions that serve in part to perpetuate themselves; they live lives that are psychologically and socially impoverished, compared with those of most others; and they live in a blatantly affluent surrounding, parts of which border on the materialistically decadent, the contrast revealing vividly and embarrassingly the hypocrisy of equalitarian and humanitarian values in our society.

Not merely the contingency of income and the essentials of

life are at issue, but also a value complex with success and achievement at the apex. We fear that by the time poverty rates have been reduced greatly (the present rates of reducing poverty are estimated at about 2 percent per year as of 1964 [138]), the overly revered values of success and achievement will have ceased to be very functional. The problems of tomorrow, in a world in which automation will have relieved us of most of the menial and not so menial jobs, will force the evolution of different values—of the good and worthwhile. Leisure will be more abundant; the society, hopefully, will be more affluent; and the division of labor will probably call for more service jobs and tasks calling for complex intellectual and interpersonal skills. This will be a profoundly different world than the settling of a frontier and the industrializing of a nation which characterized our country when the values of work, success, and achievement were most essential. The society's task is no longer that of getting everyone to work hard, long, and diligently at relatively manual activities.

Now for the problem of motivation to work. A work-income contingency system is not essential to get productive effort from individuals, contrary to most of the contemporary ideology. Studies in industrial productivity have revealed for years that even in the present work-income system, numerous other incentives and non-monetary motives are operative. Psychologists who study behavior have long known that money was not the only generalized secondary reinforcer and that high performance levels, if required, may be achieved with diverse incentives.

So much for prelude. What might an assistance system based upon responsibility look like? There are numerous possibilities. One promising alternative would be to provide all families with a guaranteed annual income sufficient to cover the essentials of life.[139] (Economists assure us that the economic resources to eliminate poverty are available, if only devoted to that purpose).[140] Then, for work performed, a work-incentive system might also be adopted in which income and other reinforcers would be applicable—a limited system of exchange justice using more than income as reinforcement. At the same time, the essential tasks of providing education, behavioral modification, and socialization can proceed for those now called poor, many of whom desperately need these efforts; and the correctional-restorative obligations to those now called poor can be accomplished without having the basic essentials of life contingent upon them.

We cannot be certain that even this program would eliminate the category of the poor, but economic deprivation would be virtually eliminated and many structural supports for poverty as it now exists would be greatly weakened. Furthermore, the entire proposal involves converting the category of the poor from a mixed achieved and ascribed position to essentially a fully ascribed category containing persons less deprived economically than the present poor. The main sense of the proposal is that there is much to gain and little to lose by such a conversion of the position. But important projections for the future are essential to the rationale, these centering on a greatly increased amount of leisure, the mass reduction of manual, menial, and other jobs as well, less necessity to work in general, and greater affluence. These projections may be contradicted by future events or may come into being much more slowly than we anticipate. Without the reality of at least some of these anticipated events, the conversion of the position of the poor to pure ascription would be risky. Actually, it is as unwise to meet the sociological dilemma of this position, as it now exists, by a purely "ascriptive" treatment as by a purely "achievement" program. The purely "achievement" programs of earlier eras failed; and the same fate awaits a prematurely "ascriptive" solution, in our view.

Under *existing* conditions as projected for the future, the best general solution for poverty, we believe, is to meet its problems by facing squarely the mixed nature of the social category. This means distinguishing all relevant subtypes of achievement-ascription profiles, and for each adopting a strong program based upon either the assistance principle of exchange justice, responsibility, or, in a few cases, some sensible blend. In point 3 above we discussed the responsibility principle, and in point 4 the exchange principle, and so repetition here is unnecessary. A "conservative" rendition of the implications of this analysis, then, is to improve assistance systems based upon exchange justice and responsibility, applying each appropriately. A "liberal" rendition would be to begin now to convert the present category of the poor to an ascribed position having members with less economic deprivation than now exists for the poor, doing so by means of the responsibility principle. "Pessimists" will favor the former rendition, "optimists" the latter. Carefully wrought projections as well as future events will ultimately decide the issue, we think. In the meantime, we are among the "optimists."

6. Even if the social category of the poor were eliminated, it is well to point out that actual social inequalities would likely still prevail. We are thinking of inequalities of power and prestige, among others. While a flattening of the income distribution in our class system would undoubtedly flatten the power and prestige distributions, at least at first, inequalities in these other areas, to the extent that they would derive from factors other than the monetary criterion, would continue. Furthermore, psychological inequality would undoubtedly still prevail. As indicated earlier, psychological inequality may exist even with material equality. And with psychological inequality goes at least some dissatisfaction.

Implications for Social Psychology

In 1908 Georg Simmel was translated as saying:

> The poor, as a sociological category, are not those who suffer specific deficiencies, but those who receive assistance or should receive it according to social norms. Consequently, in this sense, poverty cannot be defined by itself as a quantitative state, but only in terms of the social reaction resulting from a specific situation.[141]

In many ways our analysis is an explication of the thought expressed by Simmel. But our approach was more general. Thus we have tried to show the specific ways in which the position of the poor is partly or largely independent of its members; the strikingly diverse personal, social, and impersonal conditions that determine differential allocation of individuals (and families) to the category; and the many features of the social-structural context of this position that serve to sustain it. In a word, the problems of poverty dealt with here help to illuminate the social, personal, and impersonal dynamics of position membership and of the very existence of the position itself.

The many specific implications for research and theory in social psychology will not be elaborated here. But we should indicate two general conclusions:

1. Despite the differences in relative potency of specific variables entering into poverty, an almost bewildering array of variables is related to poverty and may operate in intricate combinations. Oversimple psychological, economic, or sociological explanations that stress one or a few key variables (such as economic deprivation, power, class, culture, or personal defect) are most inadequate in the face of such complexity. If the results of this analysis provide any basis at all for general-

ization, we suggest that the most adequate social psychological framework is that which confronts the diverse classes of variables, their relative potencies, and their contingencies in operation (both in time and in combination).

2. The apparent diversity and complexity of the factors affecting position membership call for research designs that provide for an examination of how the variables function when taken all together. Only a few studies reviewed here even came close to meeting this standard, but, even so, they were among the most informative. Most of the studies were too restricted in the battery of variables studied, the samples of subjects examined, and in the monitoring of variables over sufficiently long periods of time. Only multi-variate research of the type recommended here will generate the findings needed for an adequate social psychological theory of complex problems such as poverty.

Notes

1. This report is based in part upon a research project in social dependency financed in its early stages by funds of the Russell Sage Foundation allocated to Edwin J. Thomas as a Rackham Research Grant of the University of Michigan. We also wish to express our gratitude to Professors Roger Lind, Sydney Bernard, and Patricia Rabinovitz, who provided bibliographic leads and thoughtful reactions as our work progessed, and to Drs. Maeda Galinsky and Warren Haggstrom, who worked on the project in its beginnings.

2. Edwin J. Thomas and Bruce J. Biddle, "Basic Concepts for Classifying the Phenomena of Role," in Bruce J. Biddle and Edwin J. Thomas, eds., *Role Theory: Concepts and Research,* New York, 1966, pp. 28-29.

3. See Robert H. Bremner, "Modern Attitudes Toward Charity and Relief," *Comparative Studies in Society and History,* I (June 1959), 377-382; and David Matza, "Poverty and Disrepute," in Robert K. Merton and Robert A. Nisbet, eds., *Contemporary Social Problems,* 2nd ed., New York, 1966, pp. 619-669.

4. For an account of sociological factors in the current visibility of the

poor, see Nathan Glazer, "A Sociologist's View of Poverty," in Margaret S. Gordon, ed., *Poverty in America*, San Francisco, 1965, pp. 12-26. Also see Herman P. Miller, "Major Elements of a Research Program for the Study of Poverty," in Task Force on Economic Growth and Opportunity, *The Concept of Poverty*, Chamber of Commerce of the United States, 1965, pp. 115-136.

5. R. A. Gordon, "An Economist's View of Poverty," in Gordon, ed., *Poverty in America*, pp. 3-11.

6. Dwight Macdonald, "The Now Visible Poor," in George H. Dunne, S.J., ed., *Poverty in Plenty*, New York, 1964, pp. 61-69.

7. See Glazer, *op. cit.*

8. *The Negro Family*, Washington, Office of Policy Planning and Research, United States Department of Labor, March 1965.

9. For further details, see Glazer, *op. cit.*

10. For further details, see, for example, Herman P. Miller, "Changes in the Number and Composition of the Poor," in Gordon, ed., *Poverty in America*, pp. 91-96.

11. For an operational definition of the poor illustrating this point, see James N. Morgan, Martin H. David, Wilbur J. Cohen, and Harvey E. Brazer, with the assistance of Norma Meyers and Barbara Baldwin, *Income and Welfare in the United States*, New York, 1962, pp. 188-190.

12. For a view of poverty based upon this point, see, among others, Warren C. Haggstrom, "The Power of the Poor," in Frank Riessman, Jerome Cohen, and Arthur Pearl, eds., *Mental Health of the Poor*, New York, 1964, pp. 205-223.

13. For a discussion of the low esteem in which the poor are held, see Matza, *op. cit.*

14. This point will be elaborated later in some detail.

15. Oscar Ornati, "The Convergence of Poverty-Linked Characteristics," in Robert E. Will and Harold G. Vatter, eds., *Poverty in Affluence*, New York, 1965, pp. 184-189.

16. Bremner, *op. cit.*, p. 377.

17. For a detailed exposition of the prejudicial consequences of suitable home policies, see Winifred Bell, *Aid to Dependent Children*, New York, 1965.

18. Matza, *op. cit.*

19. Morgan, *Income and Welfare in the United States*, p. 216.

20. Matza, *op. cit.*

21. Eugene Smolensky, "The Past and Present Poor," in Task Force on Economic Growth and Opportunity, *The Concept of Poverty*, pp. 35-67.

22. George Gallup, "Two Basically Different Views Held on Causes of Poverty," in Will and Vatter, eds., *Poverty in Affluence*, pp. 69-70.

23. See, for example, Grace Marcus, *Some Aspects of Relief in Family Casework*, New York, 1929.

24. See Milton J. Rosenberg and Robert P. Abelson, "An Analysis of

Cognitive Balancing," in Milton J. Rosenberg, Carl I. Hovland, William J. McGuire, Robert P. Abelson, and Jack W. Brehm, *Attitude Organization and Change,* New Haven, 1960, Chapter 4. For a critical discussion of "consistency" theories in general, see Roger Brown, *Social Psychology,* New York, 1965, Chapter 11.

25. John W. Thibaut and Henry W. Riecken, "Some Determinants and Consequences of the Perception of Social Causality," in Eleanor E. Maccoby, Theodore M. Newcomb, and Eugene L. Hartley, eds., *Readings in Social Psychology,* 3rd ed., New York, 1958, pp. 117-130. See also Albert Pepitone, "Attributions of Causality, Social Attitudes, and Cognitive Matching Processes," in Renato Tagiuri and Luigi Petrullo, eds, *Person Perception and Interpersonal Behavior,* Stanford, 1958, especially pp. 264-268.

26. Marvin E. Shaw and Jefferson L. Sulzer, "An Empirical Test of Heider's Levels in Attribution of Responsibility," *Journal of Abnormal and Social Psychology,* LXIX (July 1964), 39-46; and Elaine Walster, "Assignment of Responsibility for an Accident," *Journal of Personality and Social Psychology,* III (January 1966), 73-79.

27. Leon H. Keyserling, *Progress or Poverty,* Washington, Conference on Economic Progress, 1964, p. 34.

28. Some noteworthy exceptions are S. Michael Miller and Martin Rein, "Will the War on Poverty Change America?" *Trans-action,* II (July/August 1965), 17-23; and Richard M. Titmuss, *Essays on "The Welfare State,"* New Haven, 1959, especially Chapter 2, pp. 53-54.

29. J. Stacy Adams, "Toward an Understanding of Inequity," *Journal of Abnormal and Social Psychology,* LXVII (November 1963), 422-437.

30. *Ibid.,* p. 424.

31. Adams' theory owes an acknowledged debt to the theory of cognitive dissonance. For example, see Leon Festinger, *A Theory of Cognitive Dissonance,* Stanford, 1957. Also related are theories of relative deprivation. See Robert K. Merton, *Social Theory and Social Structure,* revised ed., Glencoe, 1957, pp. 227-250.

32. For a recent study demonstrating this empirically in a welfare context, see W. G. Runciman, *Relative Deprivation and Social Justice: A Study of Attitudes to Social Inequality in Twentieth-Century England,* Berkeley and Los Angeles, 1966.

33. Adams, *op. cit.*

34. Matza was so impressed with this that he proposed a category of the economically deprived called the "disreputable poor." See Matza, *op. cit.,* pp. 628-657. For related types of deviance having a stigma attached, see Erving Goffman, *Stigma,* Englewood Cliffs, 1963; and Eliot Freidson, "Disability as Social Deviance," in Marvin B. Sussman, ed., *Sociology and Rehabilitation,* Washington, 1966, pp. 71-99. Also, for a general statement, see Howard S. Becker, *Outsiders,* New York, 1963.

35. Robin Williams, *American Society: A Sociological Interpretation,* 2nd ed., New York, 1960.

36. For varieties of such approaches, see Sidney E. Zimbalist, "Drawing the Poverty Line," *Social Work*, IX (July 1964), 19-26; S. M. Miller, "Poverty and Inequality in America: Implications for the Social Services," in Riessman, *et al.*, eds., *Mental Health of the Poor*, pp. 11-15; and John T. Dunlop, "Poverty: Definition and Measurement," in Task Force on Economic Growth and Opportunity, *The Concept of Poverty*, pp. 93-111.

37. Herman P. Miller, "Changes in the Number and Composition of the Poor," p. 94.

38. Herman .P. Miller, "The Dimensions of Poverty," in Ben B. Seligman, ed., *Poverty as a Public Issue*, New York, 1965, p. 26.

39. Jane C. Kronick, *Family Life and Economic Dependency: A Report to the Welfare Administration*, Bryn Mawr, Pa., Graduate Department of Social Work and Social Research, Bryn Mawr College, unpublished manuscript, 1965.

40. Caplovitz, in his study of low-income consumers, found that 95 percent owned at least one television set, more than three out of every five owned a phonograph, more than two in every five owned a sewing machine, and more than two in every five owned an automatic washing machine. See David Caplovitz, "The Problems of Low-Income Consumers," a paper prepared for the 57th Meeting of the American Sociological Association, September 1962, p. 3.

41. Theodore W. Schultz, as quoted in Herman Miller, "Changes in the Number and Composition of the Poor," p. 95.

42. Despite small changes in segments of the distribution, the gross categories have changed little if at all in recent decades. See Keyserling, *Progress or Poverty*. For details on the more segmented changes, see the review by S. M. Miller, "Poverty and Inequality in America: Implications for the Social Services."

43. Research by Ruth Mack, as reported in part by Herman Miller, "Changes in the Number and Composition of the Poor," pp. 97-98.

44. Smolensky, *op. cit.*

45. Keyserling, *Progress or Poverty*, p. 17.

46. Ralph Linton, *The Study of Man*, New York, 1936, p. 115.

47. Edwin J. Thomas and Bruce J. Biddle, "Basic Concepts for the Properties of Role Phenomena," in Biddle and Thomas, eds., *Role Theory: Concepts and Research*, p. 50.

48. For a more general treatment of these problems, see Edwin J. Thomas, "Social Role, Personality, and the Individual," in Edgar F. Borgatta and William Lambert, eds., *Handbook of Personality Theory and Research*, New York, in press.

49. For the related concepts of "fractional selection" and "massive generation," see Matza, *op. cit.*, pp. 657-668.

50. John T. Dailey, "Education and Emergence from Poverty," *Journal of Marriage and the Family*, XXVI (November 1964), 430-434.

51. Erdman Palmore, "Dropouts, Delinquency, and Lower-Class Children," in Will and Vatter, eds., *Poverty in Affluence*, pp. 139-140.

52. Willard Wirtz, "Income and College Attendance," in Will and Vatter, eds., *Poverty in Affluence*, pp. 135-139.

53. See Martin Deutsch, "The Disadvantaged Child and the Learning Process," in Louis A. Ferman, Joyce L. Kornbluh, and Alan Haber, eds., *Poverty in America*, Ann Arbor, 1965, pp. 353-370; Basil Bernstein, "Social Class and Linguistic Development," in A. H. Halsey, J. Floud, and C. A. Anderson, eds., *Education, Economy and Society*, Glencoe, 1961, pp. 288-314; and Robert D. Hess and Virginia Shipman, "Early Blocks to Children's Learning," *Children*, XII (October 1965), 189-194.

54. For a discussion of the relationship between job skills and unemployment in the wake of automation, see Charles C. Killingsworth, "Automation, Jobs, and Manpower," in Ferman, *et al.*, eds., *Poverty in America*, pp. 139-152.

55. Walter A. Pruitt and R. L. Van deCastle, "Dependency Measures and Welfare Chronicity," *Journal of Consulting Psychology*, XXVI (December 1962), 559-560.

56. Robert C. Stone and Frederic T. Schlamp, "Characteristics Associated with Receipt or Nonreceipt of Financial Aid from Welfare Agencies," *Welfare in Review*, III (July 1965), 1-11.

57. See Catherine S. Chilman, "Child-Rearing and Family Relationship Patterns of the Very Poor," *Welfare in Review*, III (January 1965), 9-19; Elizabeth Herzog, "Some Assumptions About the Poor," *Social Service Review*, XXXVII (December 1963), 389-402; Paul H. Glasser and Elizabeth L. Navarre, "The Problems of Families in the AFDC Program," *Children*, XII (July-August 1965), 151-156; and Esther S. Battle and Julian B. Rotter, "Children's Feelings of Personal Control as Related to Social Class and Ethnic Group," *Journal of Personality*, XXXI (December 1963), 482-490.

58. C. LeRoy Anderson, "Development of an Objective Measure of Orientation Toward Public Assistance," *Social Forces*, XLIV (September 1965), 107-113; Thomas R. Ford, "The Passing of Provincialism," in Thomas R. Ford, ed., *The Southern Appalachian Region*, Lexington, Ky., 1962, pp. 9-34.

59. Leonard Schneiderman, "Value Orientation Preferences of Chronic Relief Recipients," *Social Work*, IX (July 1964), 13-18.

60. Harold L. Sheppard, "The Young Who Are Poor," in Seligman, ed., *Poverty as a Public Issue*, pp. 102-117; Mollie Orshansky, "Counting the Poor: Another Look at the Poverty Profile," in Ferman, *et al.*, eds., *Poverty in America*, pp. 42-82; Alvin L. Schorr, "The Family Cycle and Income Development," *Social Security Bulletin*, XXIX (February 1966), 14-26.

61. For a recent study supporting this point, see Bruce K. Eckland, "Academic Ability, Higher Education, and Occupational Mobility," *American Sociological Review*, XXX (October 1965), 735-746.

62. For a penetrating analysis of these relationships, see Schorr, *op. cit.*

63. *Ibid.*

64. See *ibid.*; Orshansky, *op. cit.*; Kingsley Davis, "Some Demographic

Aspects of Poverty in the United States," in Gordon, ed., *Poverty in America*, pp. 299-319; and Lee Rainwater, *And the Poor Get Children*, Chicago, 1960.

65. For example, see Catherine Chilman and Marvin B. Sussman, "Poverty in the United States in the Mid-Sixties," *Journal of Marriage and the Family*, XXVI (November 1964), 391-395; and Herzog, *op. cit.*

66. See Paul Glasser and Elizabeth Navarre, "Structural Problems of the One-Parent Family," *Journal of Social Issues*, XXI (January 1965), 98-109.

67. Evidence for this statement may be found in Joan McCord and William McCord, "The Effects of Parental Role Model on Criminality," *Journal of Social Issues*, XIV (1958), 66-75.

68. Matza, *op. cit.*

69. Henry Miller, "Characteristics of AFDC Families," *Social Service Review*, XXXIX (December 1965), 399-409.

70. *Ibid.*, pp. 406-407.

71. Robert D. Hess, "Educability and Rehabilitation: The Future of the Welfare Class," *Journal of Marriage and the Family*, XXVI (November 1964), 422-429; Hess and Shipman, *op. cit.*

72. Norma Radin and Paul Glasser, "Maternal Attitudes of a Negro Culturally Deprived Population," unpublished paper, November 1965.

73. See Vaughn J. Crandall, "Achievement," in H. W. Stevenson, ed., *Child Psychology*, Chicago, National Society for the Study of Education, 1963, pp. 416-459; Leonard Berkowitz, *The Development of Motives and Values in the Child*, New York, 1964.

74. The first author conducted a review of the literature on motivation to work, and this was one of his conclusions. For relevant discussions, see Morris Viteles, *Motivation and Morale in Industry*, New York, 1953; E. Wight Bakke, *The Unemployed Worker*, New Haven, 1940; and Robert S. Weiss and Robert L. Kahn, "Definitions of Work and Occupation," *Social Problems*, VIII (Fall 1960), 143-151.

75. Walter B. Miller, "Focal Concerns of Lower-Class Culture," in Ferman, *et al.*, eds., *Poverty in America*, pp. 261-270.

76. Hyman Rodman, "The Lower-Class Value Stretch," in *ibid.*, pp. 270-285.

77. *Ibid.*, p. 277.

78. *Ibid.*

79. Elizabeth Douvan, "Social Status and Success Strivings," *Journal of Abnormal and Social Psychology*, LII (March 1956), 219-223; Martin L. Hoffman, Spiro B. Mitsos, and Roland E. Protz, "Achievement Striving, Social Class, and Test Anxiety," *Journal of Abnormal and Social Psychology*, LVI (May 1958), 401-403.

80. Glenn Terrell, Jr., Kathryn Durkin, and Melvin Wiesley, "Social Class and the Nature of the Incentive in Discriminative Learning," *Journal of Abnormal and Social Psychology*, LIX (September 1959), 270-272.

81. Hylan Lewis, "Child Rearing Among Low-Income Families," in Ferman, *et al.*, eds., *Poverty in America*, pp. 342-353.

82. *Ibid.*, p. 347.

83. Oscar Lewis, *Children of Sanchez*, New York, 1961; Oscar Lewis, "The Culture of Poverty," *Trans-action*, I (November 1963), 17-19.

84. For example, see Herzog, *op. cit.*; Hylan Lewis, *op. cit.*; Kronick, *Family Life and Economic Dependency.*

85. Kronick, *ibid.*

86. Hylan Lewis, *op. cit.*

87. Matza, *op. cit.*

88. Jack E. Weller, *Yesterday's People*, Lexington, Ky., 1965; Thomas R. Ford, "The Passing of Provincialism," *op. cit.*; Harry M. Caudill, *Night Comes to the Cumberlands*, Boston, 1962.

89. See David C. McClelland, *The Achieving Society*, Princeton, 1961.

90. For more details, see Weller, *Yesterday's People.*

91. Dailey, *op. cit.*

92. As of 1961, some 60.2 percent of non-white families were below the $4,000 total income level. Contrast this with a figure of 27.7 percent of white families below the same level. See Tom Kahn, "The Economics of Equality," in Ferman, *et al.*, eds., *Poverty in America*, pp. 153-172, for these and other relevant statistics.

93. Among those who have discussed the poverty-sustaining features of assistance programs are Schorr, *op. cit.*; Nathan E. Cohen, "A National Program for the Improvement of Welfare Services and the Reduction of Welfare Dependency," in Gordon, ed., *Poverty in America*, pp. 278-298; and Charles Lebeaux, "Life on A.D.C.: Budgets of Despair," in Ferman, *et al.*, eds., *Poverty in America*, pp. 401-411. See also Elizabeth Wickenden and Winifred Bell, *Public Welfare: Time for a Change*, New York, 1961.

94. Among the latest in a series of studies that fail to demonstrate the effectiveness of selected, existing face-to-face services is Henry J. Meyer, Edgar F. Borgatta, and Wyatt C. Jones, *Girls at Vocational High*, New York, 1965. Also, for the effects of a training program to provide improved welfare services, see Edwin J. Thomas and Donna L. McLeod, with the assistance of Pauline Bushey, *In-Service Training and Reduced Workloads: Experiments in a State Department of Welfare*, New York, 1960.

95. See Bell, *Aid to Dependent Children.*

96. For example, see Haggstrom, *op. cit.*

97. For additional details, see Schorr, *op. cit.*

98. See Wickenden and Bell, *Public Welfare*, pp. 30-31, 78-79.

99. For comments regarding "malingering" on welfare in Appalachia, see Caudill, *Night Comes to the Cumberlands*, Chapter 18.

100. David Caplovitz, *The Poor Pay More*, New York, 1963.

101. Elton F. Jackson and Harry J. Crockett, Jr., "Occupational Mobility in the United States: A Point Estimate and Trend Comparison," *American Sociological Review*, XXIX (February 1964), 5-15.

102. Otis Dudley Duncan, "The Trend of Occupational Mobility in the

United States," *American Sociological Review*, XXX (August 1965), 491-498.

103. See Peter M. Blau, "The Flow of Occupational Supply and Recruitment," *American Sociological Review*, XXX (August 1965), 483, fn8; Killingsworth, *op. cit.*; and Kahn, *op. cit.*

104. Kahn, *ibid.*

105. Orshansky, *op. cit.*

106. Chilman and Sussman, *op. cit.*

107. M. Elaine Burgess and Daniel O. Price, *An American Dependency Challenge*, Chicago, American Public Welfare Association, 1963.

108. Will and Vatter, eds., *Poverty in Affluence*, pp. 191-193.

109. See, for example, Charles V. Willie and Walter E. Riddick, "The Employed Poor: A Case Study," in Seligman, ed., *Poverty as a Public Issue*, pp. 139-151.

110. Chilman and Sussman, *op. cit.*; Burgess and Price, *An American Dependency Challenge*.

111. Burgess and Price, *op. cit.*

112. Morgan, *Income and Welfare in the United States*, p. 211.

113. See Haggstrom, *op. cit.*; *The Negro Family*, *op. cit.*; and Thomas F. Pettigrew, *A Profile of the Negro American*, Princeton, 1964. Also, for discussions of strategies in community action programs, see Frances Piven, "Participation of Residents in Neighborhood Community Action Programs," *Social Work*, XI (January 1966), 73-80; and Martin Rein and Frank Riessman, "A Strategy for Antipoverty Community Action Programs," *Social Work*, XI (April 1966), 3-12.

114. John C. Leggett, "Uprootedness and Working-Class Consciousness," *American Journal of Sociology*, LXVII (May 1963), 682-692; John Kosa and Clyde Z. Nunn, "Race, Deprivation and Attitude Toward Communism," *Phylon*, XXV (Winter 1964), 337-346; Hallowell Pope, *Economic Deprivation and Social Integration in a Group of "Middle Class" Factory Workers*, unpublished Ph.D. dissertation, University of Michigan, 1963.

115. See Nathan Glazer, "Paradoxes of American Poverty," *The Public Interest* (Fall 1965), pp. 71-81.

116. For example, see Richard C. Wilcock and Walter H. Franke, *Unwanted Workers*, New York, 1963. This study provides comparative unemployment data for separate communities experiencing plant shutdowns.

117. Morgan, *Income and Welfare in the United States*, p. 38.

118. *Ibid.*

119. Harold L. Sheppard, "Poverty and the Negro," in Seligman, ed., *Poverty as a Public Issue*, p. 127.

120. Ornati, *op. cit.*

121. Burgess and Price, *op. cit.*

122. *Ibid.*, p. 176.

123. Edwin J. Thomas, "Psychological Dependency and Its Relationship to Economic Deprivation," *Social Welfare Forum of 1966*, New York, in press.

124. Morgan, *Income and Welfare in the United States.*

125. Thomas, "Psychological Dependency and Its Relationship to Economic Deprivation," p. 16.

126. Stone and Schlamp, *op. cit.*

127. State Social Welfare Board, *First Annual Report*, Sacramento, Department of Social Welfare, State of California, January 1965, p. 10.

128. Schorr, *op. cit.*

129. Several studies bear on this. "Class crystallization" at the highest status level, at least, was found by Werner S. Landecker, "Class Crystallization and Its Urban Pattern," *Social Research*, XXVII (Autumn 1960), 308-320. There were higher correlations between income and education for each extreme occupational status, and between education and occupation for each extreme income level in the study by Godfrey Hochbaum, John G. Darley, E. D. Monachesi, and Charles Bird, "Socioeconomic Variables in a Large City," *American Journal of Sociology*, LXI (July 1955), 31-38. There is greater consensus on the prestige of occupations at the extremes, according to Joseph A. Kahl, *The American Class Structure*, New York, 1957. And consensus on the prestige of families at the extremes was greatest in August B. Hollingshead, *Elmtown's Youth*, New York, 1949, p. 37.

130. See Robin Williams, *American Society.*

131. Titmuss, *Essays on "The Welfare State,"* Chapter 2, pp. 53-54.

132. Richard Titmuss, "Poverty vs. Inequality: Diagnosis," *The Nation*, CC (February 8, 1965).

133. Indeed, Bremner says philanthropic approaches to poverty in the early history of this country never intended to eliminate poverty. See Bremner, *op. cit.*

134. See George Caspar Homans, *Social Behavior: Its Elementary Forms*, New York, 1961.

135. Alvin W. Gouldner, "The Norm of Reciprocity: A Preliminary Statement," *American Sociological Review*, XXV (April 1960), 171. For an interesting rationale for a formal assistance system based upon the principle of reciprocity, see Bertha Reynolds, *Social Work and Social Living*, New York, 1951. For the operation of this principle in informal assistance systems, see Peter H. Kropotkin, *Mutual Aid: A Factor in Evolution*, New York, 1902. For a conception of the assistance relationship based implicitly upon an informal model of reciprocity, see Dora Peyser, *The Strong and the Weak*, Sydney, Australia, 1951.

136. For an experimental approach to the "norm of responsibility" as opposed to that of reciprocity, see Leonard Berkowitz and Louise R. Daniels, "Responsibility and Dependency," *Journal of Abnormal and Social Psychology*, LXVI (May 1963), 429-436; and John Schopler and Nicholas Bateson, "The Power of Dependence," *Journal of Personality and*

Social Psychology, II (August 1965), 247-254. For what comes close to a sociological statement of the norm, see Georg Simmel, "The Poor," translated by Claire Jacobson, *Social Problems,* XII (Fall 1965), 118-140.

137. State Social Welfare Board, *First Annual Report, op. cit.,* p. 13.

138. Keyserling, *Progress or Poverty,* p. 17. Lampman gives a figure of 1 percent per year in this regard. See Robert J. Lampman, "Income Distribution and Poverty," in Gordon, ed., *Poverty in America,* pp. 107-108.

139. See Robert Theobald, ed., *The Guaranteed Income,* New York, 1965.

140. For example, see Lampman, *op. cit.,* pp. 102-114; and Edward E. Schwartz, "A Way to End the Means Test," *Social Work,* IX (July 1964), 3-12.

141. Simmel, *op. cit.,* p. 138.

William J. Goode
A Policy Paper for Illegitimacy

Nearly a century ago Marx based his accusations against capitalism on the detailed studies by British investigating commissions into the impact of the factory on social and economic life. He argued not only that the factory owner profited from the exploitation of women and children, the destruction of family relations, and the expulsion of laborers from the land, but that the system permitted no choice: if one factory owner did not take advantage of the helpless, others would, and he would become bankrupt.

Over half a century ago Lincoln Steffens startled his readers not merely by demonstrating widespread corruption in American cities but also by showing that every reform movement was bound to fail: crime was supported by an alliance of respectable businessmen, professional criminals, and venal politicians. Like Marx, Steffens had learned that many people profited from a social problem.

A generation ago Willard Waller commented that "social problems are not solved because people do not want to solve them." [1] On the psychological level, Freud's daring intellectual explorations into the unconscious showed that the neurotic and the psychotic cannot cope with their environments because

The writing of this paper was partially supported by NIMH grant 11389-01.

fundamentally they do not want to do so: the costs are too great.

Whether the social analyst is a muckraker or prophet, or refuses to take a moral stand, the data are similar. If a sociologist studies some of the evils in a penitentiary system, as Gresham Sykes does in *The Society of Captives*, or criminality among corporations, as Edwin A. Sutherland does in *White Collar Crime*, or the racial and ethnic ghettos of American cities, he must record that ordinary citizens have no clear wish to solve these problems. To solve them would cost too much. The necessary changes would violate some of the people's *values* (for example, criminals *should* be severely punished, or Negroes *should* be kept in their place), or would reduce some of their social or economic profits.

But though such reports reveal the strength of forces that maintain the system, they also become part of a major attack on it. In the dialogue between knowledge and action, discovery and decision, fact-finding and fault-finding, social inquiry has taken on increased political importance since World War II. The volume and widespread distribution of sociological studies have introduced a new factor in modern social change, a new pressure toward the solution of social problems.

This pressure is felt along two main axes: (1) the advantaged are forced to see how they maintain the very problems they deplore, and (2) the disadvantaged learn more precisely how the exploitative system operates.

It is much easier, for example, for the white U.S. citizen to do nothing about the racial ghetto and the poverty of the Negro as long as he can avoid knowing that he helps create that ghetto as well as the cultural and social deprivation, the poor educational system, the lack of job opportunities, the higher disease rates, and even the marital instability of the Negro. On the other hand, it is difficult to avoid that knowledge when hundreds of studies proclaim it in monographs and the popular press. Psychologists have also contributed to this growing awareness by proving that the lower achievement of Negroes on various types of I.Q. tests is a function of the deprivations which the white society has forced on the Negro. By doing so they have sharpened the essential historical irony of racist ideology and barriers to Negro advancement: if the Negro were fundamentally inferior to the white man by endowment, as the ideology asserts, then the barriers would not be necessary; he could not compete with whites anyway.

But if those who profit most from the system are forced to learn about it, those deprived by it also learn eventually what such studies contain. The modern criminal may offer a social or psychological explanation of his career. The leaders of the Negro revolution of the 1960's can buttress their claims with scientific data as well as emotional appeals. As the imperialist nations have discovered, many natives have also learned to read. The spreading mood of dissent and rejection among the very poor in the United States presses toward political and social reform and grows in part from our growing knowledge about how the present system operates. The disadvantaged will not concede that the better-off deserve their advantages, and the latter cannot claim legitimacy as wholeheartedly as before, because much research undercuts that claim.

Illegitimacy: Personal or Social Problem?

Perhaps nowhere is this dialectic of forces more apparent than in the area of illegitimacy. Until recently, illegitimacy was a personal problem and a family problem, but not a social problem. If at times it was treated as a social problem—in that many deplored or disapproved of the phenomenon—it was not viewed as a *problem* for the society to solve. Few were concerned with it.

Of course, illegitimacy occurs in all societies. Indeed, as Crane Brinton has pointed out, illegitimacy is inseparable from legitimacy. The only way we could eliminate illegitimacy entirely would be to eliminate marriage. To the extent that there are marriage rules, and some definition of a socially acceptable family relationship, there will always be some who do not conform. Thus there will be some illegitimate mothers, fathers, and children in any society. Kingsley Davis, too, has analyzed the possible "solutions" to the problem and concluded that they would have to be so radical as to undermine the family system itself.[2]

In most societies the supports for legitimacy have been so strong as to make illegitimacy a personal catastrophe rather than a widespread social problem. In his analysis of these supports, Bronislaw Malinowski enunciated what he called the "Rule of Legitimacy"—that every society has a rule disapproving childbirth outside of marriage and requiring that every child have a legitimate father. Every society has a set of rules stating who may marry whom, and under what circumstances. Subsequent research has modified Malinowski's formulation somewhat, but it has not negated his finding.

Several consequences flow from Malinowski's "rule." The child is socialized from the earliest years to want to marry and to produce children, and to socialize those children in turn to live within a family system. The child is taught to prefer one type of marriage as against another, and to look with disapproval on childbirth outside of marriage. Marriage itself is made the occasion of public ceremony as well as celebration. Typically, the young man is not viewed as a full adult until he has become a husband and father, and the young woman does not achieve full adulthood in society until she has taken on the responsibilities of wifehood and motherhood. Legends, tales, folk wisdom, and daily social pressures force almost everyone into these role activities, and away from promiscuity and a wide range of extra-familial activities that might lead to childbirth outside marriage. In these complex processes, threats and rewards interact to produce in most societies a high degree of conformity. If a woman violates the rule, she suffers social stigma and usually must assume a much greater burden of work and punishment than is the lot of those who conform.

By and large, these forces prevent the typical individual from even making a decision about having an illegitimate child. Conformity is assured by many social mechanisms which prevent most young adults from even considering alternatives. For example, in most of the world's societies until fairly recently, marriages were arranged relatively early, and prior to marriage young women were guarded reasonably well. If (as in many societies) young men and women in the lower social strata did engage in some premarital sexual activities, others knew who was going with whom, and marriage could be arranged in time to prevent scandal.

Traditional Explanations of Illegitimacy

The middle and upper social strata of the Western countries have controlled the sexual and mating behavior of their children far more effectively than have members of the lower social strata. Since they have also written most of the commentaries, in novels and essays, their attitudes toward the problem of illegitimacy in the past have been clear.

Until possibly the period of the 1930's, when a large increase in knowledge about the poor became available, the attitude of the social leaders in the middle and upper classes in Western nations seems fairly consistent. Perhaps it can be best expressed by comparing it to that of the traditional Southerner in the United States who believes that somehow the Negroes are "just like animals," and that their lives are simply a result of inherited characteristics. A few outstanding reformers—among others, Zangwill, the Webbs, and Booth—actually felt some compassion for the poor and had some understanding of the forces that created their social behavior. By and large, however, the public attitude before the 1930's was highly moralistic and exhorted the poor to give up their bad behavior, to improve their characters, to become thrifty and virtuous, for, after all, their own actions alone created the misery in which they lived.

Many novels sentimentalized over the illegitimate mother, usually an innocent betrayed, permitting the author both to titillate his reader with a vicarious participation in sex, and to pay virtue the usual flattery of hypocrisy that Oscar Wilde noted, of having the betrayed mother die in squalor and degradation. This literary version accords well with the presumably objective essays and commentaries about illegitimacy in accounts written before the 1930's: immorality, bad companions, and perhaps even mental deficiency cause illegitimacy and thus the society is not really responsible. Naturally, we need not do anything about it, but we may permit ourselves the indulgence of feeling charitable and compassionate for those who suffer this fate.

SOCIAL SCIENCE EXPLANATIONS

The ideas offered by social scientists to "explain" illegitimacy are those which common sense has thought of first. One explanation grew out of the great surge forward of detailed social investigation in the 1930's, under the leadership of the Chicago school of sociology. These included both ecological studies and detailed analyses of social interaction in primarily underprivileged areas. These investigations did not focus especially on illegitimacy. Perhaps their most important achievements were the establishment of actual field investigation as a requirement for making statements about social facts, and the accumulation of a substantial body of data about many aspects of social disorganization, including illegitimacy, juvenile delinquency, various forms of criminality, and mental disease. The importance of poverty, broken homes, and the disorganized neighborhood was underlined by these investigations.

Another thread of common-sense explanation is that illegitimacy is due to various types of psychological or personality disturbances. Thus, Leontyne Young's perceptive analysis, *Out of Wedlock*, concludes that the illegitimate mother "wants to have the child," though not consciously; that the girl is not really interested in men; that her only sexual experience is likely to be the one that resulted in pregnancy; that at some point of stress in the girl's life she actually seeks out a man for the purpose of having the child; and, indeed, that because she has carried out a strong unconscious, neurotic wish to have a child without a husband, she is usually contented during the pregnancy.[3]

The psychiatric social worker especially looks for such explanations, but in fact most people who prefer to find *individualistic* interpretations of *social* patterns that are created in large part by major *social* forces may find this psychiatric interpretation plausible. On the other hand, without at all deprecating the importance of the psychodynamic as a precipitating set of factors or, in some cases, a major determinant, it is at least worthwhile to examine, as we shall later in this essay, the types of social structure in which exposure to illegitimacy might appear to be not the irrational act of a neurotic but perhaps the best possible choice among a range of bad alternatives.

Another thread of explanation has perhaps been most widely purveyed by anthropologists: that among Negroes and, to some extent, lower-class whites there is a "subculture" with its own harmony, legitimacy, and internal supports, and in which illegitimacy is "normal" and fully accepted. The child and mother, we are told, suffer no stigma, and a union without marriage is ranked as high as any other union.

This type of interpretation has been most widely applied to

illegitimacy in the Caribbean area, but its close kinship with the traditional Southern racist view noted earlier is quite clear. Its origins are, however, very different. The racist view asserts that Negroes or lower-class whites will always have high rates of illegitimacy because of their genetic endowment. They are unable to control their impulses or to act responsibly. By contrast, the anthropological view has a sentimental origin, arising from the cultural relativism that is part of both sociological and anthropological training. In this view, however strange or foolish the natives seem to be, their culture must be respected and understood within its own terms. For example, if young men refuse to work for a copra plantation where they could earn good wages, which they could then exchange for yams, it is necessary to examine the total situation in their own terms. They may be required by their culture to grow their own yams as an index of adulthood. It is not, then, "irrational" for them to cultivate yams on their own territory.

By immersing himself in a native culture, the anthropologist comes to understand it and to sympathize with it. But not all villages with a low level of technology are integrated cultures. More important, a group of people may exhibit a fairly stable set of social patterns without feeling normatively or emotionally committed to them. Accustomed to cultures in which most people do believe in the norms that support their social patterns, anthropologists have sometimes failed to ask whether, for example, in a given lower-class community in the Caribbean or in a lower-class stratum in the North or South, people actually *desire* to live the way they live, or feel that it is the best or "right" way to live—and these data are all indices of whether these social patterns genuinely have cultural support. Indeed, the contemporary Negro revolution in the United States is a rather ample refutation of such a sentimental view.

The Social Problem as a Concern of the Society

All of these explanations continue to be offered, and all of them contain some part of the truth. They are, however, essentially unconnected with the recent increase of *interest* in illegitimacy, and more especially with the emergence of illegitimacy as a genuine *concern* of society, or at least of its leaders. Within the past decade the problem of illegitimacy has moved to the forefront, and within the past five years especially, the public has become increasingly concerned with illegitimacy, as it has with poverty.

This concern differs from that of previous periods in the history of this nation, and is part of a genuinely new social phenomenon in the world. For the first time in the history of the world, major nations have come to feel a moral responsibility for nations less advantaged than they. For the first time there is a growing recognition that at some levels and in some degree the nations of the world form a moral community. The cynical explanation—power politics—is simply inadequate, and fails to explain the wide range of help being given to less powerful nations.

Similarly, the cynical interpretation that, within the nation, poverty has become "big business," just as it has been "good politics" for many generations, is not entirely adequate. Rather, the separation of the classes in the United States is less than perhaps at any time in the past. It is now also more difficult morally than at any other time for the members of the middle or higher social strata to say in effect that they are not their brother's keepers. It has become impossible for them to assert that those at the bottom are qualitatively different from themselves, so different that one might help them out of compassion or give them charity out of goodness, but should protect oneself from them out of simple caution. This new view is supported by sociological and psychological evidence from much research, which has shown all too clearly that those who are advantaged were in infancy very much like their brothers at the bottom; and that millions of those at the bottom could have been trained to do perfectly well the jobs now held by those in the middle or higher social strata.

THE LOSS OF CREDENCE

The advantaged social strata also feel the loss of *legitimacy*, of credence. They feel increasingly that those toward the bottom do not really believe that those above *are* superior in fundamental or essential ways. To some extent, of course, the belief in equality of endowment has been a national characteristic from the founding of the republic. In a curious and ironic way, it is the very essence of a society in which money counts so much. If money does count so much, then the central point is whether one has it or not. But this means in turn that the man who is poor does not really believe that the rich man has fine spiritual qualities or has inherited some imponderable and powerful essence from his distinguished ancestors.

It is this loss of credence and legitimacy which makes the advantaged strata somewhat more frightened in our time. No one can say that there is more violence now than a hundred years ago in New York City, to take an example that is much criticized elsewhere. Nor is this true of any other major American city. What has happened, however, is that the advantaged neighborhoods are no longer inviolate. Nor are the middle and upper social strata inviolate when traveling about. The poor not only fight among themselves nowadays but also express some of their violence in casual encounters and vandalism. The upper and middle social strata feel themselves to be the target of their wrath far more than in the past.

THE CONCERN WITH ILLEGITIMACY

Several forces, then, seem to make both illegitimacy and poverty important matters to the leaders of this society. Illegitimacy in particular has come to be the focus of much attention because it has come to be increasingly expensive, and this is once again a paradox. In every state, public leaders and political figures have risen to denounce the "rising tide of illegitimacy," to accuse women of having children deliberately in order to enjoy the benefits of relief, or to denounce the softhearted social worker for allowing the illegitimate and promiscuous mother to live in lavish splendor.

These denunciations are precisely an index of how far we have changed over one generation. These attacks are primarily against the fact that we have actually begun to help the illegitimate mother in some ways, and that to do so costs money. Such denunciations were not possible at the turn of the century because, in fact, little money was spent on illegitimate mothers. Suggestions have been made in several states that a woman who has more than one illegitimate child should be penalized by a fine or jail sentence, or submit to sterilization. Although one may deplore the callousness of these and many other proposals, they all attest to the hostility aroused by genuine concern about and help for the illegitimate mother.

Perhaps the middle and upper social strata also feel threatened because of their growing sense that their own children are engaging in precisely the kinds of activities which they once thought to be the exclusive properties of the lower classes: illegitimacy, teen-age marriages, juvenile delinquency, and narcotics addiction. If the lower classes are becoming similar to the middle classes in dress, automobiles, and house furnishings, then perhaps, in turn, middle-class children have taken on some of the patterns of the lower classes. Indeed, this is one interpretation of the "hipness" of the modern beatniks: they are imitating the lower classes, and especially the Negroes.[4]

In any event, the increasing concern with illegitimacy is fairly clear. We find, for example, such articles as "My Daughter Is in Trouble" dealing with the problem of teen-age illegitimacy.[5] Another article investigates the rising illegitimacy rate and the attacks on the Aid to Dependent Children program, under the title "Paying an Illegitimacy Bonus?"[6] The *Christian Century* wonders whether the rules of the Aid to Dependent Children program are not excessively harsh in refusing any help, for example, if an employable man lives in the household, thus perhaps stimulating some fraud and even marital instability by encouraging a legal but jobless husband to leave.[7] In "Mother Without Joy" we are warned that "the number of illegitimate babies born in America is reaching alarming new heights."[8] We are also told that the illegitimacy rate has more than tripled in the last twenty-five years, while the total birth rate (in fact, the total *number* of births) has increased by only 60 percent. A New Jersey legislative committee reports that "the number of cases in the state involving public financial assistance to children rose 214 percent from 1956 to 1961," and the net grants under the program for Aid to Dependent Children rose tenfold from 1948 to 1963.[9] In 1964 Governor Paul B. Johnson of Mississippi signed a bill to make the parents of a second illegitimate child guilty of a misdemeanor, subject to a jail sentence and a fine.[10]

The concern with illegitimacy has also been reflected in the reprinting of reports from other parts of the world, such as the Soviet law to make an unmarried father responsible for his children, the rising illegitimacy rate in London, and the protest from Sweden against claims that the Swedish illegitimacy rate is extraordinarily high.[11] A broader social welfare concern can be found in the recurring attention paid by the United Nations Commission on Human Rights of the Economic and Social Council to the discrimination against children born out of wedlock. Every one of the Iron Curtain countries has rewritten its family code in part to attempt to solve the problem of illegitimacy.[12] Such efforts began in the Scandinavian countries half a century ago.

A Rising Tide of Illegitimacy?

Before considering some of the forces creating illegitimacy, we should first see how large the problem is and whether it has in fact been growing larger.

If we accept the fact that there will always be some illegitimacy as long as there is a marriage system, then our question must be, Is the present rate extraordinary compared to other countries, and is its rise (if any) excessive? If we take a world perspective, we are struck by the fact that generally the illegitimacy rate has been *dropping* throughout most of the world over the past half-century, or at least the differences are so small—considering the poor data available—that we cannot be sure that any rise has occurred.[13] In regions with very high

Illegitimacies per Hundred Live Births in Selected Countries, 1890-1960

	1890	1910	1920	1940	1960
Germany	9.1	9.1	11.4	9.8	
Japan	8.2		8.2	4.1	
England and Wales	4.4	4.1	4.7	4.3	4.7 (1956)
Sweden	10.2	14.3	15.7	11.8	11.7 (1961)
Italy	7.3	4.9	4.7	4.1	2.3 (1961)
France	8.5	8.7	10.0	7.3	6.6 (1955)
United States				4.0	4.8

illegitimacy rates, such as most New World countries, the rates either have not changed or have dropped.

In a period when family systems over the world have been breaking down to a considerable extent and certainly losing much of their control over the young, and when in many countries the amount of sexual freedom has increased while the concern with illegitimacy has grown, we must conclude, as noted earlier, that there has been a qualitative change in attitudes toward illegitimacy in those countries with high rates. That is, more people have come to feel that illegitimacy is a problem to be attacked.

HAVE U.S. ILLEGITIMACY RATES INCREASED?

The question may nevertheless be raised, whatever the stability of illegitimacy rates in other parts of the world, is it not true that illegitimacy rates in the United States have sharply increased? In paricular, as a major focus of emotional attention, has the illegitimacy rate among Negroes risen? The answer to the first question is unclear, but the unequivocal answer to the second is that in fact the illegitimacy rate among Negroes has *dropped*. Since both answers run contrary to the opinion of many contemporary analysts, a brief comment is in order.

From 1938 to the present, the number of births out of wedlock has more than doubled, from somewhat less than 100,000 per year to more than 200,000 per year. The number of births out of wedlock per thousand unmarried women of childbearing age has perhaps tripled during the same period. On the other hand, if we consider all live births, illegitimate births made up 4 percent of the total in 1940 and about 4.8 percent in 1960 —*a rise of less than 1 percent*. During the same period there has been a more than an 80 percent increase in the number of registered live births, because the U.S. population itself has grown.

As Elizabeth Herzog has noted, the public does not know that these are all estimates, based on reports from thirty-five states.[14] The central statistical point here is not that the data even now come from only thirty-five states, for in fact these states comprise most of the population of the United States, but that in earlier years the number of states reporting was still smaller, and the completeness of the reports still less. Even more important, in the earlier period, illegitimate children were *least likely* to be reported, so that a *mere increase in registration effectiveness* would increase the apparent illegitimacy rate. Herzog also notes that:

> Doubts about the rise have been with us for a long time. About 70 years ago a study of illegitimate births in Massachusetts reported a gradual increase in rates of illegitimacy over the preceding 40 years, but warned that the increase may be more apparent than real and might, in fact, be due to improvements in reporting. (p. 342)

Another aspect of this possible exaggeration is that the *absolute* number of illegitimate births has increased greatly over the past twenty years, because both the general birth rate in the United States and the *total population* have increased. This especially affects the *number* of teen-age mothers, who now represent some 40 percent of all unmarried mothers, the largest proportion for any age group.[15] Still more striking, in recent years teen-age illegitimate mothers form the *one* age group that has not increased its *rate* of illegitimate births, i.e., percentage illegitimate among all live births to this group. Over time, the trend is even more striking. In 1938 the rate for teenagers was higher than that for any other age group except those twenty to twenty-four years old. Now, however, the rate for teenagers is lower than for any other age group under thirty-five.[16]

THE TREND IN NEGRO ILLEGITIMACY

At present the data available cannot be used to demonstrate whether the illegitimacy rate among Negroes has dropped over the past twenty years. Without question, over the past fifty to one hundred years the illegitimacy rate has *dropped*, and I believe the coming decade will show a drop in the illegitimacy rate.

The reasons for the *apparent* increase over the past generation are quite clear. Throughout most of the South, and to a lesser degree in the North, the Negro was not important enough to public officials to be recorded when his status changed. Many marriages were unrecorded; divorces were often not recorded and, indeed, did not go through the official courts. Instead, an official or a man in authority simply told a Negro couple that they were divorced. An illegitimate child born to a sharecropper family in Alabama would very likely not be recorded at all, or the child would be recorded as having a father, whether or not the man was married to the child's mother. The public official was uninterested in these facts. It is indeed a measure of the Negro's entrance into the mainstream of American society that illegitimacy rates are probably more accurate now than they formerly were. Births are now actually recorded, creating an *apparent* rise in Negro illegitimacy rates.

It is certain, in any event, that before the 1930's the rate was still higher. Only a tiny minority of Negroes were married under slavery. Though doubtless the percentage rose in the post-slavery period, it seems likely that at the turn of the century, when most Negroes lived in the rural South, a majority of Negro children were born to parents who had not legally been married, whatever the couple thought their status was. It is very probable that in the period between the Civil War and the turn of the century, the illegitimacy rate was as high as that in many Caribbean countries, from 50 to 70 percent. We shall never know exactly what the percentages were, but there is no question but that by and large the legal—but not officially known—rate was much higher than at present.

In the mid-1960's the trend seems unmistakable. More and more Negroes are entering the mainstream of American life and are taking on the values and social patterns of their white peers. As a consequence, I predict that when the data are fully recorded for this decade, they will exhibit a decline in the rate of

Negro illegitimacy. In any event, at the beginning of this decade the illegitimacy rate among Negroes ranged between 18 and 30 percent of live births, and among whites it was a little over 2 percent.

Such harsh facts are important, for they tell any sensitive observer that the real problem does not lie in some obvious and catastrophic increase in the illegitimacy rate, here or elsewhere. Rather, the apparent problem is an index of much deeper and more complex processes, particularly the response of some people to widespread efforts to do something about illegitimacy. That is, illegitimacy was much less of a "social problem" when everyone could take it for granted as another of the self-caused miseries of the lower classes. But as long as no one seriously tried to *do* anything about illegitimacy, it could be deplored without becoming a great concern to anyone except the suffering parties. It is once more a vindication of Lincoln Steffens' insight, that if anyone tries stubbornly to reform a situation, those who have derived advantage from the evil will make a public outcry. For the first time, the middle and upper social strata must recognize that they are paying a very substantial bill for illegitimacy. By 1960 the Aid to Dependent Children Program, founded under the Social Security Act of 1935 in order to keep fatherless families intact, cost over a billion dollars a year.

Of course, the personal and psychological costs of illegitimacy to the participants was never a serious concern of the advantaged social strata, except to the extent that they could indulge in sentimentalizing and compassion for those who lived in misery—or, occasionally, when a member of their own family got into the same trouble. This relative lack of interest has not basically changed as yet, but it is changing, and official concern has increased greatly.

Nor has there been much increase in awareness on the part of the public of the really very high, hidden costs of illegitimacy. Penologists and social workers have been pointing out for over a generation that the expense of confining a criminal or juvenile delinquent, caring for a child from a broken home, paying the social costs of an illegitimate child, or more broadly, paying the bill for various kinds of social services in a delinquent neighborhood, might amount in purely financial terms to far more than a program of prevention. Such arguments have carried relatively little weight in the past, and they are not persuasive to the ordinary American even now. Doubtless, Americans are like people in other countries, in that they can face and handle the crisis or catastrophe, but planning to prevent it does not seem very "practical." A river must overflow many times, perhaps over many generations, before a valley region will finally attempt to pay the relatively smaller cost of controlling floods. Money is now being spent to clean up some polluted rivers in the United States, but no important river was kept clean from the beginning by adequate planning.

Since the Aid to Dependent Children Program is more properly to be considered in the section on social services offered to the illegitimate mother and child, we shall only comment here that we believe the public outcry about illegitimacy over the last ten years has been raised primarily because more people have become aware that someone else's illegitimacy is being paid for out of their own pockets.

In any event, whether the illegitimacy rate is less than 5 percent or double that, and whether it is rising or falling, and even though the rate among teenagers has been dropping for the past quarter of a century, it is a serious social problem both because society at large has become much more concerned with it and because its costs are very high financially as well as personally. It therefore deserves our serious attention. Let us consider some further simple but basic facts about illegitimacy as a social phenomenon to be found in every part of the world.

Legitimacy and Social Structure

The crucial link between the biological survival of the helpless human child and the social system of the family is, of course, the socialization of the child and his transformation from an animal to a human being, motivated to follow the patterns of his own culture. This can be achieved only if each generation is taught not merely to rear children but also to transmit to them the desire to reproduce and in turn to socialize their own children. Individual people, not society in general, must accept this responsibility. Because of its slow maturation, the child cannot survive unless others are motivated to care for it and to transmit to it the necessary social and intellectual tools for survival.

Just when the evolution of this particular unit, the family, occurred in the history of mankind can never be known, but the form that it came to take is fairly clear: the *community* controls the choice of mate as well as the family behavior of the couple. Specifically, the community—in all societies—disapproves of casual unions which create a child without a family unit that will be responsible for it. Those who procreate must either be adult enough to support themselves and their children, or be part of some larger family unit with enough adults in it to care for the next generation of children. Rules of legitimacy generally state who has the right to mate and to rear a fully accepted member of the society, that is to say, *the rules of legitimacy determine the social placement of the child.*

More particularly, the rules of legitimacy define the obligations of adults to the children they bear. At the same time, these rules also specify the many obligations of kinfolk to one another. A man may not have a child outside of the family because he would necessarily fail in some of his obligations to either the mother or the child. One consequence of these rules is that, although some two-thirds of the societies of the world permit some premarital sexual intercourse among young people, societies disapprove of casual unions in which children are born. Thus, even if society concedes a great amount of sexual freedom to its members, it will still concern itself with legitimacy.

The rules then are concerned with social *placement, descent,* or where the child is located in the kinship network. One consequence of this central importance of the rules of legitimacy and illegitimacy is that in all societies there is much less con cern with illegitimacy when it occurs in the *lower* social strata, since the position of these people, and the obligations they owe to one another, are much less important for the larger social structure. The absence of the father is most important in patrilineal societies, which contain most of the world's population, since the main line of descent is broken when the father is not part of the child-rearing unit.

The rules of marriage thus guarantee the social placement of the child and its socialization. Otherwise, an illegitimate child is a burden with no corresponding benefit to its mother's kin, since without a definite position within the kin network, the child has few socially enforced obligations to them. Social ties, not blood ties, determine whether people receive gifts from other kin. To some extent the child also represents in many societies a violation of the rules that confer on elders the right to make *decisions* about marriage.

CASTE AND CLASS DIFFERENTIATION IN ILLEGITIMACY

Clearly, then, according to the value system of those who dominate society, illegitimacy is a much more serious matter in the upper strata. There the pressures are much stronger and the resources greater for assuring control over mating and punishment for deviations from the rules. One consequence is

that in all societies from which we have any data, especially in
Western societies, "free unions," consensual unions, common-
law marriages, and illegitimacy are far more common in the
lower social strata than in the upper.

These universal differentials and attitudes toward legitimacy
may be observed in the United States, of course, and in turn
they suggest several other principles of importance. One is
that the degree of disapproval of illegitimacy depends in part
upon *where* in the social structure the illegitimacy occurs and
between *whom*. For example, if an upper-class man has an
illegitimate child by a lower-class woman, the males in his own
class will typically look with a tolerant eye on his behavior,
while the women in his class may very well disapprove, in part
because this reflects bad taste on his part and in part because
they may fear the competition. Lower-class men, on the other
hand, will feel annoyed at the upper-class man for this transgression, because he has exploited his social position and they
cannot easily punish him. Lower-class women, in turn, may
feel that the woman aspired too high or made a foolish gamble,
while perhaps wondering whether they themselves might have
fared better in the exchange. Comparable differences in behavior might be charted for various such combinations.

The caste pattern of the United States permits similar com-
parisons. In at least one area of social interaction, sexual liai-
sons, the Southern white male has not totally disapproved of
integration; indeed, many Negro women and their children were
manumitted under slavery by a white owner who had established a Negro woman as his concubine. Without tracing all
of these possible combinations and differences in attitude, we
can at least see that not only are there great differences in attitude depending on whose interests are at stake, but different
combinations of matings may arouse different degrees of disapproval at different class or caste levels.

A closer look at these combinations shows still a further

principle, that the disapproval is likely to be stronger if marriage cannot "solve" the problem of illegitimacy, either by forestalling it through an early marriage, or by marriage after the child has been born. Obviously, in a caste system cross-caste illegitimacy cannot be solved by marriage, nor can marriage solve the problem if one of the partners is already married and polygamy is not permitted. In still other combinations, such as incestuous illegitimacy, no such solution is possible, nor would it be in a society in which one of the partners is required by ecclesiastical rule to be celibate.[17] Such cases arouse far more disapproval.

Great differences in approval also grow out of substantial variations in the social structure. For example, in a period of social disorganization, such as may occur during a lengthy war or revolution, social controls and attitudes against illegitimacy may weaken, so that the rate of illegitimacy may rise. Or the social structure may be anomic for generations, as in many of the societies of the New World, and most especially in the Caribbean countries, where the illegitimacy rates range between 30 and 70 percent. There the stigma of illegitimacy is lower, and social controls are weaker.

These facts throw considerable light on the forces that create illegitimacy and also point to at least part of the solution for high rates of illegitimacy. Illegitimacy can be defined legally and formally, but the various types include (1) a wide range of socially very different patterns, (2) under different degrees of disapproval, (3) *by* different social strata, and (4) with very different consequences for the social structure and therefore for the individuals concerned. Such a ranking is presented below, arranged by the increasing degree of social disapproval, and roughly by the degree of apparent social disruption created by the illegitimacy. To some extent, this ranking also parallels (5) the amount of punishment meted out to the illegitimate partners as well as to the child.

*Increasing Social Disapproval of
Types of Illegitimacy*[18]

1. Consensual union
2. Concubinage where it is institutionalized (traditional China and Japan)
3. Lower-class illegitimacy
4. Liaison of nobleman with mistress in pre-industrial Western society
5. Childbirth during betrothal
6. Casual relationship, followed by marriage
7. Adulterous, only the man being married
8. Union of a person in a celibate status with either another celibate or a non-celibate
9. Adulterous, only the woman being married
10. Adulterous, both parties being married
11. Union of upper-caste woman with lower-caste man
12. Incestuous, brother-sister
13. Incestuous, father-daughter
14. Incestuous, mother-son

One further consequence of these criteria needs to be pointed out, and, though the principle may be derived from the foregoing discussion, in fact data from Clark Vincent's study, *Unmarried Mothers*,[19] confirm it in large part. Precisely because an illegitimate birth is more scandalous in the upper or middle social strata, it creates far less of a *social* problem. That is, families in these strata can deal with it as a personal problem. They are better able to afford an abortion and to make such arrangements. They can muster far more social pressure to force a marriage, so as to forestall a childbirth outside of marriage. They are more likely to send the girl a considerable distance away to a private nursing home for the childbirth itself, and they are more likely to turn the child over to an adoption agency. It is more likely that the girl became pregnant as a result of a fairly serious emotional involvement, so that marriage will not seem so unwise a solution as it might be among the lower social strata. For these reasons, an illegitimacy in such strata is likely to be socially far less conspicuous, since it is so well hidden. Finally, even the child will suffer less from it, since he is more likely to be ultimately adopted.

Forces that Affect Illegitimacy Rates

All societies attempt to persuade their members that virtue will be rewarded and vice punished: "Crime doesn't pay, very much." Aside from attempting to generate a rational fear of the consequences when the individual deviates from the straight and narrow, societies also try to develop internal controls which make the individual feel that it would be morally wrong to transgress.

There are also many layers or networks of social control by which the individual is warned that he is approaching areas of forbidden behavior. Thus, no society can easily punish an individual for falling in love with another man's wife, but social controls operate to prevent most such people from getting into the types of situations in which falling in love is likely. No society succeeds fully in preventing delinquencies, but everyone has experienced some of these pressures.

On the other hand, the techniques of *social control* do vary from one society to another. In some Western societies in the past, and in many Latin societies until very recently, a chaperone system was used to prevent a nubile girl from ever being alone with an adult male, except for close kin or perhaps a respected old man. Married women were given much more freedom. The social cost of a chaperone was not possible for lower-class families, but in most Western countries lower-class men were responsible for guarding the women of their family until they were married.[20]

Very few societies have attempted to rely heavily upon internal controls or strong moral repression. Among these may be included the Puritans of the seventeenth century. Coupled with this strong socialization was a pattern of high social visibility: they snooped on one another a great deal. Moreover, the punishment for transgression was very high.

In India, where the illegitimacy rate has perhaps been as low as in any area of the world, marriages were until recently arranged by elders, and it was the duty of a man to marry his daughter before the age of puberty. Although the age was not equally low in Arab countries, the girl was supposed to be married early and was guarded very carefully before that time. A similar pattern existed among the upper classes in classical China and in Japan until the modern era.

Only recently have we discovered that another pattern of social control has been extremely widespread in the past, distributed throughout much or all of Europe and Japan and perhaps most primitive societies.[21] In the peasant groups of these societies, much courtship and even premarital sexual intercourse took place without any close supervision and without direct disapproval of such intimacy. Although ideally a marriage took place before conception, scattered evidence suggests that there has been a *fairly high rate of premarital conception* in Western countries for many centuries. In the United States today, more than one-fifth of all marriages are preceded by conception, but this rate was probably higher two hundred years ago in France or Sweden.

Note, however, that the social controls were nevertheless strong. Only young men and women who formed part of the same social circle or class associated together. No young man could afford to run away, for he would thus abandon his only means of livelihood, the family farm. In some areas, the number of births occurring less than nine months after the actual wedding ceremony was relatively high, resulting in a rate of illegitimacy as high as 20 percent, but even then the couple would eventually settle down to legal domesticity. In this widespread pattern of control over illegitimacy, it is clear that some substantial number of children were born who were *legally* but not *socially* illegitimate, since the responsibiilty was clearly fixed, and the pressures toward marriage were so great as to make it almost a certainty.

ILLEGITIMACY IN THE NEW WORLD

On the other hand, the pattern among the Negro population of the United States is very different, even though the actual rate of illegitimacy among Negroes has been equalled in many regions or counries of Western Europe in past generations.

The precise position of the American Negro can be best understood by placing it in proper historical and contemporary perspective. The Negro population in the United States is not set apart by having a fairly high illegitimacy rate. Much more significantly, illegitimacy rates are high in *all* the New World countries south of the United States, whether or not they are predominantly Negro. This suggests that to some degree these populations have had a common fate, but that race has not been the most significant variable. On the other hand, the rates are highest in those countries in which the descendants of Negro slaves are numerically dominant. Even here, however, interesting variations in social structure show that race is not the prime factor.[22] In the table on page 288 a few of these rates are given.

Although scholars have focused much of their attention on illegitimacy in the Caribbean because the rates are so high, some have thereby been led to either erroneous or partial interpretations of the larger phenomenon, i.e., high illegitimacy rates in *all* the New World countries south of the Rio Grande, and in

Selected New World Illegitimacy Rates [23]

Country	Percent Illegitimate of All Live Births
Guatemala (1963)	68
Venezuela (1963)	54
Mexico (1963)	25
Argentina (1963)	25
Peru (1963)	43
Jamaica (1961)	73

the disorganized population segments north of the Rio Grande.

Some have supposed, for example, that since the Caribbean populations are largely descendants of Negro slaves, the illegitimacy patterns are a remnant of "native customs," perhaps older African customs. But African family patterns did not approve of childbirth outside of marriage. Among the New World Indian tribes, similarly, no such tolerance of illegitimacy existed. Indeed, among the African and Indian ancestors of the present populations, hundreds of kinship patterns existed, but they did not share the special trait of high illegitimacy rates.

IS ILLEGITIMACY APPROVED AMONG THE LOWER CLASSES?

Other field workers, beguiled by their assumption that the villages they entered were somehow comparable to a "primitive society," morally committed to their own behavior patterns, have supposed that they were in the presence of a "subculture," in which a consensual union is the "moral equivalent" of a legal marriage and is fully approved by the community. They supposed, further, that since most children were born outside a legal union, the illegitimate child had the same status as that of a child born of a legal marriage.

This opinion has been so widely stated as to become almost a truism among some Caribbeanists, just as it is among some

U.S. Southern interpreters of Negro family life. But *every* field researcher who has reported such a generalization in a full-scale study has always included sufficient details to disprove it. Whenever values and attitudes are reported, they invariably give a higher evaluation to legitimacy and marriage—and this is true for the American Negro and white population at lower-class levels as well. Many behavioral indices are reported which disprove the researcher's own generalization: mother and child *do* have a lower rank when they are outside a legal marriage; women attempt to marry, and if they enjoy some personal advantages of family or property, they can do so without first entering a consensual union; most people eventually marry; and children may even push their parents to marry legally. Such behavioral indices show clearly that the consensual union and illegitimacy are not so highly valued as legitimacy.

ILLEGITIMACY AND THE NEW WORLD CONQUEST

What is so striking and unusual about the New World in this connection is that the European conquest was not a mere political or military domination, or a system of heavy exploitation by conquerors, as occurred in India, Indonesia, Egypt, or Manchu China. More fundamentally, it was a social and cultural destruction. Most of the major centers of civilization in the New World were crushed by 1600, and a variety of pressures was applied by the Europeans to undermine the cultural and social patterns of the inhabitants. In the Caribbean the Indians were almost completely destroyed, and Negro slaves were introduced. The Negroes could not maintain their cultural systems, because people from the same tribes were not permitted to live and work together. Thus their social systems were destroyed as well. After they had been "seasoned" in the Caribbean, they might be moved to the United States, where similarly repressive measures followed. Their religions were supplanted, their languages were wiped out, and, except for a few interesting survivals here and there—polytonality and polyrhythm in music, the use of certain African foods, and so on—their descendants became and are Western in culture.

Though the cultural and social destruction of the Indian population outside the Caribbean was not so complete as this, throughout most of the New World the cultural and social patterns of the Indians were undermined. Except for tribal pockets here and there, for example, in northwestern Guatemala and the Andean Highlands, these populations have also become Westernized.

The assimilation of these populations to Western patterns was not complete, however, since in all these countries a near-caste system prevailed. Consequently, individuals did not receive the kinds of rewards which white immigrants to the United States received for becoming Americanized. Thus they did not develop a deep normative commitment to Western family patterns or courtship values. Nor could they, dominated as they were by Western white elites, develop their own social controls by which some small pride in family honor might be supported or created. The upward mobility that was the reward of the Americanized white immigrant was generally forbidden to both Indian and Negro populations of the New World countries for nearly three hundred years.

Thus the Indians could not adequately train their young to believe strongly in their own traditional values, for their social, political, and economic structures were dominated by their conquerors. They came to accept the superiority of European values, religious conversion, and submission to the dominant political system, and they experienced the failure of their own social system to support their older, traditional values. On the other hand, they did not come to accept fully the European values, because the normal rewards that are necessary for full cultural assimilation were always withheld.

The application of this complex analysis to the Negro population of the United States is fairly obvious and needs no lengthy exposition. By comparison with the Iberian conquest, the slavery systems of the United States and the Caribbean were even more destructive of traditional Negro social and cultural patterns. No towns, villages, or societies, except a few created by escaped slaves, were composed of people from a single tribe. It must be concluded:

> Consequently, for many generations the majority of these populations lived in *cultures* that were not internally integrated, *or* integrated fully with the dominant culture of the rulers; and in *social systems* that were not integrated socially, *or* fully integrated with the dominant social system of the rulers.[24]

After all, it is the community, not primarily the individual or the family, that by paying or withholding prestige and honor can persuade or compel people to conform to the norm of legitimacy. The individual must be trained to believe deeply in the norm, and the social controls must be relatively strong in support of that norm.

THE PERSONAL BARGAIN OF ILLEGITIMACY

Such a broad sketch must, however, be sharpened by a further analysis of the interpersonal situation in which illegitimacy takes place. For even though we can expect a lower norm commitment to legitimacy in the lower strata (whether white or Negro) in all major societies of the world, we must still examine the immediate social context within which the social interaction takes place.

The primary factor in this context is that within the lower social strata, especially among Negroes but to a striking degree among whites as well, the young woman in her courtship behavior has to make her *own role bargain*.

In any interaction between individuals, both are restricted to some degree in what they agree to do for one another by the expectations of others. Even if both are willing to agree to certain obligations to one another—sex, the cooking of meals, or even darning socks—there are others in their role networks—a "third layer" or a network of "third parties"—who also expect role performances from these individuals and who will object to some kinds of bargains they may wish to make. Thus, even if a mother is willing to indulge her son, and the son may wish to seduce his mother, other people within the family or neighborhood, or even individuals at school, may object to this relationship.

This is most evident in courtship behavior, for young people may be willing to accept a wide range of obligations to one another, to which their families might object. In many societies in the past, elders have controlled marriage arrangements, in part because young people would not be willing or able to drive the kind of hard bargain that the elders might desire. The youngsters might be willing, for example, to choose mates who are considered improper because of age, race, religion, class, and so on.

Thus, even if a young girl is wildly in love with her high school sweetheart, her girl friends and her boy friends, her kinfolk and family, as well as neighbors, might object to her having sex relations or living unmarried with the young man. If she becomes pregnant, some of these people will intervene to insist upon a marriage or to hide the pregnancy.

In the lower strata in the United States, such social pressures are less compelling because individuals have much less to bargain with, fewer resources with which to punish or reward. Parents are less able to assert their authority over the young because the young have less to lose if they incur their parents' displeasure. Dating is far more likely to occur anonymously, without the knowledge of parents or relatives. If the young man arouses the annoyance or anger of the girl's parents or even of the neighborhood, they have less power to force him to conform. The girl's first love and sex contacts are more likely to occur away from home, and without the knowledge of the family.

As a consequence, the best bargain the girl can make will depend upon her own resources, with relatively less support from her own family. Thus the lower-class girl in the United States, white or Negro, may be able to demand marriage without any great concessions to the boy's demands if she has unusual qualities or if the boy is especially in love with her. On the other hand, and this holds far more for Negro girls than for white, she may have relatively little chance at marriage, early or late, unless she is willing to gamble that a more permanent union may grow from one of her relationships with boys. Just how far she goes, what risks she takes, will depend on how much support she gets from her kin and friendship network and on her own bargaining power. The decision to marry is likely to be the boy's rather than hers, and she gains more from the marriage than he does. He can escape more easily from the consequences of a casual relationship, and, in any event, the social structure yields him little basis for feeling the adult male dignity that in other strata rewards the founding of a family.

Intensifying this set of interpersonal forces is a fairly widespread masculine value, called "machismo" in Latin countries. Precisely because the economic and social structures do not offer the opportunity for a young man to obtain a job that will pay enough to found a family, or yield enough prestige to permit him much self-respect, he must find his self-esteem in other areas, notably physical bravery and violence among men, and the active seeking of sexual conquest. Specifically, the norm asserts that a man proves his masculinity by physical courage and by being able to command or persuade women to engage in sex relations with him and to bear his children.

Consequently, the young male adopts an exploitative attitude toward women, seeking to gain as much pleasure from them as possible while paying as little as he can. The young woman is in no position to demand very much.

CONTRACEPTIVES AND ILLEGITIMACY

But sex alone does not produce babies. Why do young people not use contraceptives? A full answer to this question would require more data than are now available. Certainly some illegitimacies result from simple ignorance, though I am inclined to believe that this is a very small percentage, confined primarily to a minority of Catholics and illiterate whites and Negroes. By and large, most young Americans in their teens know about contraceptives, even when their physiological and anatomical knowledge is somewhat limited. Doubtless, too, Leontyne Young's interpretation applies to some minority of illegitimacies—the young girl unconsciously wills the pregnancy and simply has no interest in taking any precaution.

Among lower-class male Americans, the use of contraceptives is practiced as a concession to the girl or to the threat of community reprisal, and is thus viewed at least partially as an expression of weakness. The young man is likely to view the use of a condom, the most likely contraceptive, as equivalent to sexual intercourse while wearing rubber boots. Indeed, that is a common male phrase. Sexual intercourse while using a condom is considered less pleasurable for both parties. Most fundamentally, however, it is an expression of middle-class caution which the lower-class male rejects, while the lower-class female often feels she cannot insist on it without endangering the relationship.

The lower-class male in the United States does not feel the same solicitude for the welfare of his sexual partner as does the middle-class male, nor is he forced to do so by her kin, family, or community. Since he has less to lose, he is willing to take risks that men in other class positions would fear to take, while his female partner is forced to share them if she is eventually to establish a permanent relationship with some man.

PSYCHODYNAMIC VARIABLES AND CLASS

The foregoing analysis places relatively little emphasis upon psychological forces, especially psychopathology. Leaving aside the more serious psychiatric problems, I am inclined to believe that an illegitimacy arising from neurotic forces is far more likely to occur in the middle or upper social strata than in the lower. In simple terms, the behavior that leads to pregnancy in the middle and upper strata is far more likely to have irrational sources. The costs of illegitimacy are greater, and accurate knowledge about preventing pregnancy is more widespread. Certainly, some percentage of the illegitimate pregnancies in the upper strata are caused by the processes that are described above as common in lower social strata, especially when the participants evaluate incorrectly their relative bargaining powers. That is, many girls believe their boy friends will abandon them if they do not agree to sexual intercourse (and to at least some extent they are correct), while the boys out of bravado and a superficial masculinity are willing to take the risks which they know rationally will lead to trouble.

In this connection, Clark Vincent has examined in considerable detail the value contradictions within middle-class society, specifically the high emphasis upon sex and permissiveness coupled with very severe punishment if transgressions become known or an illegitimacy results. What is missing from his analysis, and what will remain missing for a while, is why, in view of severe sanctions, so many young people fail to use contraceptives. The very differentials in this respect between Negroes and whites, and between middle-class whites and lower-class whites, suggest that we must lay greater stress on the broad social factors sketched above, rather than idiosyncratic psychological weaknesses. One can at least see that the consequences of the failure to use contraceptives are far more catastrophic for the girl in the middle and upper social strata than for the

white or Negro girl in the lower social strata, and that, corre-
spondingly, the suspicion of irrationality seems much better
founded.

In any event, social science cannot explain why each individual engages in a given type of act. We can only outline the
types of forces which produce a higher percentage of certain
types of individuals who might carry out such acts. We must
state probabilities rather than explanations of unique events.
We can only point out that, given a set of social and cultural
patterns, the chances of illegitimacy are maximized in one group
rather than in another.

Care for the Unmarried Mother and Child

If there is no established home for the child, and the father is
absent or is unable or unwilling to contribute, the mother and
child need a wide range of services. Some mothers do not want
to take care of their child, or cannot, and foster family homes or
adoption services are then needed to give adequate physical
and emotional attention to the child. While the mother is going
through pregnancy, some type of maternity home care or medical care may be necessary. In some instances, the mother needs
to be advised about her legal rights. And because most unwed
mothers are relatively poor and untrained, vocational counseling or training may be in order. States vary in the amount of
such care they offer to unmarried mothers or children, but the
following table [25] indicates roughly the types of services now
available.

This summary table overstates the *amount* of care available,
since many states give this help to only a small percentage of
their unmarried mothers, or the services available are found in
only a few counties. Moreover, special services such as medical
care or legal counseling may be available only under special
circumstances. Moreover, private agencies are all voluntary, that

Types of Services Offered	Number of States in Which Service Is Offered, by Type of Agency	
	Public	Private
Foster family home services	50 states	43 states
Adoption service	47	47
Maternity home care	41	46
Social casework	50	45
Medical care	40	44
Foster family homes	50	43
Legal services	22	27
Vocational services	15	20

is, the mother and her family must themselves seek out professional help. Of course, not all public agencies attempt a thoroughgoing case-finding operation either, so that many young mothers receive none of these services at all. Finally, as noted earlier, some substantial but unknown percentage of mothers want to avoid attention from any agency, public or private.

From a more fundamental view, however, such services cannot "solve the problem." No amount of public service can create a father where there is none. The most competent professional cannot, except rarely, remove the mother from the same kinds of social influences she was under when she first began to run the risk of pregnancy. And the most skilled practitioner cannot change the social circumstances that produced both the mother and the father, and will in turn produce still more young people who will produce still more illegitimate children.

Indeed, it is difficult to prove that the availability of skilled services has *any* effect on the *rate* of illegitimacy. Denmark, Sweden, and Norway, with far more tolerant attitudes toward the illegitimate child, attempt in a much more thoroughgoing way to furnish services, to guarantee an income, and to care for the illegitimate child. The social stigma is much less, and the support given is much greater, but these gradual developments over the past half-century or so have not created higher illegitimacy rates. As noted earlier, the rates may have dropped during this period, though very likely not as a *result* of these changes.

In the countries behind the Iron Curtain, the official ideology is that the welfare of the child is most important, that the future of the nation depends upon the adequate care of the child, and that all children must be equal before the law.[26] So laudable an aim must be admired, though the illegitimate mother in all of these countries experiences shame, and no system has been able to erase the basic fact that the father is missing.

In Russia, a new Family Law was drafted in 1964 which provided that the unwed father be responsible for his own children. A strong effort to force the father to contribute to the welfare of the child may be found in all the more enlightened civil codes, though usually the contribution is minimal. In any event, to name the state as guardian, even when the state is relatively efficient in furnishing foster or orphan homes or in giving support to the mother, does not basically change the child's status while he is growing up.

In the United States, over the past generation social services to the unmarried mother have been widened, and the social worker has become more skilled. The American public has become more willing to pay for social welfare, because most people have come to believe that at least part of the misery and failure that people experience is not entirely their own doing, and that even when it is, compassion requires that help be given.

THE AID TO DEPENDENT CHILDREN PROGRAM

In no area has this concern been more evident than in the development of the Aid to Dependent Children program. Originally developed in 1935 in order to aid families without fathers, in recent years it has been increasingly seen—and attacked—as a program to help illegitimate mothers and their children. Indeed, legislators have charged in several states that loose women deliberately have illegitimate children in order to live off the taxpayers.

In fact, however, only about one out of five ADC families is on the rolls because the mother is not married to the father of the child, and less than 10 percent of white surviving illegitimate children and about 10 percent of Negro illegitimate children are in ADC families in which the father has not married the mother.[27]

Moreover, if we consider only the child welfare services to illegitimate mothers, without considering the continuing payments made under the ADC program, about one-third of the girls under fifteen years of age receive some child welfare services from public or voluntary agencies, but only about one-seventh of those over nineteen years old do so.[28]

Nevertheless, the contrast between fact and outcry over the supposed facts is sociologically instructive. It tells us that we must look for other factors to interpret the outcry. Doubtless the primary factor is the large increase in the *number* of families served by welfare agencies generally and by the ADC program in particular. This increase is not so much due to a growth of illegitimacy as it is to the rapid increase in the *child* population and the total number of *families* in the entire country. In addition, it is a consequence of the larger *relative* increase in the number of families headed by women because of divorce, separation, or death. Still more important, as noted earlier, the major increase in the number of families served by welfare

agencies arises from a growing concern on the part of all
Americans about the underprivileged, and from the conviction
that we should care for children, whatever the failure or errors
of their parents.

But this expansion of services to unfortunate families angers
many because it is a social reform. The social reformer angers
us more than the charity fund raiser, because the fund raiser
merely reminds us that we are our brother's keeper. The
reformer, by contrast, is rude enough to insist that the unfortunate really are *our brothers.* He adds injury to simple insult
by asking respectable people for money, to improve matters
we would rather ignore.

It is not surprising, then, that public officials, private citizens,
legislators, newspaper columnists, clergymen, and even social
researchers have cried out against financing "the rising tide of
immorality" in the form of federal grants to aid illegitimate
children. After all lower-class Negro and white "immorality"
once seemed to cost us nothing, and respectable people could
even be amused by the supposed liberal sex practices of the
bottom social strata. They were a steady source of off-color
jokes in this country. Formerly, the Negro woman who had an
illegitimate child got no help from anyone except her own kins-
men, and she continued to support herself as well as possible
by domestic work. But now the ADC program suggests in
principle that her higher duty is to stay at home to take care
of her children, and even offers her financial assistance toward
that end.

Every serious study of the families on the ADC rolls—and
there have been many, in response to the outcry—shows that
although there are frauds here and there, few ADC parents are
cheats, and the amounts the mothers get are small. Three-
fourths of ADC families with illegitimate children have only
one or two children, and three-fourths of the illegitimate children were born before the families began receiving ADC payments. The funds are largely paid out during the years when

the children are young and need a mother's care, so that the average time on ADC is 2.4 years for even the families with illegitimate children.

In the United States, state and local payments for ADC to the 13 percent of all illegitimate children who get any help at all averaged only about $45 per child in 1959. An ADC mother with one child got a little more than $30 assistance a month in Arkansas, and $95 in Wisconsin. These amounts are *less* than the costs of taking care of the children in an institution or in foster homes.

The more important but contrary criticisms that should be made against the ADC program are that it pays so little, and that its severe rules have so often been drawn up in response to misplaced emotionalism, that they handicap the effective rearing of children. For example, the widespread rule that there must not be a man in the house sometimes means that a husband who has deserted will not return to the home, since he does not yet have a job and his presence there would remove the family from this steady benefit. Or, a woman might be able to benefit from some type of vocational help or a part-time job, but some interpretations of rules make it difficult for her to accept such opportunities. The ADC grant may be reduced if she attempts to work.

Obviously, if we withhold the *means* which are necessary for individuals to live a stable family life, we cannot expect them to accept our ends or goals as entirely worthwhile.

What Can Be Done to Reduce the Illegitimacy Rate?

Although the public clamor about illegitimacy is based largely on misinformation, and the amount of money spent for services given to illegitimate children and their mothers is small compared to the need, the problem is an important one. Moreover, it will cost the society an increasing amount in money, not to mention the personal anguish suffered by illegitimate mothers, children, their families, and their kin. In spite of the growing permissiveness regarding sexual behavior, there seems to be no greater tolerance of illegitimacy in our time. Can anything be done to reduce the rate of illegitimacy?

ADOPTION AS A SOLUTION

Widespread adoption would not, of course, reduce the rate of illegitimacy, but it would create a more salutary home environment for illegitimate children and reduce the financial burden on federal, state, and local governments. Adopted parents would then take over the tax burden shouldered by other citizens. There seems little likelihood, however, of any major changes in this area. About 70 percent of white children now born out of wedlock are adopted, but only about 10 percent of non-white children. The assumption is widespread that Negro couples are less willing to adopt than are white couples, but the data run to the contrary. The rules for adoption are strict in most states and set rather stringent requirements for adopting couples. If, then, one compares only those husband-wife families with husbands under 45 years old, and with incomes over $3,000 a year—the most eligible category—there are fewer Negroes in this group and more whites, while the adoption rate for Negro couples is higher than it is for whites.[29]

If Negro income were to rise substantially, a slightly greater absorption of Negro illegitimate children might occur. But the basic discrepancy between the possible "market" for such children and the very large supply will remain unless the birth and illegitimacy rates themselves are reduced substantially. Needless to say, changes in the present rules would also facilitate adoption somewhat: Negro couples may not adopt white children, Protestant couples may not adopt Catholic children (whether or not they have actually "chosen" a religion), and so on. Without question, this rigidity is being relaxed here and there, and will be relaxed more in the future, but the process moves slowly. Thus the probable changes in the near future will not increase the absorption rate for illegitimate children very much.

THE PREVENTION OF NEUROSIS

Clearly, the prevention of illegitimacy is the task to be faced, not merely the care and feeding of illegitimate children after they are born. But one source of prevention cannot be engineered: we cannot easily prevent that part of illegitimacy due to neurotic sources.

If we suppose that the rate of neurosis would be reduced if our society were to be more harmonious and less stressful, less tense and straining; or if parents as individuals would become well adjusted, mature, and warm human beings, in either case the illegitimacy from neurotic sources is not likely to change much in the near future.

Although many essayists and social scientists have asserted that Western, and especially American, society produces a high rate of psychosis and neurosis, the facts are inconclusive so far. The myth of the happy peasant, the Rousseauvian savage, the idyllic primitive society, is attractive, but little evidence has been uncovered to show that industrial societies—American, Russian, Japanese—produce more neurosis or psychosis. In any event, social scientific knowledge is much too undeveloped to offer a blueprint for creating out of the present society a social system that would generate fewer neurotic personalities.

As to the parents themselves, we cannot easily or soon make each child feel contented with the amount of parental love he receives, so that each will have a healthy, well-adjusted psychic structure. Children cannot choose their parents either, so as to escape the destructive ones. And parents themselves cannot suddenly transform themselves into wise, loving persons.

This is not to say that efforts at therapy are useless or may not help in individual cases. Unfortunately, all the psychiatry and psychiatric social work now available is far too little to lower by much the daily production of neurosis in our society, and thus is far too little to change greatly the next generation of youngsters who will soon use illegitimacy as one expression of their own neurotic problems.

CONTRACEPTION

Although it is only common sense to note that a reduction in the rate of exposure to sexual relations among the unmarried would also decrease the illegitimacy rate, it is not wise to expect such a change. The weight of evidence runs to the contrary. More young people now engage in sexual intercourse before marriage than in generations past, and a higher percentage of widowed or divorced adults have sexual relations outside marriage. The dire warnings of moralists—that we live in a decadent era which precedes the downfall of civilization—may be incorrect, but there is little reason to expect that the illegitimacy rate will decline because the unmarried people in our society are going to remain celibate outside marriage. Consequently, the major possibility of such a reduction will be the wider use of contraceptives among the unmarried.

After many years of shilly-shallying, the more enlightened American city governments have finally taken a step which will reduce the illegitimacy rate, at least among mothers and wives already on social welfare rolls. The public welfare agencies have agreed to give contraceptive help to mothers on relief, whether or not they are Catholic.[30] It seems likely that Catholics, both organized and unorganized, have recently opposed this step less strongly than in the past because of a change in the polemic about the use of contraceptives.

For some years a majority of American Catholics have favored the use of contraceptives, and it is obvious from mere observation that most Catholics use some type of birth control. After all, not all Catholic mothers continue to have children throughout their childbearing years. The terms of the debate about contraception did not change, however, until the advent of the contraceptive pill. This is not the place to debate either the biological or the theological aspects of "the pill," but it is important to note that the pill not only has been viewed as more "respectable" than other forms of contraception, but it has also permitted for the first time some public and even private conversation about contraceptives, formerly a taboo topic. Neighbors can discuss contraceptives by introducing the subject of the pill. Many Catholics now eagerly look for a pronouncement from the Church that the pill is theologically permissible. Whether or not such a statement is forthcoming, many Catholics feel morally easier about using the pill than they did about using other forms of contraceptives. Moreover, the use of contraceptives is spreading still more widely, among Catholics and non-Catholics.

This change in the attitudes of all groups has reduced somewhat the tension about the use of contraceptives, increased the readiness to consider new types of techniques, and undermined the former vigorous opposition to giving contraceptive advice to the poor. Now there is only token resistance to this step. Sometimes it means help only when the woman asks for it; on the other hand, most social workers will probably manage to bring up the subject for discussion with clients who need this help, even in agencies in which a formal restriction has been imposed.

Resistance to the giving of contraceptive advice has also been lowered by the growing awareness that a considerable part of U.S. illegitimacy occurs among Negroes, and that illegitimacy costs money—a good bit more than contraceptive advice.

Note that "the pill" solves the problem of masculinity, or "machismo," noted earlier. If the woman takes contraceptive pills, the lower-class male need not take any precautions or abandon his self-image as a daring and wild fellow. More important, the pill permits some communication between young men and women about the topic. This means, in turn, that if— as seems likely now—the intra-uterine loop proves to be a more useful technique for all these goals, young people are more likely to adopt it quickly. That is, even if the pill is not used, they are now more likely to discuss other forms of contraception.

Both the loop and the pill give some help in an area where social change is needed but is unlikely to occur quickly. Those with little education and poor jobs live very much in the present. They plan only little for the future and are often willing to take risks (such as purchasing on credit far beyond the realities of their income) which middle-class people would not take. The consequences of this pattern for illegitimacy are fairly obvious. The pill and the loop both eliminate the impact of such a pattern on illegitimacy, for both require little planning. One may even say of the pill that it also fits in with the national pastime of taking pills.

The comments in this section apply, it should be underlined, to both the ever-married and the unmarried. That is, to be effective, contraceptive advice and help must be given to those who need it, whether adult or youngster, white or Negro, male or female. There is no evidence that more than a tiny percentage of women want illegitimate babies, and society can help all the rest by this single important step.

ABORTION

Although governmental support of contraceptive advice and help will substantially reduce the illegitimacy rate in the future if vigorously administered, still other steps are necessary. One important change in the social rules must be the repeal of almost all abortion laws in the United States, so as to legalize abortion in all hospitals. Abortion should be a decision made by the persons it affects most: first, the potential mother, and second, her family. Anyone who wants an abortion should be able to obtain one from trained physicians in good hospitals.

The present repressive laws and the outdated attitudes of physicians (as Mary Jean Huntington and Sidney Spivak have shown, doctors' attitudes are outdated even with respect to giving contraceptive advice) create a vast array of social and personal problems. The callousness and heartlessness of the present rules are in glaring contrast to the relative generosity of the American people in responding to human needs. The family or individual who faces the far-reaching difficulties of illegitimacy could avoid most of them if abortion were easy.

The operation is not difficult or dangerous and need not be expensive. What makes abortion dangerous now in the United States is the restrictive laws and customs themselves, for they force those who need abortions to seek out incompetents, quacks, or marginal physicians who must work under difficult operating conditions. Often, the woman is not even permitted a day or so of convalescence, but must leave immediately so as to protect the abortionist. The situation generates corruption: wherever the abortionist operates, he must pay off a network of others who might otherwise turn him over to the authorities.

The laws and customs of the United States are, of course, not unique. Even in Sweden, which has more liberal laws, many young women must travel to Poland to obtain an abortion. In this respect Japan has been far more enlightened than the United States. One salutary result there—which the United States might well attempt to achieve—has been a considerable drop in the birth rate, to a point where it is only about two-thirds that of the United States.

The very modest cost of abortion compared with the staggering costs society must bear in order to support the illegitimate mother and her children (not to mention the later cost to society when the illegitimate child grows up and must suffer the typically higher chances of disease, early death, educational dropout, and occupational failure), should make the argument fairly persuasive.

As against these great financial and human costs of the insistence that a woman bear the illegitimate child, when abortion would be both practical and easy, the theological argument has been that the destruction of the fetus is evil. It is interesting in this respect that for some seven centuries the Catholic Church itself taught that a fetus during the early months of pregnancy was not a human being. The Roman canonists from the twelfth century until 1869 held that abortion before the child "quickened" was not a crime. The modern rule has, of course, held that abortion is evil. If we consider the argument fully, however, we must see that forcing a woman to have a child she does not want is also an evil act against her, and an evil the more unnecessary and cruel because the child that is eventually produced will also suffer.

In any event, the use of contraceptives alone is not sufficient, because failures do occur. It is also necessary to repeal the present abortion laws so that women who are not prepared to bear an illegitimate child may at least have the human choice of not doing so. As an aside, it should be kept in mind that both here and abroad the great majority of women who undergo abortions are *wives*.

INTEGRATION OF THE DISADVANTAGED

Finally, a much more fundamental change in our social structure is necessary, one which is within our capacity: the integration into the larger society of precisely those lower social strata which generate high illegitimacy rates. Those who live among the bottom social strata of any society have a lower stake in it. Every study of attitudes and values shows that those who derive the least benefit from the society are also less likely to be committed to its norms and values. As noted earlier, this general principle holds not only for Negroes in our society but in other New World countries as well, and generally for all major nations. Granted that no society will be created in which everyone is fully committed to the norms of the dominant groups, but it is not overwhelmingly difficult to give the less advantaged a greater stake in its operation and a richer share of its product.

As we have increasingly been forced to recognize over the past decade, the Negro segment of our society *can* be integrated more fully into the larger social structure. It *is* possible to give them economic opportunities. It is not necessary for them to be culturally deprived or barred from jobs that they can handle adequately. It is both immoral and uneconomical for Negroes to be confined to ghettos in the North and South, to attend ill-equipped schools that are badly staffed, or to suffer diseases which are easily preventable.

The Negro revolution of our time is the most significant social change in the United States of the last hundred years, and it has great relevance for illegitimacy rates. It is only by assimilating the Negro into American life that he can feel the same stake and interest in it that the white person does. Those who have made so vociferous an outcry against the ADC program are most likely to be those who have been least active in facilitating the Negro revolution. Those who claim that Negro illegitimacy is "natural" are those whose repressive actions against integration are likely to maintain a high rate of Negro illegitimacy.

Indeed, this is one area in which natural, human needs, on both a large scale and at the private level, coincide very closely.

For to the extent that we make every effort to open the doors of American life to Negroes and other disadvantaged people in our society, to the extent that we take all possible steps to speed the process of accepting Negroes as full citizens in every social and legal sense, we are not only living up to the ethical principles that are the source of the United States Constitution but will be gaining the benefits from the full participation of these people in American life. The financial and moral costs of segregation are too great to bear any longer. It is perhaps trivial, considering the implications of this revolution, to note that one of its further benefits will be a lowering of the illegitimacy rate, but for those who have had to shoulder the burden of illegitimacy the problem is substantial. To reduce the costs in money and personal misery cannot be a small gain.

Nor must it be forgotten that the Negro shares the deprivations of white men at the bottom, though the heavier load has been the Negro's. How far American leadership can reduce the economic and social poverty of the white lower social strata is not even theoretically clear at this time, but perhaps the pragmatists can lead the way—doing it while the social scientists ponder whether it can be done. It is safe to say, however, that only if it is done will a large part of the illegitimacy among lower-class whites be eliminated.

Notes

1. Willard Waller, "Social Problems and the Mores," *American Sociological Review*, I (December 1936), 928.

2. See his "Illegitimacy and the Social Structure," *American Journal of Sociology*, XLV (1939), 215-233.

3. Leontyne Young, *Out of Wedlock*, New York, 1954.

4. In this connection, perhaps the most perceptive writings have been those of Norman Mailer and James Baldwin.

5. *Look*, August 14, 1962.

6. *Saturday Evening Post*, January 30, 1960.

7. October 17, 1962.

8. *Saturday Evening Post,* March 23, 1963.

9. *New York Times,* April 4, 1963.

10. *New York Times,* May 28, 1964.

11. *New York Times,* February 17, 1964; December 11, 1963; March 27, 1962.

12. For a summary of these legal provisions, see Virginia Wimperis, *The Unmarried Mother and Her Child,* London, 1960, Chapters 14 and 15.

13. Data from official sources.

14. Elizabeth Herzog, "Unmarried Mothers: Some Questions to Be Answered and Some Answers to Be Questioned," *Child Welfare,* XLI (October 1962), 341.

15. Herzog, p. 342.

16. For these and other relevant facts of illegitimacy, see *Illegitimate Births: Fact Sheet,* Washington, D.C., National Office of Vital Statistics, April 15, 1960, and Joseph Schachter and Mary McCarthy, *Illegitimate Births: United States, 1938-1957,* Washington, D.C., National Office of Vital Statistics, 1960.

17. In this connection, see Kingsley Davis, "The Forms of Illegitimacy," *Social Forces,* XVIII (October 1939), 77-89; and "Illegitimacy and the Social Structure," *American Journal of Sociology,* XLV ((1939), 215-233; as well as Robert K. Merton, "Intermarriage and the Social Structure," *Psychiatry,* IV (1941), 361-374.

18. William J. Goode, *The Family,* New York, 1964, p. 23.

19. New York, 1962.

20. See my analysis, "The Theoretical Importance of Love," *American Sociological Review,* XXIV (February 1959), 38-47, for a fuller exposition of such controls.

21. William J. Goode, "Illegitimacy, Anomie, and Cultural Penetration," *American Sociological Review,* XXVI (December 1961), 912, and *The Family,* pp. 26-28.

22. This problem has been extensively analyzed in my two articles, "Illegitimacy in the Caribbean Social Structure," *American Sociological Review,* XXV (February 1961), 21-30; and "Illegitimacy, Anomie, and Cultural Penetration," *op. cit.,* pp. 910-925.

23. Source: Personal communication with United Nations Statistical Office, January 1967.

24. Goode, *The Family,* p. 30.

25. Material summarized from Hannah M. Adams, "Social Services for Unmarried Mothers and Their Children Provided Through Public and Voluntary Child Welfare Agencies," *Child Welfare Reports* No. 12, Washington, D.C.: Children's Bureau, 1962, pp. 3-15.

26. Wimperis, *op. cit.,* Chapters 14 and 15.

27. *Illegitimacy and Its Impact on the Aid to Dependent Children Program,* Washington, D.C., Bureau of Public Assistance, 1960, pp. 32-35.

312   *William J. Goode*

28. "Social Services for Unmarried Mothers and Their Children, Provided Through Public and Voluntary Child Welfare Agencies," *op. cit.,* p. 26.

29. Elizabeth Herzog and Rose Bernstein, "Why So Few Negro Adoptions?" *Children,* XII (January-February 1965), 14-18.

30. After some years of avoiding the topic, the World Health Organization has recognized the importance of contraception as a health measure (*New York Times,* May 23, 1965).

Selected Bibliography

This bibliography is provided primarily for laymen interested in wider reading on the major topics of this book. The list includes basic textbooks, major empirical and theoretical monographs, and anthologies of articles on related themes. In some cases we have divided the topics differently than in the text. For example, several of the essays discussed problems of organizational analysis; in this bibliography we have a separate section on organizational analysis.

SOCIOLOGY AND SOCIAL WELFARE POLICY

Alvin Gouldner and S. M. Miller, ed., *Applied Sociology: Opportunities and Problems*, New York, 1965.

Robert K. Merton and R. A. Nisbet, ed., *Contemporary Social Problems: An Introduction to the Sociology of Deviant Behavior and Social Disorganization*, New York, 1963.

Marvin B. Sussman, ed., *Sociology and Rehabilitation*, Washington, D.C., American Sociological Association, 1966.

Richard M. Titmuss, *Essays on "The Welfare State,"* New Haven, 1962.

Harold Wilensky and Charles N. Lebeaux, *Industrial Society and Social Welfare*, New York, 1958.

Barbara Wootton, *Social Science and Social Pathology*, London, 1959.

AMERICAN SOCIETY AND COMMUNITY STRUCTURE

Edward C. Banfield and James Q. Wilson, *City Politics*, Cambridge, Mass., 1963.

Robert Dahl, *Who Governs? Democracy and Power in an American City*, New Haven, 1961.

Leonard Duhl and John Powell, *The Urban Condition: People and Policy in the Metropolis*, New York, 1963.

Scott Greer, *The Emerging City: Myth and Reality*, New York, 1962.

Scott Greer, *Governing the Metropolis*, New York, 1963.

Martin Meyerson and Edward C. Banfield, *Politics, Planning and the Pub-
lic Interest: The Case of Public Housing in Chicago,* New York, 1965.
Maurice Stein, *The Eclipse of Community: An Interpretation of Ameri-
can Studies,* Princeton, 1960.
Arthur Vidich and Joseph Bensman, *Small Town in Mass Society,* Prince-
ton, 1958.
Roland Warren, *The Community in America,* Chicago, 1963.
Roland Warren, ed., *Perspectives on the American Community,* Chicago,
1966.
Robin Williams, *American Society: A Sociological Interpretation,* New
York, 1951.
Robin Williams, in collaboration with John Dean and Edward A. Such-
man, *Strangers Next Door: Ethnic Relations in American Communities,*
Englewood Cliffs, 1964.

ORGANIZATIONAL ANALYSIS AND CHANGE

Peter M. Blau and W. Richard Scott, *Formal Organizations: A Compara-
tive Approach,* San Francisco, 1962.
Amitai Etzioni, *A Comparative Analysis of Complex Organization,* New
York, 1965.
Elliott Jacques, *The Changing Culture of a Factory,* New York, 1952.
Ray Johns, *Confronting Organizational Change,* New York, 1963.
Philip Selznick, *Leadership in Administration: A Sociological Interpre-
tation,* New York, 1957.
David Sills, *The Volunteers,* New York, 1957.
David Street, Robert Vinter, and Charles Perrow, *Organization for
Treatment: A Comparative Analysis of Institutions for Delinquents,*
New York, 1966.
James D. Thompson and others, ed., *Comparative Studies in Administra-
tion,* Vol. 1, Pittsburgh, 1965.

COMMUNITY ORGANIZATION PRACTICE AND CHANGE THEORY

Saul Alinsky, *Reveille for Radicals,* Chicago, 1946.
Arthur K. Dunham, *Community Welfare Organizations: Principles and
Practice,* New York, 1958
Ronald Lippitt, Jeane Watson, and Bruce Westley, *The Dynamics of
Planned Change: A Comparative Study of Principles and Technique,*
New York, 1958.
Albert K. Mayer and associates, with the collaboration of McKim Mar-
riott and Richard Parks, *Pilot Project India: The Story of Rural De-
velopment in Etawah Uttar,* Berkeley, 1958.
Murray G. Ross, *Community Organizations: Theory and Principles,* New
York, 1955.

PROBLEMS OF EDUCATIONAL INSTITUTIONS

Aaron V. Cicourel and Joseph I. Kitsuse, *The Educational Decision Makers*, Indianapolis, 1963.
James S. Coleman, with the assistance of John W. C. Johnstone and Kurt Jonassohn, *Adolescent Society*, New York, 1961.
James S. Coleman, Ernest Q. Campbell, et al., *Inequalities in Educational Opportunities in the United States*, Washington, D.C., United States Office of Education, 1966.
Ronald G. Corwin, *A Sociology of Education: Emerging Patterns of Class, Status and Power in the Public School*, New York, 1965.
Edgar Z. Friedenberg, *The Vanishing Adolescent*, Boston, 1959.
Jean Dresden Grambs, *Schools, Scholars, and Society*, Englewood Cliffs, 1965.
A. H. Halsey, Jean Floud, and C. A. Anderson, ed., *Education, Economy and Society*, Glencoe, 1961.
Bel Kaufman, *Up the Down Staircase*, Englewood Cliffs, 1965.
Martin Mayer, *The Schools*, New York, 1961.
Mathew Miles, ed., *Innovation in Education*, New York, Bureau of Publication, Teachers College, Columbia University, 1964.
A. Harry Passow, ed., *Education in Depressed Areas*, New York, Bureau of Publication, Teachers College, Columbia University, 1963.
Patricia Cayo Sexton, *Education and Income*, New York, 1961.

MENTAL ILLNESS AND COMMUNITY PROCESS

Howard Becker, *The Outsiders*, London, 1963.
Elliot Freidson, *Patients' View of Medical Practice*, New York, 1961.
Erving Goffman, *Stigma*, Englewood Cliffs, 1963.
Erving Goffman, *Asylums*, Garden City, 1961.
Milton Greenblatt, Daniel Levinson, and Richard II. Williams, *The Patient and the Mental Hospital*, Glencoe, 1957.
Gerald V. Gurin, *Americans View Their Mental Health*, New York, 1960.
A. B. Hollingshead and F. Redlich, *Social Class and Mental Illness*, New York, 1958.
Frank Reissman, Jerome Cohen, and Arthur Pearl, ed., *Mental Health of the Poor*, New York, 1964.
Thomas Scheff, *Being Mentally Ill*, Chicago, 1966.

POVERTY

Winifred Bell, *Aid to Dependent Children*, New York, 1965.
David Caplovitz, *The Poor Pay More*, New York, 1963.
Louis Ferman, Joyce Kornbluh, and Alan Haber, ed., *Poverty in America*, Ann Arbor, 1965.

Margaret S. Gordon, ed., *Poverty in America*, San Francisco, 1965.
Oscar Lewis, *The Children of Sanchez: An Autobiography of a Mexican Family*, New York, 1961.
James M. Morgan, Martin H. David, Wilbur J. Cohen, and Harvey Brazer. *Income and Welfare in the United States*, New York, 1962.
Thomas F. Pettigrew, *A Profile of the Negro American*, Princeton, 1964.
W. G. Runciman, *Relative Deprivation and Social Justice: A Study of Attitudes to Social Inequality in Twentieth Century England*, Berkeley, 1966.
Alvin Schorr, *Slums and Social Insecurity: An Appraisal of the Effectiveness of Housing Policies in Helping to Eliminate Poverty in the United States*, Washington, D.C., U.S. Department of Health, Education and Welfare, 1963.
Ben B. Seligman, ed., *Poverty as a Public Issue*, New York, 1965.
Arthur Shostak and William Gomberg, ed., *Blue Collar World: Studies of the American Workers*, Englewood Cliffs, 1964.
Robert Theobald, ed., *The Guaranteed Income*, New York, 1965.

ILLEGITIMACY AND FAMILY PATTERNS

Bernard Farber, *Family: Organization and Interaction*, San Francisco, 1964.
William J. Goode, *World Revolution and Family Patterns*, New York, 1963.
William J. Goode, ed., *Readings on the Family and Society*, Englewood Cliffs, 1964.
Charles S. Johnson, *Shadow of the Plantation*, Chicago, 1934.
Lee Rainwater, with Karol Kane Weinstein, *And the Poor Get Children*, Chicago, 1961.
Robert W. Roberts, ed., *The Unwed Mother*, New York, 1966.
Clark Vincent, *Unmarried Mothers*, New York, 1961.
Leontyne Young, *Out of Wedlock: A Study of the Problems of the Unmarried and Her Child*, New York, 1954.